Alternative Masculinities in Feminist Speculative Fiction

Alternative Masculinities in Feminist Speculative Fiction

A New Man

Michael Pitts

LEXINGTON BOOKS
Lanham • Boulder • New York • London

Published by Lexington Books
An imprint of The Rowman & Littlefield Publishing Group, Inc.
4501 Forbes Boulevard, Suite 200, Lanham, Maryland 20706
www.rowman.com

6 Tinworth Street, London SE11 5AL, United Kingdom

British Library Cataloguing in Publication Information Available

Library of Congress Cataloging-in-Publication Data Available

ISBN 978-1-7936-3660-7 (cloth)
ISBN 978-1-7936-3662-1 (pbk)
ISBN 978-1-7936-3661-4 (electronic)

To my grandmother for her greatly missed monthly phone calls. To my parents, who allowed me to explore and idly people-watch as a child. And to those women and men I observed in ballparks, skating rinks, and churches who impressed upon me the myriad ways masculinity may be challenged, altered, and reinvented.

Contents

Acknowledgments

Special thanks are due to Dr. Robin Roberts, Dr. Steven Rosales, and Dr. Susan Marren. My gratitude to Jeff Northrup, Dr. Geoffrey Wright, and Dr. Bruce McComiskey for their guidance over the years. Finally, love and thanks to Alicia and our sweet feline companion, Cat Stevens, for their endless encouragement throughout this endeavor.

Introduction

Alternative Masculinities in Feminist Speculative Fiction: A New Man traces the ways masculinities are framed and valued in genre fiction, focusing on science fiction written by U.S. women from 1971 to 2017. Since gender and national identity are mutually constitutive concepts, products of popular culture such as science fiction novels act as rich sites for analyzing representations of gender reflective of the society in which such works are produced.[1] This project, therefore, continues the work of scholars mining "theatre, film (narrative and documentary), literature, music, advertising, internet content, television, photography, politics, and current events—to posit questions about the processes of gender creation" (Shaw and Watson 2011, 1), but applies such an approach specifically to American science fiction. This study adds to scholarship at the intersection of gender studies and contemporary American literature by analyzing these novels' portrayal of new radical ideals of manhood. In her landmark text *Gender Trouble: Feminism and the Subversion of Identity*, Judith Butler (1990) sets out "to trace the way in which gender fables establish and circulate the misnomer of natural facts" (xxxiv). *Alternative Masculinities in Feminist Speculative Fiction: A New Man* examines the ways feminist speculative authors, reversing the process Butler highlights, utilize their fiction to challenge naturalized, patriarchal conceptions of gender privileging whiteness and heteronormativity.

By tracing the changes in the depiction of masculinities in feminist utopian novels, these chapters further illuminate the role of gender within this segment of American literary history. Feminist speculative fiction from 1971 to 2017 contains numerous instances of alternative masculinities that these authors present as crucial to the improvement of society. Presenting such altered ideals of manhood, these utopias signal shifts in how masculinity is depicted in contemporary American science fiction. In describing American

1

literary histories, Stacey Olster (2017) explains that the task of literary critics is to push "what follows the 'since' in the subtitles of earlier scholarship . . . further along chronologically so as to explore the changes and continuities, additions and alterations, displayed by American fiction" (8). Departing from established scholarly interests in examining the role of women in such utopias, I examine the evolutionary qualities of feminist speculative novels as they signal key changes in the representation of masculinities. As my analyses demonstrate, these works of earlier genre fiction offer valuable sources of new masculinities in a cultural milieu marked by a resurgence of traditional, American ideals of manhood. Drawing on masculinity studies, contemporary fiction, and speculative literature contributes to ongoing discussions of manhood and the possibility of transforming patriarchal gender scripts. These novels more specifically focus upon the conversion of traditionally masculine men by depicting the radical disruption of normative masculinities.

Since the inception of masculinity studies as an organized subset of feminist theory in the 1990s, newly developed theories of manhood have been applied to diverse cultures. Originating in the 1970s in opposition to the anti-feminist men's right movement, critical men's studies initially focused predominantly upon normative scripts of manliness in the United States and Europe. Such approaches were problematic in the way they overlooked important factors such as race and sexuality and did not analyze the experiences of men marginalized according to these and other nonnormative identity elements. What followed in the 1990s was the introduction of complexity and nuance to this burgeoning field. Notable texts such as Raewyn Connell's *Masculinities* (1995) and Michael Kimmel's *Manhood in America: A Cultural History* (1996), for example, consider the connection of cultures and masculinity, tracing links between performances of manhood and a greater system of power or gender order. According to these scholars, analyses of manliness should consider both those masculinities idealized by a culture and the alternative versions with which they compete (Kimmel 2006, 4). Building upon this scholarship, I apply the sociological apparatus developed within masculinity studies to cultural products of the contemporary United States, feminist utopias published from 1971 to 2017.

In mining feminist utopian fiction for new ideals of manhood at a time in which traditional gender scripts are experiencing a resurgence, this research is invaluable to current discussions concerning twenty-first-century American masculinities. Two events are considered central in this recent reemergence of traditional masculinities and their attending crisis: the attacks on and events surrounding September 11, 2001, and, more recently, the 2016 U.S. election of Donald Trump. Victor J. Seidler (2006) in *Transforming Masculinities: Men, Cultures, Bodies, Power, Sex and Love* identifies events following September 11, 2001—specifically the war in

Iraq and the resulting protests across Europe—as exemplifying "a struggle that involved diverse global masculinities being locked into terrifying relationships with each other" (1). In an updated preface to *Angry White Men: American Masculinity at the End of an Era*, Michael Kimmel (2017) highlights the importance of the Trump presidency to hegemonic masculinities: "Trump's election underscores" how "white men's anger comes from the potent fusion of two sentiments—entitlement and a sense of victimization" (x). In examining a fictional version of such traditionally masculine attitudes from a feminist perspective, this research locates new insights into the possibility of transforming manhood that are derived from the lived experiences of women.

Focusing on such portrayals of manliness in contemporary American speculative fiction fits within masculinity studies and the ongoing project of deconstructing cultural representations of manhood. This project builds directly upon the work of other scholars within masculinity studies who locate and analyze, for example, how various parts of popular culture (film, television, music, photography, theater, and literature, to name a few) portray normative and marginalized ideals of manliness. These chapters specifically locate and analyze utopian masculinities in the works of influential American feminist science fiction writers. This analysis builds, therefore, upon the current interest within masculinity studies in "representation and its connection with wider questions of change and continuity in contemporary, and in some more historical, masculinities and identities" (Edwards 2006, 3). Analyzing these literary representations introduces questions about the role of feminist writers in presentations of manhood in American science fiction.

This analysis examines an intersection often overlooked in scholarship: that of masculinity studies and contemporary American fiction. Following the development of masculinity studies, American literary scholars gradually applied these analytical tools to disparate writers and literary traditions.[2] Building upon such analyses of American fiction, *Alternative Masculinities in Feminist Speculative Fiction: A New Man* expands the application of masculinity theory to women science fiction writers. This research contributes to ongoing discussions within masculinity studies of popular culture as a valuable site both for identifying radical, new conceptions of manhood and noting older, residual masculinities beneficial to patriarchy. My analysis focuses upon the framing of traditional and alternative masculinities in feminist science fiction and builds upon a theoretical foundation informed both by literary studies and masculinity studies. I identify as fundamental to these feminist speculative writers' portrayals of new performances of masculinity the presentation of utopian male characters exemplifying ideal performances of manhood. This analysis, therefore, joins conversations within masculinity studies and literary studies and seeks to highlight in such discussions the ways utopian feminist novels reveal new conceptions of manhood that reject interests in power and control.

These chapters uniquely contribute to discussions surrounding changing gender scripts and specifically reveal the way these feminist writers address old and new conceptions of manhood. While Bryant, Le Guin, Piercy, Butler, and Jemisin positively portray traditional ideals of manhood such as honor, bravery, loyalty, and strength, they disconnect such attributes from male biology and instead frame them as ideal attributes of masculinity. In this way, the positive aspects of male characters such as the unnamed, transformed narrator in *The Kin of Ata Are Waiting for You* (1971), Shevek in *The Dispossessed*, Jackrabbit in *Woman on the Edge of Time* (1976), Akin in *Adulthood Rites* (1988), and Schaffa in *The Stone Sky* (2017) illustrate aspects of these authors' representations of masculinity widely considered traditional. These writers imagine that these same characters lack the traditionally masculine, negative desires for power and control and possess instead interests in community and equality that are historically identified as feminine. Feminist writers, therefore, present in their works portraits of masculinity that possess traditional traits of manliness such as bravery, loyalty, and strength but diverge drastically from the negative aspects of these historic gender scripts such as desires for control and power over others. Though scholars have historically examined these novels' portrayals of female experience, *Alternative Masculinities in Feminist Speculative Fiction: A New Man* moves from this focus to note how these feminist writers address and examine masculinities in their utopias and offer new, transformed conceptions of manhood vital for ongoing discussions about the future of masculinity.

These novels and their new conceptions of manhood coincide with some key shifts in American science fiction and utopian writing from 1971 to 2017. More specifically, the novels I discuss illustrate the importance of a new type of utopia, the critical utopia, for feminist writers seeking to critique masculinities in ways not made available to them by realistic fiction. In *Demand the Impossible: Science Fiction and the Utopian Imagination*, Tom Moylan defines critical utopias as those that negate "the negation of utopia by the forces of twentieth century history." As critical utopias, each of these feminist novels are aware of the "limitations of the utopian tradition" and, therefore, challenge it, imbuing it with revolutionary, feminist reframings of the good society. They also "dwell on the conflict between the originary world and the utopian society opposed to it so that the process of social change is more directly articulated" (Moylan 1986, 10). Since, as previously mentioned, nationality and masculinity are mutually constitutive concepts, a central source of this friction between these imagined feminist and patriarchal polities is the transformation of masculinities. The critical utopia is crucial to the feminist project of highlighting particularly important social changes—in this case, those to masculinity—necessary for the improved society to be realized.

This application of masculinity studies contributes to science fiction studies. Analyzing how feminist novelists utilize the speculative genre and the possibilities it allows for imagining new formations of gender, this analysis connects with and owes a great deal to the scholarship of Justine Larbalestier. In *The Battle of the Sexes in Science Fiction*, Larbalestier (2002) examines speculative texts from 1926 onward "that are explicitly about the 'sex war' between men and women and which posit as a solution to this conflict that women accept their position as subordinate to men" (1). Informed by this analysis of anti-feminist science fiction texts preoccupied with such a conflict of the sexes, my analysis notes a significant development beginning in the 1970s: the advent of new, feminist-oriented portrayals by female American writers of and solutions to such a battle. Such works written by women propose new, egalitarian conceptions of manliness as central to their solutions meant to dismantle white supremacist patriarchy. These novels present alternatives to conceptions of manhood that privilege, for example, whiteness and heteronormativity. *Alternative Masculinities in Feminist Speculative Fiction: A New Man* offers an overview of feminist engagement with masculinities, focusing on nine American speculative novels produced in the late twentieth and early twenty-first centuries: Dorothy Bryant's *The Kin of Ata Are Waiting for You*, Ursula K. Le Guin's *The Dispossessed: An Ambiguous Utopia*, Marge Piercy's *Woman on the Edge of Time*, Octavia E. Butler's *Lilith's Brood* trilogy, *Dawn* (1987), *Adulthood Rites*, and *Imago* (1989), and N.K. Jemisin's *Broken Earth* series, *The Fifth Season* (2015), *The Obelisk Gate* (2016), and *The Stone Sky*.

This research at the intersection of gender and science fiction research necessitates the utilization of theoretical frameworks and terms pivotal to these fields. Central to *Alternative Masculinities in Feminist Speculative Fiction: A New Man*, for example, is the figure of the *self-made man*, theorized by Michael Kimmel (2006) as the idealized American male whose value is based upon "activities in the public sphere" and "measured by accumulated wealth and status, by geographic and social mobility" (Kimmel 137). Capitalism's impact on American masculinities is foundational to critiques of imagined societies in speculative fiction. As analyses of these feminist utopias illustrate, these writers present such profit-driven male characters in a negative light, illustrating their complicity to racist, patriarchal systems of power to consolidate their power and social influence.

These chapters similarly consider a literary character type characterized by racist and patriarchal desires for control and power, the *supermen* of the so-called golden age of science fiction. Ubiquitous in midcentury American speculative fiction, the superman of science fiction, exemplified by characters such as Jommy Cross in A.E. van Vogt's *Slan* (1946) and John Pollard in Edward Hamilton's "The Man Who Evolved" (1931), is detached from societal concerns and, instead, focuses upon his own evolution and the possibility of consolidating power. Opposing the utopian project, he sees no value in "schools, governments, families, political groups, media," (Attebery 2002, 67) and other such communal organizations. He is instead hierarchical, individualistic, exploitative, selfish, and uninterested in community-building. Joanna Russ similarly characterizes the white male hero of pulp, space opera, and other subsets of science fiction during its so-called golden age as the "Master of the Universe." He "is invulnerable. He has no weaknesses. Sexually he is super-potent. He does exactly what he pleases, everywhere and at all times. He is absolutely self-sufficient. He depends on nobody, for this would be a weakness. Toward women he is possessive, protective, and patronizing; to me he gives orders. He is never frightened . . . he is never indecisive and he always wins" (Russ 2007, 210). In short, the masculinities of earlier science fiction oppose liberty, equality, and fraternity and espouse instead the accumulation of power and control through aggressive acts and domination. In contrast to the superman character type who "evolves apart from, or even in opposition to, his society," the men populating the 1970s feminist utopias seek to nurture strong communal bonds and reject all hierarchical systems of power including racism, homophobia, and capitalistic patriarchy (Attebery 2002, 67). These new portraits of masculinity by feminist science fiction writers specifically challenge earlier depictions of men as violent dominators seeking to subjugate others. Feminist science fiction writers critique traditional gender scripts supporting the traditional hero, reject essentialist conceptions of problematic masculinities, and present traditional performances of manhood in a new, negative light within their fiction. In reenvisioning masculinity, Bryant, Le Guin, Piercy, Butler, and Jemisin present new men who replace the Masters of the Universe or supermen and their desires for dominance and influence with interests in community and fraternity. *Alternative Masculinities in Feminist Speculative Fiction: A New Man* emphasizes the vital importance of such utopian works and their alternative masculinities to ongoing discussions surrounding American conceptions of manhood.

In my analyses of these pivotal feminist utopias, I utilize Raewyn Connell's theorization of mechanisms or *patterns of masculinity* by which patriarchal societies reward or punish subjects according to masculinities. Connell identifies four patterns in the contemporary Western gender order—hegemony, subordination, complicity, and marginalization—that function so that traditional performances of manhood are granted power while alternative masculinities are subjugated or sent to the social margins. As Connell outlines, the proximity of men from power in the patriarchy is based upon their ability to match hegemonic conceptions of manhood. If they are not able to attain a position within hegemony, they are subordinated to it and granted limited power according to their complicity to traditional masculinities. Those who are unable or unwilling to comply with this system of power are relocated to the societal margins. Applying Connell's theorization of masculine patterns to these feminist utopias shows how these authors posit new, egalitarian performances of maleness in opposition to traditionally masculine characters and the societal patterns of power and marginalization benefiting them.

In discussing masculinity as an ideology influenced by and influencing such social systems of power, I draw upon the research of Todd Reeser and his conception of the *gendered nation*. In *Masculinities in Theory: An Introduction*, Reeser (2010) posits that "masculinity can be thought of both as created by institutions and as creating them, and the process of the construction of masculinity as a constant back-and-forth movement between masculinity and institutions" (20). According to Reeser, images, myths, discourses, and practices produced by public and private entities and individuals construct and reinforce patriarchal conceptions of manhood (21). Entertainment platforms such as television, for example, are capable of constructing new masculinities while also revealing current forms widely accepted in a society and involve public and private organizations. Such a mutually constitutive relationship between masculinities and institutions leads to the gendering of the nation. As my analysis of contemporary feminist utopian fiction reveals, central to these novels and the alternative masculinities they present is the interpellation of normative masculinities in the traditionally patriarchal, gendered nations populating these texts and the polity they represent, the contemporary United States.

Since this analysis focuses upon how these speculative novels "provide insight into the role of women in science fiction, literally and textually" (Larbalestier 2002, 1), it emphasizes the role of female writers in developing this wave of feminist utopias and contributes, therefore, to the extratextual interests of science fiction studies. Authors such as Sally Miller Gearhart, Joanna Russ, Dorothy Bryant, Suzy McKee Charnas, Marge Piercy, and Ursula K. Le Guin, for example, produced feminist utopias that to varying degrees challenge traditional masculinity through the use of speculative fiction tropes and second-wave feminist theoretical frameworks. It is no coincidence that these texts appear in "the period of the greatest optimism and inventiveness in the women's movement of the late twentieth century" (Magarey 2007, 326). Stirred by this activism, these writers signaled a paradigm shift in science fiction through both their success as female genre fiction writers and the inclusion in their novels of critiques concerning the condition and social position of women. They imagined new societies that are nonhierarchical, directly rejecting traditionally masculine interests in authoritative societal networks. As utopias directly opposing normative masculinities, they outline the changes masculinities must undergo for the better, feminist society to be realized and, while challenging essentialism and the overlooking of race and sexuality within feminist circles, generally reflect second-wave feminism. New masculinities within contemporary feminist utopias reveal significant shifts within the genre that reflect both radical and intersectional feminist paradigms. These novels illuminate, therefore, the trajectory of feminist writers from narrow, essentialist conceptions of gender toward broader, more encompassing understandings of gender and its interaction with race and other identity elements. As *Alternative Masculinities in Feminist Speculative Fiction: A New Man* uniquely demonstrates, this development is significant since it facilitated a greater understanding of masculinities and the possibility of radically transforming them.

Positing that central to the strength of these feminist utopias is their exposure of patriarchal conceptions of manhood and their presentation of alternative masculinities, I examine the texts' uses of speculative generic conventions to correctly frame traditional and alternative masculinities, demonstrate their malleability, and emphasize connections between traditional masculinity and other ideologies of oppression and between gender and the nation. These novels offer alternative and traditional conceptions of manhood at a time in which the public visibility of harmful, traditionally masculine qualities, framed as ideal, are prevalent. As Michael Kimmel (2017) explains, a significant factor in the anxiety and anger surrounding the so-called crisis of manhood "is that we still don't really know how to talk about masculinity in the United States" (2). This failure, Kimmel outlines, is due substantially to the misframing of positive and toxic masculinities in media and the blurring or mislabeling of these categories. Applying this approach to the realm of fiction, I consider how feminist utopias ideally frame masculinities, both patriarchal and egalitarian, through characters whose masculinities are demonstrated to have significantly positive or negative impacts upon others.

The chapters of *Alternative Masculinities in Feminist Speculative Fiction: A New Man* are organized chronologically and thematically. They demonstrate a general move by feminist utopias from the periphery to the mainstream as their popularity grew over time; they also illustrate a thematic trend in which feminist utopias moved away from the experiences of white male characters and toward those of characters marked by nonnormative sexualities, racial identities, or genders. In these two decades, feminist speculative writers gradually gained a larger readership, relocating them from the obscure margins to mainstream acceptance, indicated in part by literary and other awards, and their continuing availability in print. Progressing from Dorothy Bryant's *The Kin of Ata Are Waiting for You* to N.K. Jemisin's *Broken Earth* trilogy, this analysis illustrates the growing recognition of feminist utopias as legitimate and valuable sources for reconceptualizing gender. While briefly mentioned in Bryant's novel, race and ethnicity, for example, are more prominent in Le Guin's text and are fundamental to the works of Piercy, Butler, and Jemisin. In addition to chronology, these chapters are organized according to movements from the margins to the mainstream and illustrate developments within feminist activism as characters marked by different racial, gender, and sexual identities are gradually relocated to the center of these texts.

The first chapter of *Alternative Masculinities in Feminist Speculative Fiction: A New Man* focuses upon the earliest of these novels, Dorothy Bryant's *The Kin of Ata Are Waiting for You*, published as *The Comforter* in 1971. This text did not receive wide attention upon its release, though it has remained in print for more than forty years. Its publication history—initially published privately before being purchased and distributed by Random House—illustrates the growing popularity of feminist utopias during the 1970s. This utopia is the first discussed in this analysis since it marks, as the earliest published and least widely distributed, the early position of feminist utopias as far from the mainstream or popular.

In addition, its focus on the unnamed patriarchal narrator and his oppression of others according to identity markers such as race in addition to sex signifies Bryant's early rejection of a trend within 1970s radical feminism: the privileging of white, straight women and their needs above those of women of other races and sexualities among other marginalized identity elements. Through her protagonist, Bryant, for example, illustrates how patriarchal masculinities connect to racism when, prior to raping, Augustine, a female inhabitant of the utopia, the novel's male protagonist reflects on how he had "had black women before, but they'd never lived up to my expectations of primitive passion" (53). Told from the perspective of this protagonist who, as the unnamed narrator of the novel, looks back at his earlier, patriarchal self with disgust, Bryant's novel aligns its audience against traditional masculinities and their symptomatic racism. Though Bryant consistently connects patriarchy with related forms of oppression in similar scenes throughout her novel, her presentations of intersectionality are not as extensive as those of later feminist utopian writers such as Piercy, Butler, and Jemisin. The novel, therefore, exemplifies the productive if limited ways in which early feminist utopias dealt with race and sexuality and serves as a reference point against which increased presentations of intersectionality in later feminist novels may be compared.

In her novel, Bryant also exposes the dangers of essentializing gender. As pointed out by scholars such as Audre Lorde, essentialism manifests in the radical feminist branch since such activists often view women as having innate and common attributes, interests, or traits producing universal sisterhood and uniting them in their struggle.[3] This conception of a uniform female experience ignores important differences across racial, sexual, and gendered lines and contributes, therefore, to the privileging of misogyny in discussions concerning social inequality. Bryant presents through her novel a political tract that, while often in agreement with the theories of radical feminism, challenges ideals attributed to this movement—such as essentialist conceptions of gender—in significant ways. She, for example, presents in her novel the interlocking social mechanisms that uniquely subjugate the aforementioned female Atan, Augustine, when she departs from the utopia. Rejecting simplistic, essentialist conceptions of female experience as uniform irrespective of race, Bryant emphasizes the distinct ways women are marginalized from power according to unique combinations of identity markers.

The core argument I present in chapter 1 is that such important challenges to essentialism, and especially those concerning manliness, make the novel a vital source for positing new ideals of manhood in the current so-called crisis of masculinity. A male conversion novel told from the perspective of an abhorrent patriarch, *The Kin of Ata Are Waiting for You* is invaluable to discussions of masculinity because it gives a voice to traditional masculinities themselves, represented by the unnamed narrator. As a successful writer—through whom Bryant comments on the toxicity of successful male American authors—he acts as a symbol both of patriarchal and hegemonic conceptions of manhood. His initial perspective and gradual transformation, I assert, benefit ongoing conversations about how manliness may be positively altered for the betterment of society. In addition, his position as a profiting writer of misogynistic fiction adds considerable depth to discussions surrounding the intertwined nature of capitalism and patriarchy.

Bryant uniquely comments on masculinity through a radical assertion she embeds within the plot of the text. She argues in her novel that, through reeducating and socializing men in a transformed society based upon fundamental feminist principles, even the most violent patriarch may undergo meaningful change. This often-overlooked aspect of her novel marks her work as unique among feminist utopias. Unlike these other feminist utopias, it intensifies its revolutionary message by presenting the extreme end result of patriarchal masculinities. The protagonist, having gained the wealth and power made available to hegemonic men, continues consolidating further power over others until he ultimately resorts to extreme acts of violence to accumulate further control. Having repeatedly killed and raped, he undergoes a gradual, dramatic transformation as a resident of the feminist utopia that renders him a new, egalitarian man. By focusing on a toxic, criminal male protagonist and ultimately imagining how such a violent individual may transform, Bryant radically challenges her audience to consider the implications of nonessentialist theories of gender.

It is Bryant's social constructionist presentation of gender and, more specifically, the rejection in her novel of manliness as necessarily violent that makes *The Kin of Ata Are Waiting for You* a rich source for mining new masculinities. Depicting the most toxic products of patriarchy, violence including rape and murder, Bryant highlights for her audience the potential for changing traditional masculinities. Based on this understanding of gender, she compels her reader to consider if and how men performing heinous acts tied to their traditional gender roles may be converted. Her novel, therefore, presents pathways by which men may move toward feminist-informed conceptions of manhood. *The Kin of Ata Are Waiting for You* provokes key questions concerning gender and whether the most extreme, misogynistic men may be altered through feminist influence and is, for this reason, critical to ongoing conversations surrounding the possibility of recovering men from toxic masculinities.

The second chapter focuses on Ursula K. Le Guin's *The Dispossessed: An Ambiguous Utopia*, a text that illustrates the pattern of feminist speculative novels moving from the margins to the mainstream. Unlike *The Kin of Ata Are Waiting for You*, Le Guin's utopia received enthusiastic and positive attention upon its release. It was awarded the Nebula, Hugo, and Locus awards and received a nomination for the John W. Campbell Memorial Award. The enduring widespread interest in the novel is further illustrated by the 2017 publication of a special edition of Le Guin's complete *Hainish Cycle* (including *The Dispossessed*) by the Library of America. Its lasting importance and mainstream popularity make it an influential and valuable source for locating new masculinities standing against patriarchal ideals of manhood.

Published three years after Bryant's utopia, the novel shares some key elements with that earlier text. *The Dispossessed*, for example, similarly marks a limited departure from the radical feminist privileging of female oppression. The novel specifically portrays the marginalization of others according to sexuality and class in a way that signals a growing recalibration of radical feminist authors in the 1970s to include the experiences of others similarly oppressed by patriarchal masculinities. *The Dispossessed*, for example, follows the experiences of Shevek, a male scientist of the anarchic and feminist-oriented nation of Anarres, as he visits Urras and spends a great deal of time within a capitalistic patriarchy on this planet, A-Io. The novel centers around a queer male anarchic protagonist whose open attitude toward nonnormative sexualities and opposition to capitalistic class oppression exemplifies new masculinities. Also, like Bryant's novel, *The Dispossessed* is interested in the transforming masculinities of its protagonist. Le Guin's novel stands as a significant, materialist presentation of patriarchal and utopian masculinities.

The Dispossessed is vital to discussions concerning masculinity due to its presentation of gender as subject to transformation. This importance is increased by its commentary on the mutually constitutive relationship between masculinity and the nation and the need to transform the socioeconomic aspects of a society in order to produce significant changes in gender. Like *The Kin of Ata Are Waiting for You*, Le Guin's text concerns the experiences of a man whose masculinity is informed by his nationality. The novel follows the attempts of Shevek, a male scientist whose feminist masculinity is informed by his upbringing in an anarchic nation, to build upon a mathematical theory enabling communication across vast distances. Shevek resists the attempts of the capitalistic patriarchy he visits to control and exploit this information. Unlike Bryant's novel, the text does not end with the protagonist adopting a new concept of manliness in direct contrast to one held at the beginning of the text. Instead, Le Guin's protagonist temporarily adopts toxic masculine traits after being exposed to and seduced by capitalism and patriarchy, which are fundamental elements of the nation he visits. This adoption of traditional masculinities produces in him a predatory view of others and especially women, which culminates in sexual assault. Le Guin, like Bryant before her, presents an ethically complex story focused upon the transformation of men. Instead of centering her utopia around the alteration of a hypermasculine misogynist, she is concerned with the continuous struggle of men possessing alternative masculinities to reject capitalism and patriarchy, their promises of power and control, and the brutality that results.

This interest in the precarious status of improved masculinities makes Le Guin's novel unique. In highlighting the dynamic nature of gender and, more specifically, ideals of manhood, her text resists a common pitfall of utopian writing: the presentation of imagined resolutions to social conflicts as conclusive and static. Avoiding such a tendency, Le Guin's text presents, as the subtitle suggests, a resolution to the crisis of masculinity that is, like the utopia of the novel, ambiguous. While the new masculinities Le Guin presents are ideal alternatives to traditional American masculinities, the introduction and normalization of them in a society requires, in addition to the removal of capitalism and patriarchy, the constant reassessment of social norms surrounding manhood. *The Dispossessed* is distinct in its centering of a male protagonist who initially subscribes to feminist-inspired masculinities but later succumbs to and eventually resists patriarchal masculinities. The novel distinctively outlines what is required for traditional American ideals of manliness to be deposed and, to a greater extent, the attentiveness required for their disempowerment to be maintained.

The novel is important to this analysis of new masculinities in contemporary feminist utopian novels for two reasons. *The Dispossessed* highlights an issue foundational to the current crisis of masculinity, the relationship of American patriarchy to capitalism. The text demonstrates, for example, an underlying complication for young American men seeking new ideals of manhood: attempts to reject traditionally masculine desires to consolidate power and control over others are difficult in a nation whose economic system rewards these patriarchal values. In addition, by presenting a character who, instead of modeling perfectly a utopian performance of manhood, falters to a very significant degree, sexually assaulting a woman as a result, Le Guin illuminates the vigilance and constant self-reflection required of men adopting feminist-informed masculinities. By avoiding the tendency among utopian writers to simplify and make conclusive resolutions to sources of friction in their plots, Le Guin offers in *The Dispossessed* a rich, nuanced map of new, egalitarian conceptions of manliness.

Marge Piercy's *Woman on the Edge of Time*, upon which chapter 3 of this analysis focuses, illustrates the continuously growing popularity of feminist novels in the 1970s. While it did not receive the immense acclaim of *The Dispossessed*, it was a literary and commercial success, remaining in print since its initial debut. *Woman on the Edge of Time* received instant recognition in academic circles as an important text of feminist science fiction. Noted for belonging to a branch of literature that combines "traditional fictional devices with specific information" from academic fields such as anthropology and mixes "both the normal concerns of social realism and verisimilitude in the choice of details from daily life . . . with the moral fervor of utopian fiction and social reform," Piercy's novel was quickly and widely recognized among scholars and mainstream audiences alike as an important speculative work (Olderman 1978, 500). When compared to Bryant's earlier novel, *Woman on the Edge of Time* signals a vital development in popular culture: as the 1970s and second wave of feminism progressed, utopias grounded in the principles of feminist theory gained a larger audience.

Reflecting discussions within radical feminist circles during the 1970s, *Woman on the Edge of Time* is substantially informed by a Marxist analysis of sex and, more specifically, the theoretical approach of Shulamith Firestone. Firestone's (1970) "materialist view of history based on sex" directly manifests in Piercy's novel, as is illustrated by the societal norms of the utopia and its use of technology to eliminate the sex distinction Firestone identifies as foundational to patriarchy (5). As Susan Archer Mann outlines, there are multiple commonalities located in both Firestone's theory and Piercy's novel. The nuclear family, for example, "is viewed as a major site of women's oppression" by Firestone and does not exist in the utopia of the novel (Mann 2012, 90). In addition, schools are abolished (allowing the complete integration of children and women into society), cultural diversity is valued and ubiquitous, and advanced technology is used in the novel to make "ex-utero reproduction possible and" enable "people to live comfortably in a communal lifestyle" that is ecologically conscious (Mann 2012, 91). Finally, the novel, like Firestone's theoretical apparatus, presents androgyny and pansexuality as crucial qualities of the feminist utopia. Piercy presents in her text a utopia grounded in radical feminism and, more specifically, the materialist feminism espoused by Firestone.

Chapter 3 argues that, though Piercy's utopia is built upon Firestone's theoretical foundation, it signals through its focus on intersectionality a development in feminist utopias. Her novel anticipates theories of intersectionality and focuses on how identity markers such as race and biological sex produce distinct experiences of oppression within patriarchy. The text—more than those of Bryant or Le Guin—specifically considers how American hegemonic masculinities are predicated upon ethnicity. While left unspoken, men classified in this network of power must necessarily, in addition to being straight, be or pass as white. Piercy's novel imagines how racism, like and in addition to misogyny, may be eradicated through the development of an improved, feminist society. Piercy makes as her protagonist a Mexican American woman subjugated according to both her racial makeup and biological sex. Outlining the toxic qualities of patriarchal masculinities in the dystopian setting of the novel, the contemporary United States, Piercy exposes her audience to a range of male characters whose masculinities, like their social positioning in relation to power, are predicted upon their racial makeup. A significant aspect of her novel is its strong emphasis on race as an influencing factor in configurations of masculinity and power.

Piercy's utopia is unique narratively in that it centers the perspective and experiences not of a male character negotiating masculinities but of a woman of color historically found on the margins of American novels. While the utopias of Bryant and Le Guin follow the interactions of men possessing traditional and new conceptions of manhood, Piercy's utopia aligns the reader with a female character additionally marginalized according to her identity as a Mexican American. Giving power to those women such as Connie and Augustine in *The Kin of Ata Are Waiting for You* and Vea in *The Dispossessed* who are abused at the hands of patriarchal protagonists, the novel centers their experiences and illuminates for the reader the ways toxic masculinities harm women of color in unique, intersectional ways. Chapter 3, therefore, posits that Piercy's novel marks a significant development in contemporary feminist utopias in its focus on the experiences of a woman of color.

Woman on the Edge of Time is therefore an important speculative text for ongoing discussions of masculinity since it asks its male readers to align themselves with a protagonist unlike them in two ways, race and sex, that have a profound effect upon her social positioning and experiences. By placing readers inside the mind of a woman of color, Piercy's novel asks them to experience vicariously the oppressive forces of patriarchy and racism that uniquely subjugate women of color in the contemporary United States. In positioning the reader alongside such a character traditionally at the margins of utopian texts, Piercy's novel calls attention to how alternative and patriarchal conceptions of manliness positively and negatively impact the lives of such women, respectively. *Woman on the Edge of Time* is, therefore, an invaluable literary resource for masculinity studies in two distinct ways: it asks pivotal questions concerning the mutually constitutive relationship of racism and patriarchy and it offers for the reader's consideration new, feminist masculinities characterized by interests in community and opposition to control and power and presented as necessary for the development of an improved society. By emphasizing the ways women of color uniquely suffer as a result of patriarchy, her novel broadens and complicates considerations of manhood and illustrates the opportunities the utopian genre grants for feminist writers to imagine new, egalitarian masculinities.

Chapter 4 focuses upon the novels making up Octavia E. Butler's *Lilith's Brood* trilogy, *Dawn, Adulthood Rites*, and *Imago*. These novels and the author's career more generally illustrate the continually growing importance and popularity of feminist utopias in the 1980s. Achieving mainstream acclaim, each novel was nominated for the Locus Award for Best Science Fiction Novel. Signaling a newfound public interest in female speculative writers of color, the Hugo and Nebula awards were additionally bestowed upon Butler during her career. Butler's work demonstrated the cultural importance of speculative fiction when she was awarded the MacArthur Fellowship, making her the first science fiction writer to receive it.[4] Tracing developments across these decades from the marginal positioning of Dorothy Bryant, the success of Marge Piercy, and the widespread acclaim of both Ursula Le Guin and Octavia Butler demonstrates how feminist utopias and science fiction more generally grew significantly in mainstream popularity and academic interest.

Besides this marked growth in public and academic valuations of speculative fiction, these novels also signal key shifts within feminism in the 1970s and 1980s. Specifically, Butler's texts mark a trend in feminist utopias away from radical feminism and toward intersectional theory and the broader consideration of intermingling identity categories. Butler's trilogy is the most radical representative of these developments. Her novels and this trilogy more specifically comment directly upon patriarchal social forces that distance subjects from power in ways unique to their combination of identity markers such as race, biological sex, gender, and sexuality among others. Though she stated, "I avoid all critical theory because I worry about it feeding into my work," her texts are informed by her experiences as a woman of color, a perspective brought further to the center of feminist thought during the 1980s by the development of intersectional theory (Potts 1996, 331).

Initiated in many ways by the Combahee River Collective's landmark "Black Feminist Statement," intersectional theory owes a great deal to that group's concept "horizontal oppressions," which refers to the differences dividing "women on the bases of gender, race, class and/or sexual orientation" (Mann 2012, 172). Starting in the 1980s, feminists marked by their non-normative races and sexualities among other factors felt themselves excluded from the centralized power of white women within mainstream feminism and developed this theory of differences. Critical race and feminist theorists such as Kimberlé Williams Crenshaw and Audre Lorde, for example, utilized intersectional theory to consider the unique experience of African American women. In key works such as Cherrie Moraga's *Loving in the War Years* (1983), Gloria Anzaldúa's *Borderlands/La Frontera: The New Mestiza* (1987), and the landmark anthology they edited together, *This Bridge Called My Back* (1981), Chicana feminists continued this work, bringing from the margins to the center the unique voices of women representing various races and sexualities. As a theoretical framework that recognizes the unique ways such disparate identity markers position individuals further from or closer to power, intersectional feminism added necessary complexity theretofore missing from feminist models. Regardless of Butler's level of interest in these developments in contemporary feminism at that time, her fiction reflects the lived, intersectional experiences of women of color and is therefore significant to both speculative fiction and feminist theory.

Her novels are uniquely groundbreaking in their centering of issues such as race, sexuality, and gender in relation to feminist theory and masculinities. Like Piercy's text, the first of these novels, *Dawn*, privileges the perspective of a woman of color, Lilith. She encounters and negotiates patriarchal masculinities linked with racism (presented as speciesism) in both a new society of aliens and among the survivors of a previous one, the contemporary United States. She, for example, is viewed by her alien captors, the Oankali, as easier to control due to her biological sex and as irrational due to her species (race) and is therefore tasked with awakening her fellow human survivors and convincing them to join the alien species, a role that results in her human counterparts marginalizing her as a traitor. A significant portion of her fellow human survivors, on the other hand, uniquely disparage her due to her identity, refusing to follow the leadership of a woman, and view her as tainted racially by what they view as her miscegenation with the Oankali. Through Lilith, Butler presents firsthand encounters with problematic masculinities and the ways patriarchy uniquely disempowers women of marginalized racial groups.

There exists, however, a time gap between this text and *Woman on the Edge of Time* and this divide is bridged by Butler's earlier novel *Wild Seed* (1980), upon which chapter 4 briefly focuses. Piercy's text, as L. Timmel Duchamp (2013) points out, shares a special kinship with Butler's novels in that it similarly utilizes the perspective of a woman of color and the tropes of science fiction to subtly present revolutionary feminist ideals (83). Like

Dawn, it utilizes a female narrator belonging to a marginalized racial group to illuminate for the reader the interlocking forces of oppression uniquely affecting such women in contemporary American society. What sets *Dawn* and *Wild Seed* apart from Piercy's earlier text are the ways Butler concludes her novels not with the radical destabilization of patriarchy but, instead, with the compromises and limited victories more closely reflecting the lived experiences of women of color.

Wild Seed focuses upon the conflict between a female protagonist, Anyanwu, a centuries-old African shapeshifter, and her male adversary, Doro, an African vampiric being who, due to the inability of those mortal bodies he possesses to sustain him for long, has for millennia bred, murdered, and inhabited the bodies of "his people." In this capacity, Doro acts as an extreme representation of patriarchal masculinity. It is significant that Butler ends her novel not with the destruction of Doro and, therefore, patriarchy but instead with a compromise that finds Anyanwu living with her subjugator as a person of special status. This departure from earlier feminist utopian narrative styles illustrates how, for Butler, "the feminist story isn't an all-or-nothing struggle; it isn't simply about overthrowing patriarchy. It's about understanding how oppression works in all its complexity and finding ways to negotiate with what can't in the particular situation be changed" (Duchamp 2013, 94). *Wild Seed* and *Dawn*, therefore, bridge the gap existing between Piercy's earlier novel, which focuses on the perspective of a woman of color who is able to significantly destabilize patriarchy, and the final novels of Butler's *Lilith's Brood* trilogy, *Adulthood Rites* and *Imago*, which center a host of diverse perspectives and further consider the commonality of compromise within the lives of people marginalized by the patriarchal economy.

The connections Butler highlights between patriarchal masculinities and the will to subordinate others is widened in the second novel of the series, *Adulthood Rites*. This novel is revolutionary in that it centers characters who, like women of color, are marginalized according to unique combinations of nonnormative genders, races, and sexualities. Centering a male protagonist (as Bryant and Le Guin do), Butler complicates this narrative approach by differentiating him by both gender, sexuality, and racial makeup. The first hybrid offspring of the human species of the novel and their alien counterparts, the Oankali, this son of Lilith, Akin, is uniquely positioned outside both societies and the masculinities they normalize. This possession of a hybrid racial identity that affords him unique experiences in both Oankali and human separatist polities compels him to rethink each nation and the masculinities each favors. By aligning her audience with a male character who experiences intersectionality due to his gender and race, Butler compels her readers to recognize the complex ways patriarchy works alongside racism to relocate nonnormative subjects—including men—to the societal margins. In addition, it marks her trilogy as a key text for materialist analyses of masculinity that recognize gender as socially situated and, therefore, susceptible to transformation. Her utilization of intersectional theory and challenges to essentialist ideals of radical feminism therefore add considerable strength to her criticism of contemporary American masculinities and those alternatives she posits as necessary for a feminist-informed utopia.

Utilizing the tools of science fiction to further explore race, gender, and their relationship to masculinities, Butler centers in her final novel of the series, *Imago*, another hybrid child of Lilith, Jodahs, who does not fit within the traditional gender binary. A member of the third Oankali gender, ooloi, it possesses both feminine and masculine traits. It, for example, performs traditional femininity in seeking to heal and connect with its human partners. It also proves susceptible to the temptations of patriarchal masculinities, consolidating power and control over others before ultimately rejecting these interests. Jodahs, representative of nonconforming gender identities, is the only hybrid ooloi and faces significant discrimination but is also capable of oppressing others. By presenting to her audience characters whose unique combinations of identity elements place them at distinct distances from societal power, Butler compels her readers to rethink masculinity as it relates to, in addition to misogyny, the oppression of others due to their genders, races, and sexualities.

In addition to her inclusion of topics related to the intersectional oppression of such subjects, she builds upon the non-essentialist themes of the earlier feminist writers included in this analysis. Through her male human and Oankali, male human-Oankali hybrid, and ooloi human-Oankali hybrid characters who all struggle to varying degrees in rejecting patriarchal masculinities, she presents a radically materialist account of gender and, more specifically, masculinity. Her extensive portrayals of patriarchal conceptions of manhood as socially situated and having a differentiated impact upon individuals according to their complex identities make *Lilith's Brood* a unique, significant work of contemporary feminist fiction.

The central argument chapter 4 presents, therefore, is that Butler's trilogy of novels, with their focus on the lived experiences of the marginalized, fantastical imagining of problematic masculinities across genders and societies, and interest in the intersectionality produced by patriarchy, significantly widen the scope of current discussions concerning manhood. They reflect intersectional feminist discussions in the 1980s in that they contain both "a critique of feminist essentialism" and "an analysis of multiple and simultaneous oppressions and their mutually constitutive features" (Mann 2012, 205). This foundation in intersectionality theory, therefore, enables more fruitful discussions about masculinity. *Lilith's Brood* highlights the broad impact traditional ideals of manliness have upon those marked *other* and the way these conceptions of gender work in concert with other oppressive ideologies such as racism and homophobia. By doing this, Butler presents to the reader myriad questions concerning the possibility of both developing and maintaining healthier masculinities. As an invaluable literary site for correctly framing toxic masculinities and mining new ideals of manliness grounded in feminist thought, it is vital to analyses of masculinity in speculative fiction.

The fifth chapter focuses upon N.K. Jemisin's *Broken Earth* novels, which demonstrate the continued mainstream success of feminist speculative fiction. Upon its release, *The Fifth Season* was nominated for the Nebula Award and World Fantasy Award for Best Novel and won the Hugo Award for Best Novel, making Jemisin the first African American to win this prestigious prize. Both the second novel in the series, *The Obelisk Gate*, and the final entry in the trilogy, *The Stone Sky*, were awarded the Hugo Award for Best Novel, making Jemisin the only writer to receive the award in three consecutive years. In addition, *The Stone Sky* garnered both the Nebula Award for Best Novel and the Locus Award for Best Fantasy Novel. Such widespread appreciation for the *Broken Earth* trilogy illuminates the continuing relocation of feminist utopian fiction from the margins to the mainstream and makes the series a valuable resource for reenvisioning masculinity in the twenty-first-century United States.

Signaling, like Butler's *Lilith's Brood* trilogy, a departure from the narrow focus of radical feminist texts upon the experiences of white women within the patriarchy, the novels making up Jemisin's series center characters traditionally placed on the margins of speculative fiction due to their race, sexuality, and gender among other identity markers. The *Broken Earth* trilogy, for example, continues the efforts of earlier feminist writers such as Marge Piercy to present female characters marginalized according to both their biological sex and racial makeup and the alterations to masculinities necessary for such individuals to flourish in an improved society. Building upon such efforts to trace how racism and sexism work in concert to distance women of color from power in the contemporary United States, Jemisin's novels outline, like those of Butler, how patriarchal masculinities must be destabilized to improve the lives of subjects experiencing intersectionality due also to their nonnormative gender identities. Focused upon the building of a better society, the *Broken Earth* trilogy acts as a recent, pivotal entry into the feminist utopian genre that seeks to further expand its interest in challenging the oppressive logics of patriarchy, racism, transphobia, and homophobia.

The central argument delineated in this final chapter is that Jemisin's trilogy marks a limited return of optimism to the feminist utopian genre in that, while presenting minor utopian polities riddled with compromise, they nevertheless emphasize as pivotal to the future of humankind hope-driven efforts to completely dismantle the patriarchy and its masculinities. As this chapter demonstrates, Jemisin continues the work of Bryant, Le Guin, Piercy, and Butler by presenting feminist critical utopias grounded in radically materialist conceptions of gender and, more specifically, masculinity. Providing only brief glimpses of improved societies, Jemisin's trilogy remains a crucial continuation of the feminist critical utopian trend since it, through such depictions of feminist-oriented polities and masculinities, "negates the negation of utopia" and offers her readers an optimistic vision not intentionally included in Butler's fiction (Moylan 1986, 10). As previously outlined, Butler's fiction and, more specifically, *Dawn* and *Wild Seed* are unique in that they conclude not with the radical destabilization of patriarchy but, instead, with the compromises and small victories echoing the lived experiences of women of color. Departing from Butler, Jemisin infuses in her feminist utopian texts an optimistic attitude toward the future and a hope for the comprehensive transformation of society through activism and revolution. While her utopias remain sober in their presentation of toxic masculinities and the patriarchy, they are unique in their signaling of an important return in feminist utopian fiction toward optimism and hopes for an improved society shaped in part by alternative conceptions of manhood.

The *Broke Earth* series is pivotal to ongoing discussions at the intersection of science fiction, masculinity studies, and critical race theory since it utilizes the tools of speculative and utopian fiction to emphasize the negative effects of traditional masculinities upon subjects possessing nonnormative racial, sexual, and gender identities. A successor of the feminist utopian fiction of Piercy and Butler, Jemisin adds considerable complexity to these topics, emphasizing the historical contextualization of patriarchal masculinities, the impact of patriarchy upon ecological systems, and the necessity of comprehensively deconstructing and replacing the patriarchy and its masculinities. Her trilogy illustrates the opportunities science fiction grants for imagining improved societies and masculinities and are crucial for discussions concerning the future of genre fiction and the continuing destabilizing of its historical focus upon heteronormative, white, male characters and authors.

Focused upon feminist utopias of the late twentieth and early twenty-first centuries as rich sources for developing alternative conceptions of manhood, *Alternative Masculinities in Feminist Speculative Fiction: A New Man* uniquely contributes to discussions of manliness and gender by tracing key changes within contemporary American science fiction. As it demonstrates, there was a significant repositioning of these authors from the periphery to the mainstream as speculative fiction gained newfound recognition within literary scholarship. Coinciding with this development was the proliferation of feminist utopian novels that both reflected and challenged radical feminism and brought new ideals of masculinity eventually to widespread audiences. Central to these challenges to radical feminism are their materialist presentations of masculinity and increasing interest in extending this non-essentialist attitude toward those like women of color whose subjugation by patriarchal masculinities is differentiated according to their identities. These novels therefore reveal both the harmful effects of patriarchal masculinities and the pathways by which men may realize and adopt better scripts of manliness. As *Alternative Masculinities in Feminist Speculative Fiction: A New Man* illustrates, such novels, in their presentation of the ideal feminist society, are increasingly important to discussions surrounding the so-called crisis of twenty-first-century American masculinities.

NOTES

1. In *Masculinities in Theory: An Introduction*, Todd Reeser (2010) notes the significance of analogies drawn between the nation and gender: "One might gender a nation by analogy with the gender of its leader, or a leader may act in a certain gendered manner in order to gender the nation by analogy. Conversely, if a leader's gender is seen as not ideal, the nation's gender may be a source of concern by extension" (173). Since, as Reeser further explains, the gender of a nation and its attending "cultural codings affect everyone in a nationally based context," national identity and gender shape and are in turn shaped by each other (171).

2. Keith Clark in *Black Manhood in James Baldwin, Ernest J. Gaines, and August Wilson* (2004) investigates, for example, how these African American writers present characters whose "notions of community, space, and healing-the lexicon of intimacy" (4) stand in opposition to hegemonic conceptions of black masculinity. Other literary critics have examined the relationship of masculinities to sexuality and class among other topics. In *Aging Masculinity in the American Novel* (2016), Alex Hobbs considers the intersection of masculinities with gerontology while Josef Benson in *Hypermasculinities in the Contemporary Novel* (2014) examines the influence of American expansionist ideals upon contemporary American conceptions of manhood.

3. Derived from comments given at the "Personal and the Political Panel" at the Second Sex Conference on September 29, 1979, in New York, Audre Lorde's widely cited "The Master's Tools Will Never Dismantle the Master's House" (1984) illuminates the tendency among white radical feminists to overlook or minimize the divergent experiences of women based upon their racial makeup. According to Lorde, "Difference is that raw and powerful connection from which our personal power is forged. As women, we have been taught either to ignore our differences, or to view them as causes for separation and suspicion rather than as forces for change" (112).

4. Awarded annually, the MacArthur "Genius Grant" is bestowed upon individuals noted for their "extraordinary originality and dedication in their creative pursuits and a marked capacity for self-direction" ("About the MacArthur Fellows Program").

Chapter 1

Recovering Men in Dorothy Bryant's
The Kin of Ata Are Waiting for You

The centering of male experience unites the first two novels upon which this analysis focuses, Dorothy Bryant's *The Kin of Ata Are Waiting for You* and Ursula K. Le Guin's *The Dispossessed*. *The Kin of Ata Are Waiting for You* is unique, however, in that it follows the gradual, positive transformation of a vile male protagonist who is both a murderer and a rapist. In this utopia, Bryant, therefore, presents the evils of traditional masculinities by center-ing a hyperviolent narrator and imagining the possibility of him adopting a feminist-informed conception of manliness. Bryant's novel acts as the start-ing point for this analysis because, while it is traditional in its centering of a male protagonist, it radically explores the underpinnings of social construc-tionist theories of gender by presenting the conversion to feminist values of a repellent traditionally masculine character to whom audiences are utterly unsympathetic.

A significant source of power for *The Kin of Ata Are Waiting for You* and its commentary on masculinity is its use of the utopian genre. In utilizing the conventions of utopian writing such as the journey to an isolated, ideal soci-ety as a backdrop to this radical male conversion narrative, Bryant contrasts twentieth-century American masculinities and their alternatives. Since mes-sengers from utopia such as the protagonist are charged with presenting to the outside world the benefits of non-patriarchal performances of manhood, the novel predicates the proliferation of new gender conceptions upon the acts of transformed men. Bryant, therefore, escapes what is often identified as a failure of utopian writing, its adoption of ahistorical, static qualities.[1] The unique power of this feminist novel is derived from its presentation, through this framing of the utopia as a powerful dream experienced by citizens of the patriarchal dystopia, of the better society as possible and dependent upon

the actions of men in the present and, more specifically, their adoption of
feminist-oriented masculinities.

The utopias imagined by feminist writers such as Bryant make up an egalitarian response to problematic, misogynistic, earlier imagined polities. As
Brian Attebery (2002) outlines, contemporary feminist utopias act as intaglio
versions of these patriarchal predecessors, meaning that "the relationship
between" them is "not one of simple contradiction but of reversing values
while retaining the basic configuration" (116). Attebery demonstrates this
phenomenon by contrasting an earlier patriarchal utopia, Robert Heinlein's
Space Cadet (1948), with Suzy McKee Charnas's *Walk to the End of the
World and Motherlines* (1974), a feminist dystopia published three years after
Bryant's novel. While the polities of these texts are similarly "ritualized, hierarchical, homosocial, legalistic" and "misogynistic" (Attebery 2002, 121), the
nation of Heinlein's text is presented as a utopia while that of Charnas's novel
is portrayed as a nightmarish dystopia. Such an intaglio effect similarly exists
in the relationship between the male characters inhabiting feminist utopias
and those depicted in earlier, patriarchal speculative texts. The alternative
masculinities Bryant imagines in her novel represent a significant departure
from the traditional gender ideologies of earlier speculative fiction and this
radical reconceptualization of manhood is fundamental to her feminist utopia.

Part of Bryant's success in subverting traditional assumptions of gender
is due to her drawing upon another subgenre of science fiction: the lost
world narrative. Specifically, she utilizes the form of these earlier texts but
supplants their patriarchal values. Since such novels, for example, valorize
imperialistic, patriarchal men who triumph over the other identified by marginalized identity markers such as race and sex, Bryant radicalizes the lost
world tradition by presenting a similar character, her unnamed protagonist,
but causing him to undergo a conversion process away from patriarchy.
Male characters in earlier novels such as what is often considered the first
of this subgenre, H. Rider Haggard's *King Solomon's Mines* (1887), are traditionally masculine, exploiting forgotten lands and their native people for
socioeconomic gain. The protagonist of Haggard's novel, Allan Quatermain,
and his fellow adventurers, for example, triumph over the indigenous
female-worshipping population in this forgotten land and return home at
the conclusion of the text with a substantial fortune. Though he initially has
similar goals, Bryant's narrator, on the other hand, returns from Ata without
any fortune; instead, he gains a sense of wholeness made possible by the
adoption of those masculinities favored in the utopia. This alteration of the
lost world hero archetype signals, therefore, a departure from the norms of
capitalistic patriarchy, which values success within the free market through
self-reliance and disconnection from society. In defiance of this gender
script, Bryant's protagonist learns to serve his fellow subjects, to build a

community not predicated upon hierarchy and the exploitation of others, and, through writing a book about his experiences, to advocate for feminist-oriented masculinities. It is this role of the protagonist as a once murderous rapist and a current proselytizer for alternative ideals of manhood that distinguishes *The Kin of Ata Are Waiting for You* from other contemporary feminist utopias.

Bryant presents her unnamed male narrator's role as an activist through the incorporation of a framing device. More specifically, *The Kin of Ata Are Waiting for You* is presented as a didactic, nonfiction text written by the protagonist. In this way, it acts as a warning crafted by a recovering patriarch for misogynistic men and guidelines for how they may escape the toxicity of traditional masculinities. Though addressing all readers regardless of their sex, race, and so on, the writer, in looking back at his violent and misogynistic past, tacitly acknowledges how this work will significantly impact like-minded men: "think that if I, a murderer whose murders were the least of his crimes, if a man like me could find himself in Ata and could re-learn the dream, and further, could glimpse for a moment the reality behind the dream . . . then how much easier it might be for you" (220). Previously, a well-paid and famous author of sexist fiction now convicted of murder, the narrator utilizes his literary skills, along with both his former social influence and current notoriety, to spread a message condemning patriarchy and its masculinities. In this way, writing is central to Bryant's utopian novel and the finished product, the didactic text the protagonist hopes to distribute, acts as a rejection and replacement of his earlier, misogynistic publications.

The protagonist's project of educating men through his writing aligns with Lorde's (1984) solution to how the master's house—in this case, patriarchy—may be disassembled (112). Importantly, Lorde, in her comments made at the Second Sex Conference in 1979, condemns attempts to achieve equality for women that ignore the unique experiences and identities differentiating them. She accuses radical feminists of reproducing the faults of the patriarchy and being therefore ill-equipped to attack it. She notes, for example, a tendency among white radical feminists to expect women of different races, sexualities, and so forth to teach them about their experiences and needs. Lorde draws a parallel between this practice of expecting "women of Color to educate white women—in the face of tremendous resistance—as to our existence, our differences, our relative roles in our joint survival" and that of men placing the responsibility upon women "to stretch across the gap of male ignorance and to educate" (Lorde 1984, 113) them. Bryant's narrator uses writing to combat his own previous misogynistic fiction and to educate other patriarchal men about the need for transformation. By presenting a manifesto of a misogynist's conversion, Bryant offers a model of a way to ask men to assume the responsibility for presenting alternative masculinities.

The protagonist writes this account of his experiences to compel his male readers to, among other things, decrease their estimation of language as the optimal tool for recording reality and to consider other, traditionally feminine sources of knowledge such as intuition. As a result of his visit to Ata, he learns to no longer emphasize language as a tool capable of accurately and conclusively symbolizing reality and to accept knowledge gained via seemingly contradictory information. Desiring, for example, to draft a record of dreams commonly recited by the Atans, the protagonist illustrates this trait of hegemonic men and struggles against his utopian counterparts, rejecting their acceptance of such dreams as contradictory and mutable. Clinging to his patriarchal belief that language may accurately decipher and record truth, he divides dreams into categories such as "Great Dreams" and "Sabbath Dreams" but soon recognizes the shortcomings of his approach. Such a recording, he discovers from studying a similarly ill-fated past attempt, are liable to cause disputes concerning which are "the best versions of the dreams, and as to whether the mark," or series of linguistic symbols he has developed, gives "the correct meaning" (201). This previous approach disallowed change to transform these cultural artifacts: "'even more serious was the effect that writing had upon the words of the story. It froze them. People began to mistake the word for the unknown behind it. Instead of expressing the unknown, the carved world became a thing between the people and the unknown which it should symbolize.' 'All was'" ill-fitted for dreaming, it was "donagdeo" (201). In this way, Bryant illuminates the inadequacy of patriarchal language, which controls and dominates, and presents as alternative dreams, which are fluid and flexible. A central message of *The Kin of Ata Are Waiting for You*, therefore, is that traditional approaches to manhood and their commitment to language and communication as tools for symbolizing reality are problematic in their desire to control and stabilize such experienced phenomena.

This patriarchal use of language also does not allow for intuitive knowledge gained via seemingly contradictory recitations. As pointed out in the novel by one of the residents of the utopia, Augustine, such dreams "are all true" (168). Linguistic methods of recording such intuitive truths, on the other hand, "'are all untrue, as words are always untrue'" (168). Such a conception of language directly opposes its valuation by hegemonic masculinities. As a writer, the narrator is a patriarchal male whose socioeconomic success is tied to his presentation of traditional gender ideologies as fact in his novels. In this encounter with utopian masculinities, he demonstrates the tendency of the traditional man to seek power through language by rejecting recognitions of it as faulty and problematic. The reliance upon the written word as a means of accurately controlling and fully understanding reality both causes and reinforces the evils of traditional masculinities. The narrator's eventual understanding of the limitations of language is revealed in the conclusion of the novel when he comments on the text he has produced: "I have had to leave out many things, and even those that I have told may be misunderstood, told, as they are, in the faulty medium of words, and frozen on paper" (220). Adopting an alternative, feminist-informed conception of manhood, he rejects patriarchal emphases on language as a comprehensive tool for fully symbolizing and therefore controlling reality. While recognizing these limitations of writing, he utilizes it and composes a manifesto that functions as a bridge, offering his experience to the unenlightened, locked into traditional gender roles.

In producing this instructive text, Bryant's protagonist locates helpful tools that, though imperfect, may indeed assist in the dismantling of patriarchy through the spreading of a new masculine consciousness. Donna Fancourt identifies within feminist utopias the need for altered states of consciousness in order to achieve utopia. Fancourt (2002) contends that such "altered states, which include dreams, trances, meditation and hallucinations, are intrinsically related to the texts' visions of feminist utopianism as rooted in creating a new spiritual and political consciousness" (94). Her analysis demonstrates the need for new conceptions of manhood in these utopias since "the necessary shift in consciousness that is intrinsic to" these works is represented by a "movement away from an emphasis on sexual difference, and towards a society that promotes connection with others" (109), a value not traditionally identified as masculine. Recognizing the limitations of language and the written word, Bryant's narrator progresses with the hope that his message may resonate and bring about such a reassessment of masculinities among men occupying the contemporary American patriarchy. In this way, a source of power propelling *The Kin of Ata Are Waiting for You* is its focus on a male conversion story through which a former hegemonic man critiques traditional masculinities and offers to his readers improved, feminist alternatives.

Bryant's decision to create a male character who has committed violent, vile actions enhances the message of her novel concerning the possibility of transforming masculinity. A grotesque misogynist who, while fleeing his home after murdering his partner, Connie, transports to Ata, the narrator is utilized by Bryant to illustrate how even the most destructive forms of masculinity may be challenged and destabilized. The conversion of the protagonist begins in the utopia when he, mistaking his own visions during one of the Atan ceremonies as real treasures, threatens the utopian people with exposure to the outside world if they do not allow him to depart with what he perceives as their valuables. During an argument concerning the existence of this treasure, the narrator causes an elderly utopian citizen, Tran, to lose his balance and subsequently die. It is this second murderous act that precipitates the narrator toward a transformation that in total lasts almost twenty years (a more accurate approximation is not available since the narrator gradually loses track of time in the nonlinear, anti-patriarchal utopia).

Fleeing to an isolated hilltop due to his fear of retribution for this murder, he undergoes a psychological change that begins with his physical body, lacking food and water: "I spent three days this way. By the third day I was feverish and coughing, trembling constantly" (87). His physical state impacts his psychological condition, producing visions of those people such as Tran whom he has harmed as a result of his subscription to patriarchal masculinities. In conversation with an Atan woman, Augustine, he recognizes his toxic, traditionally masculine qualities: "I killed the old one. Before that I killed a woman. But these murders are the least of my crimes. I have never done anything good. I am an empty man. Not a real person. I gave away what was real in me long ago. I sold it. For nothing. I am nothing. I am not fit to live" (89). This confession signals the transformation central to the novel: the gradual conversion of the narrator from traditional destructive masculinities to their feminist-oriented alternatives.

This incremental adoption of new masculinities is completed at the novel's conclusion. Faced with the opportunity to avoid atoning for his actions via legal means, he ignores his lawyer's advice, rejects the temptation to levy his privileged position as a hegemonic male to escape punishment, and confesses to murdering Connie. Able to treat Ata and the masculinities it espouses as merely a dream, he ultimately maintains his belief in both Ata and its conceptions of gender and utilizes his position as a famous male writer and murderer to spread awareness of new perspectives on gender and society. Bryant's novel, as a testament of the murderous narrator to his audience about the utopian polity and its masculinities, is addressed to an audience he hopes are open to the possibility of such gender reconfigurations:

> Do not judge these words by the man who writes them. Listen, not to my words, but to the echo they evoke in you, and obey that echo. And think that if I, a murderer whose murders were the least of his crimes, if a man like me could find myself in Ata and could re-learn the dream, and further, could glimpse for a moment the reality behind the dream . . . then how much easier it might be for you. You have only to want It, to believe in It, and tonight, when you close your eyes, you can begin your journey. The kin of Ata are waiting for you. Nagdeo. (220)

In its ending, the novel therefore charges its audience of contemporary American readers with the responsibility of relearning a dream of a complete rejection of traditional patriarchy. Through the positioning of the novel as the supposedly real testament of a hegemonic masculine male to the American public, Bryant connects her utopia to the real world of twentieth-century patriarchy.

Such a connection is furthered by Bryant's delineating of toxic qualities of twentieth-century American masculinities. These qualities, which the male narrator exhibits, include, besides the aforementioned reliance upon language as a stable epistemic tool: support of societal networks of power based upon sexuality, race, gender, class, and biological sex; and negative valuations of male emotional health care through dream analysis, mystical experiences, and other approaches similarly labeled non-masculine. By imagining the positive alteration of these traits possessed initially by the traditionally masculine protagonist, Bryant presents to her audience a road map for challenging and replacing contemporary American ideals of manhood. Importantly, *The Kin of Ata Are Waiting for You* notes the limitations of such a path toward healthier masculinities. More specifically, Bryant illuminates for her readers the relationship of masculinity to the nation and the necessity to transform the socioeconomic systems of a polity for its gender ideologies to truly be improved.

Since its publication, *The Kin of Ata Are Waiting for You* has been analyzed by critics as in part a tract for political and social change. Utopias such as Bryant's novel necessitate such scholarly approaches since any work of this genre "must at least apply to, if not directly concern itself with, the institutions of persons" and the process of imagining "utopia . . . is from the outset to reconstruct human culture" (Barr 1983, 1). Many scholars, for example, recognize in feminist utopias calls for remodeling society that deal with key topics including separate spheres of life and work based upon gender, the abolishment of the nuclear family, methods for negotiating problematic citizens, the validity of embodied knowledge, and new forms of political order.[2] Lyman Tower Sargent (1983), for example, situates Bryant within a group of feminist writers such as Ursula K. Le Guin and Marge Piercy who imagine collectivist anarchies that remodel societies so they are both nonhierarchical and communal (5). As Joanna Russ (1980) delineates, Bryant's novel and those of her contemporaries such as Russ herself are "explicit about economics and politics, sexually permissive, demystifying about biology, emphatic about the necessity for female bonding, concerned with children . . . non-urban, classless, communal, relatively peaceful while allowing room for female range and female self-defense, and serious about the emotional and physical consequences of violence" (15). In an analysis of contemporary feminist utopias including *The Kin of Ata Are Waiting for You*, Lyman Tower Sargent (1983) notes that it "may not be quite impossible, but men in particular are going to have to change dramatically if a healthy society is to be possible" (30). Bryant's materialist portrayal of gender suggests the need to transform both masculinities and the nation influencing them. A crucial step in this transformative plan Bryant imagines is, in addition to the adoption of new masculinities, the challenging of the patriarchal economy.

As a capitalistic patriarchy, the contemporary United States depends upon a hierarchy or *patriarchal order* "organized by sex, race, etc." and this system of power "generates and distributes the flows of power within both social and institutional organizations," a process identified as the *patriarchal economy* (Buchbinder 2012, 69). The contemporary American patriarchal order is delineated by Bryant in the novel with the protagonist situated among its higher echelons. A central source of his power, besides his race and biological sex, is his loyalty to this phallocentric society's ideologies of sexuality. A purveyor of novels of "obscene urbanity" focused upon "ruthless, indestructible" male spies and with "equal parts of sex and violence," he acts as a cultural influence, taking part in the patriarchal economy by reinforcing heterosexual, misogynistic ideologies that view sex as a site of power and control (25). To return to Todd Reeser's (2010) theorization of the *gendered nation* outlined in the introduction to my analysis, "cultural codings affect everyone in a nationally based context" (171). As a producer through his fiction of problematic, patriarchal cultural codings concerning the masculine and feminine, the protagonist works at the intersection of the nation and gender and is rewarded for his representations of gender through increased power within the patriarchal order. Importantly, Bryant further illuminates these connections between the nation, gender, and writing in the contemporary United States by highlighting very real examples of American male writers who, like her protagonist, benefit immensely from their production of traditional cultural codings of gender.

Bryant, for example, draws key parallels between the fiction produced by her narrator and Norman Mailer's *An American Dream* (1965). The protagonist of Mailer's text, like the heroes populating the works of Bryant's protagonist, is violent and dominates those women with whom he comes into contact. Having murdered his wife, Stephen Rojack enjoys sex with several women, including a maid and nightclub singer, as he dodges the police and eventually makes a small fortune gambling in Las Vegas and escapes the country. Mailer presents in Rojack a hegemonic, masculine male hero who, like those characters populating the fiction of Bryant's protagonist, appeals to a patriarchal readership. The anti-feminist content of *An American Dream* reflects Mailer's attitudes toward women and his violent treatment of them during his life. By imagining a protagonist who initially possesses patriarchal views similar to those of Mailer but who encounters and is transformed by feminist masculinities, Bryant condemns male writers such as Mailer while positing that even they may be transformed by new ideals of manhood.

A significant similarity Bryant draws between her unnamed narrator and male writers such as Mailer is the way they profit from the patriarchal economy. The achievements of Bryant's narrator, for example, reveal his attitude toward sex as a social function by which men in power may be rewarded:

"When the book hit the top of the best seller lists, I left my wife. I turned out four more of them, released them one a year, signed film contracts, and at thirty was rich and famous" (26). In this way, he exemplifies Michael Kimmel's (2006) *self-made man* by measuring his worth by his "accumulated wealth and status" (137). Like other male writers such as William S. Burroughs, John Updike, and Norman Mailer, the narrator consolidates social influence and economic power through his reproduction and proliferation of misogynistic ideals in his writing. As outlined by Bryant, sex functions alongside wealth and popularity as a reward for the self-made men of this patriarchal, capitalistic polity and is utilized to dominate others situated further from power, namely women.

A significant portion of the narrator's tract, detailing his lengthy conversion process, is his gradual rejection of capitalistic, traditionally masculine interests in accumulated power and wealth. Outlining again the connection between the nation and gender, Bryant, through her protagonist, presents the incremental change of a man formerly living within a capitalistic patriarchy. Before his conversion to Ata's anti-capitalist values, the narrator demonstrates his interest in gaining further social power in two ways: seeking to colonize and exploit the utopia through contact with the outside world and attempting to rob the utopia of precious stones he notices in their ceremonies. He describes this first effort, typical of the traditionally masculine man, remarking how "it was easy to talk about bringing the blessings of so-called civilization to Ata. Ata would probably gain a jet-strip, a gambling casino and a set of slums from which these people could go out each day to serve the tourists" (75). Bryant, in this way, again connects normative American conceptions of masculinity, as presented in the narrator, to capitalism and economic exploitation. Beyond this strategy for colonizing Ata, the protagonist seeks to regain his position in the capitalistic patriarchy, albeit under an alias, via the appropriation of jewels he believes are used in their spiritual rituals. "My real plan was to get possession of the precious stones and metals they used in their rituals and return to the world with a new name, a new identity and plenty to live on for the rest of my life" (75). He values individualism, his own welfare and profits over others, and the possibility of upward socioeconomic mobility due to his identity makeup and assets he intends to accumulate through the exploitation of others. Over time, however, he recognizes the value of serving others and living without the drive for power and control. Through his conversion narrative, he presents to his audience the evils of patriarchal capitalism and the need to transform both the socioeconomic system and masculinities of the contemporary United States.

An important aspect of this conversion, as the protagonist emphasizes for his audience, is his realization that the same patriarchal economy providing him power due to his identity distances others from power in unique ways based upon their own complex identities. During his initial interactions with Augustine, the narrator, still subscribing to traditional masculinities, views her as subhuman. Augustine possesses "Nordic features and blue eyes" (19), she is "black, not just brown but almost a true black" (12) and this bodily difference from normalized racial markers is utilized by the traditionally masculine man, the narrator, to dehumanize her. His transformation is later noted by his understanding of how the patriarchal economy produces oppression according to the same logic he once followed. When, more than a decade later, Augustine is chosen to leave Ata to minister to those who have forgotten their utopian origin, her fellow Atans mourn the marginalization and domination she is likely to experience. The narrator, having by this time adopted the egalitarian masculinities of Ata, recognizes more overtly the nature and logic of the subordination she is destined to experience: "I thought of Augustine— black, female, in that world run by men like me" (187). Augustine does experience marginalization, isolated from social and economic power during her travels around "the world on her knees, scrubbing floors of the powerful" and "succoring the oppressed" (193). Augustine, the protagonist understands, experiences intersectional oppression and this is due to both her biological sex and race. As elaborated upon by Sally Robinson (2000), subjectivity is "inevitably grounded in the relations of power that structure a given society" and such "relations of power are embodied in persons whose differential relationships to normativity are registered, in large part, by the evidence of visible, bodily difference" (3). Alternative masculinities are posited by Bryant and her narrator as necessary for transforming both traditionally masculine men such as the narrator and those racist, intersectional societies from which he originates.

As the unnamed narrator outlines for the readers he hopes to convert, the patriarchal economy must also be dismantled since it grants the hegemonic man special opportunities to regain his socioeconomic standing should he lose it. Upon returning from Ata and being treated in a hospital for his wounds while a future trial date looms, the protagonist is confronted by his lawyer with the possibility of using his patriarchal power to avoid punishment. Recognizing the importance of public opinion, his lawyer, Spanger, reviews newspaper publications covering the case and happily informs the protagonist that his injuries have caused temporary public sympathy. Surveying these newspapers himself, the narrator notes an "underlying flavor of envy and admiration" (213), revealing the violent, phallocentric climate of the nation. In addition, he notes the intersection of capitalism and patriarchy, commenting on how newspaper opinions of his case must continue to diversify in order to maintain profit: "to sell newspapers, it was expedient to be somewhat more sympathetic to me now" (214). Such outside aid, likely unavailable to subjects further distanced from power in the patriarchal order, increases the likelihood that he may further reap the benefits of his socioeconomic position if declared innocent: "But I knew that after I got through the hearing, if there were not enough evidence to try me, there would be dozens of 'friends' and scores of women, just as there had been before . . . only a few weeks before. And I would be more famous than ever. And there would be more money. And any trash I wrote would sell, for at least the next three years, until a new sensation was found" (215). In ultimately rejecting the option of blaming Connie's murder on an unknown intruder and possibly escaping punishment, he foregoes the socioeconomic rewards allocated to hegemonic men within the capitalistic patriarchy. Through the narrator's experiences, which he presents to his readers as a warning, Bryant identifies a key threat to feminist activism: the ability of men to utilize their social power, using money and culture, to reinforce the patriarchal order.

Focusing upon this gender order, the novel initially outlines the mutually constitutive relationship between traditional masculinities and the capitalistic patriarchy before contrasting it with the alternative ideals of manhood found within the collectivist anarchy of Ata. Influencing and, in turn, influenced by the utopia's radical conceptions of manhood, this societal network of power, unlike the patriarchal economy, cultivates equality regardless of biological sex, gender, and race among other factors. According to Lyman Tower Sargent (1983), Bryant's utopia, like those of Le Guin and Piercy, presents "a new anarchism more concerned with affective than economic relationships or, to use slightly different terminology, with reproductive or nurturant rather than productive relationships" (8). These feminist utopias, he points out, "emphasize that freedom and equality go together; they are not separate or separable" (30). *The Kin of Ata Are Waiting for You* presents equality as central to the feminist utopia and absent from its capitalistic, patriarchal alternative. The novel illuminates how these divergent polities shape masculinities that reflect these contrasting attitudes toward equality. Through his male conversion story, the protagonist offers clear objectives for transforming the masculinities and socioeconomic systems of the United States in order to introduce egalitarianism to them.

The importance of these goals is emphasized by Bryant's narrator through his in-depth recounting of his former role as a violent and subjugating man of power. At the opening of the text, the protagonist delineates the manner by which he, equipped with his former, traditionally masculine views on sexuality, destroyed the lives of his female partners before his conversion. Unable to provide any details about the reason for the altercation between himself and his partner, Connie, he reflects instead upon those details related to her appearance upon which his mind was focused, reducing her to the status of a faulty commodity: "She went on screaming at me. I sat on the edge of the bed and watched her. Her breasts were full, but they hung loose, like bags over a torso on which I could count every rib. The pubic hair told the true color of her bleached head: mousy brown. Her skin, breaking through her smeared make-up, was blotchy" (1). When he at last takes note of what she is communicating, the reader is made to understand that Connie recognizes this denial of her humanity: "'I exist!' she was screaming. 'I'm a person!'" (1). Desiring only to control and maintain power over her by reducing her again to a commodity, the protagonist rejects this claim of personhood: "I yawned and looked at the clock. Four a.m. 'No,' I told her. 'I invented you, or you tried to invent yourself, right out of my latest book'" (1). His role as a self-made man empowered and made rich by his writing of exploitative novels informs his view of Connie as a mere sexual object. His horrendous acts including the murder of Connie reflect the fantasies he harbored of male domination, which are also present in the fiction he produces. Prior to his transformation, he, for example, views his partner as a mere production of the male imagination with features—"long legs, small waist, full breasts half covered by tossed blonde hair" (1)—typical of the characters from his books. This dehumanizing comment enhances the violent pitch of the altercation and the narrator ultimately chokes Connie to death. Bryant, therefore, presents in her protagonist a changed man reflecting upon his former hegemonic self and noting for his readers the ways his past acts of extreme violence including murder represented a means of control within sexual relationships and are directly linked to the patriarchal masculinities he once promulgated in his writing.

In recounting this scene, the narrator, and Bryant through him, highlights the ways capitalism and patriarchy reinforce each other. Specifically, Bryant's opening scene reveals how women are commodified and dehumanized in a capitalistic patriarchy. Through this comparison of Connie to fictional characters and the narrator's quick use of violence to silence her, the reader is made to understand how intrinsic to patriarchy is the desire to subjugate others. To him, their personhood is as valid as that of the fictional, female characters he develops in the misogynistic stories he composes for profit. This desire to overpower and control women is a key aspect of dystopian masculinities that the protagonist urges his audience to condemn.

The narrator adds to this plea by recounting to his readers his relationship to an Atan female, Augustine, that was crucial to his transformation. Through the unnamed narrator's recollection, Bryant emphasizes the toxicity of American rape culture. As described by sociologists Julia Schwendinger and Herman Schwendinger and feminist theorist Susan Brownmiller in their analyses of rape myths in the 1970s, "the cultural mythology surrounding rape" at the time served "to perpetuate male sexual aggression against women. This was thought to be achieved by simultaneously blaming the victim, absolving the perpetrator, and minimizing or justifying the aggression" (Payne et al. 1999, 28). As Bryant's narrator reflects, his reaction directly after assaulting Augustine was to minimize his attack and absolve himself of responsibility by asserting falsely she likely enjoyed the encounter. Specifically, when Augustine communicates a disinterest in his advances, he responds, "Probably she liked it a little rough, I thought, as I pushed her down to the ground and yanked up her tunic. There were stretch marks on her belly. 'You're not exactly a virgin,' I mumbled. I pulled the tunic up beyond her breasts. It covered her face, and she lay still" (54). As is made clear by this passage, he attempts to sanitize the nature of this attack in two ways: by justifying his actions on the false premise that Augustine "liked it a little rough" (54) and asserting that, since there are signs that she has given birth in the past, this rape is somehow relatively inconsequential. Placing on the periphery of this scene, Atans shocked and silent and centering Augustine, described as lying "quite still, her face still covered by her tunic, her body quivering" (54), Bryant clarifies the disgust with which the reader should contemplate the narrator's actions. In this way, Bryant presents to her audience the voice of a narrator who, once vile and hypermasculine, previously subscribed to rape myths prevalent in the contemporary United States.

In these passages, Bryant also presents through her didactic protagonist a warning concerning the toxic tendency of traditional masculinities to commit such brutalizing acts to seek revenge against those who destabilize masculinity. During the aforementioned scene of assault, the protagonist is suddenly made aware that they are surrounded by Atans who, instead of preventing this rape, stand by observing his brutality. In response, the narrator ceases his assault and is made to feel "a wave of shame" but is only able to respond in a way common to the traditionally masculine male, with "anger, sickening anger" (55). This shame challenges the valorization of control and power typical of traditional masculinities since it originates in the overwhelming, negative response of a better, feminist society to the patriarchal actions of the narrator. In response, the narrator recommits himself to his conventional gender role. Accordingly, he opts to view the silence of these onlookers as a form of mockery and decides to seek revenge, tellingly not on these bystanders but on Augustine: "I wanted revenge. I went out to the fields. I followed and I watched until she went off by herself, to one of the fallow fields. I waited while she dug a small hole, crouched over it, then filled the hole with dirt. Then I grabbed her, threw her down and rammed myself into her. I came, like a sneeze without pleasure or relief. And I felt I had lost something again" (56). Attempting unsuccessfully to restabilize his masculine identity through revenge, he finds a growing emptiness that, as Bryant's novel demonstrates, is endemic to traditional masculinities. His recognition of this emptiness, caused by patriarchal masculinities and exposed through the silent rebuke of the Atan people, propels the changes he undergoes through the recognition of the instability of patriarchal masculinities and the adoption of new ideals of manhood that eventually produce healing.

Bryant also highlights through the narrator's relationship to Augustine connections existing between twentieth-century American capitalism and the masculinities it normalizes. Following a gender script echoing the capitalistic patriarchy of which he is a subject, the contemporary United States, the protagonist sees Augustine—similar to his estimation of Connie—as a commodity that may provide relief through its consumption: "I knew who I wanted, and if things were so free and easy here, I could at least enjoy her, and probably think a lot straighter afterward" (52). The narrator's capitalistic, patriarchal perspective leads to and justifies his intention to dominate and control his sexual partners whom he views as mere objects similar to the products sold on the free market. She demonstrates this connection through the narrator's treatment of Augustine as a sexual object he "could at least enjoy" (52) and not as a person with whom he could experience mutual pleasure. In addition, his comment that "things were so free and easy" (52) in Ata reveals not merely the openness of the culture regarding sexuality but the freedom of using those commodities in which the protagonist is most interested, women. Bryant, through her radically transformed narrator, exposes the damaging intersection of capitalism and patriarchy and the cost to women of such brutalizing conceptions of manhood produced by these hierarchical ideologies.

As the narrator recounts to his audience, his new conception of masculinity involves an egalitarian approach to sex that replaces the earlier, violent attitude of the narrator endemic to hegemonic masculinities. He describes the impact of his new conceptions of manhood upon his views of sex via a memory with Augustine: "Our love-making was a kind of ceremony, like a stamp or a seal upon something. I entered her almost immediately, and as I felt myself coming, I heard a low crooning sigh from her that told me she was with me. Then we lay together on our side, her arms and legs enveloping me, our eyes looking straight into one another's. This was a ritual to cancel out the rape, a purified re-enactment" (107). This positive, empathetic attitude toward sexual partners initially causes discomfort for the protagonist due to the ways it destabilizes traditional conceptions of manhood: "She was not an adversary, nor was she simply a body to be aroused by prescribed techniques to prescribed responses. I was not fucking her. And I was afraid" (110). Afraid of his newfound vulnerability but choosing to continue his adoption of these new ideals of manhood, the protagonist opts for deeper levels of intimacy. As a result, he benefits from a meaningful connection to another human being. Through her protagonist, Bryant therefore portrays the transformation of the most violent type of patriarchal man whose previous approach to sex was one of abject violence and domination. Instead, this new man values the connection he feels with his partner, focuses upon the mutual pleasure and enjoyment of each person involved, and calls for a new attitude among men concerning sex and sexual partners. He—a once murderous rapist—represents the possibility Bryant imagines of transformed men challenging their fellow men to reject patriarchy and the exploitation of women.

Such a rebuke between men necessitates the recognition that the nation must also be transformed for new masculinities to flourish. An important quality of Ata the narrator advocates for in the United States, for example, is the societal equality of women. In his tract, the protagonist outlines such a need for change by presenting the egalitarian aspects of Ata related to the sexes. Instead of placing the responsibility of food preparation upon women, for example, the men of Ata exemplify a polity that values service over individualism and selfishness by sharing these responsibilities. Prior to his transformation, the narrator recognizes this societal norm when he selfishly seeks to take as much food offered to him as possible: "I could not resist reaching into the pot and feeding myself five or six handfuls. No one stopped me, but I was immediately surrounded by people with pots, offering me bits from their fingers. I was being indulged, like a greedy child" (100). Understanding that such an approach to food preparation and distribution is labeled immature by his utopian counterparts, he learns to serve food to his fellow citizens through his incremental adoption of the new masculinities of Ata.

Shaped by the feminist polity, these new masculinities reflect the standards Cheris Kramarae and Jana Kramer identify as common to the feminist utopias of Sally Miller Gearhart's *The Wanderground* (1979), Marge Piercy's *Woman on the Edge of Time*, and *The Kin of Ata are Waiting for You*. According to Kramarae and Kramer, there are three "values in which these societies are firmly rooted: mutual respect, personal responsibility, and trust in others." These qualities describe the new masculinities Bryant and other contemporary feminist authors present as necessary "to produce a culture without power differences" (Kramarae and Kramer 1987, 37). The narrator initially, for example, estimates incorrectly that, due to his position as a white male, he must be a prized person from whom food may be received: "I supposed that they considered it a special honor to be fed by me, until I noticed that they made the same gesture when a small child stopped feeding himself and held out food toward others" (32). What he finds is that the utopia is shaped in part by the favoring of masculinities that serve others and do not develop hierarchies of power and subjugation according to, among other identity elements, biological sex. Central to his conversion is the adoption of these values held by the feminist society and its alternative masculinities.

In his presentation of the ideal nation as it relates to sex, the narrator highlights for his audience how such a lack of a patriarchal order manifests in the society's handling of childbirth and parenting. As a collectivist anarchy, this feminist social system breaks down any separation of labor by sex.

As the protagonist witnesses, these citizens attempt to share the pain of the final experience the mother must undergo predominantly alone before sharing the responsibility of raising the child with society, childbirth: "We try to take some of the pain on ourselves, to share it. We try to give some of our strength for the hard work. We try to make the girl feel happy that, once she has done this, she need no longer carry the burden of the child alone" (149). The centrality of these utopian masculinities is made clear also in this ceremony by the presence of multiple men, the potential fathers of the child, who assist the mother without need to officially determine or recognize paternal lines. Free of patriarchal masculinities, she, instead, is "constantly attended by the fathers of the child" (150–151), a social norm that clearly delineates the need for new masculinities to deconstruct the gender order of patriarchy. The social norms of parenting and childbirth in the feminist utopia reflect and are shaped by the nation's lack of hierarchies organized according to, among other identity elements, biological sex.

This absence of the patriarchal order produces widespread effects throughout the feminist society. As outlined by Lucy Freibert (1983), the feminist utopias of which Ata is an exemplary model are egalitarian across a spectrum of aspects: they "dispense with private property but provide rooms of their own for everyone. They also furnish food, clothing, education, medical care, travel, and recreation at common expense" and offer dining and child-care facilities that "extend parenting responsibilities to all community members" (68). As the narrator outlines for his audience, the economy of Ata therefore represents the feminist ideal nation and this polity requires the adoption of masculinities favoring the abolishment of power networks based upon sex.

In addition to such calls to dismantle institutionalized misogyny, the narrator presents to his readership the necessity of opposing the gender binary and, like the Atan culture for which he advocates, presents an ideal alternative: androgyny. During his stay in Ata, the protagonist notes a significant aspect of the transformed men and women of this utopia, their possession of traits and performance of social roles traditionally viewed as both masculine and feminine. The fully androgynous nature of Ata and, more specifically, the possession of feminine traits and roles by the utopian males are noted by Bryant's unnamed narrator when he records his early experiences among these people: "the men waited on me as often as the women did, and on each other. The tent was cleaned out every few days, the fern branches shaken out, the floor tamped and brushed, but everyone helped with the work. I saw no difference of function, except the women obviously nursed the infants; but the men carried and cared for the small ones as much as the women did" (19). This lack of distinction in social function is reflected in the Atans' clothing and appearances: "Since all wore their hair long and all wore the same shapeless, kneelength tunic, only beards and body contour were definite signs. Up to the age of sexual maturity the children were naked and long-haired and unless I made a special point of looking for a little penis, they were sexless to me" (19). Bryant's novel presents a utopia closely aligned with the third type of androgynous society Pamela Annas (1978) identifies within speculative fiction: a vision of a world "in which male and female functions and roles simply are not sharply differentiated" (146). The new masculinities for which Bryant's narrator advocates, therefore, appear and take on social roles traditionally deemed both masculine and feminine.

This simple lack of differentiation by gender enables Bryant to avoid issues raised about other feminist, androgynous utopias such as Ursula K. Le Guin's *The Left Hand of Darkness* (1969). As Natalie Myra Rosinsky (1982) noted soon after its publication, "the context critical to understanding the significance of *The Kin of Ata*" is "the controversy about feminist ideology and literary practice in" (31) Le Guin's novel. Bryant avoids the problematic tendency observable in *The Left Hand of Darkness* to portray androgyny as the simple adoption of masculine qualities by female characters and not the coinciding presentation of feminine traits among male characters. Her success, therefore, is due to her centering of a character who laboriously and incrementally learns to appreciate feminine views and qualities over time. A significant source of power for Bryant's novel are the deeply androgynous qualities of the utopian nation it persuades the traditional male narrator to appreciate and recommend to his readers.

As the protagonist explains in his instructional text, such an absence of networks of power based upon sex or gender is greatly enabled by the abolishment of the nuclear family. Rejecting hierarchies within every aspect of society, the new masculinities the narrator recommends complement the feminist utopia Bryant imagines through their opposition to the patriarchal order and this central, familial network of power (Buchbinder 2012, 69). As formulated by Raewyn Connell, there are four dimensions of gender relation that produce this hierarchical family unit. Each of these dimensions—power, division of labor, cathexis, and the symbolic level—illustrates the need to replace hegemonic masculinities and the nuclear family units they bolster. The traditional male, Connell demonstrates, enjoys favorable positions of power in public and private spaces, benefits from a division of labor that grants him better access to economic opportunities, enjoys the cathexis and emotional support of women without returning that care, and is recognized symbolically as the leader of the family.

The new man for which Bryant and her protagonist advocate, in stark contrast to the patriarchal head of the nuclear family, seeks to abolish these gender dimensions: he does not value or maintain a position of power in public and private spaces, benefit from a division of labor that grants him better access to economic opportunities, enjoy the emotional support of women

without returning that care, and does not desire to be the symbolic leader of
the family. Since traditional marriage and the nuclear family do not exist in
Ata, the protagonist must, for example, learn in becoming the new man to not
desire control of Augustine or their child. This adoption of new masculinities
is complicated by his traditional perspective on the family. When Augustine
informs him that she will "be woman" (107) to him, he falls back into earlier, patriarchal practices. In response, he attempts "to replicate the racist
and gendered relationship patterns familiar to him." He eventually gives "up
his old conceptions about couples and families" and alters "his definition of
and ability to love" since Augustine "remains both loving and nonattached"
(Mebane-Cruz and Wiener 2005, 315). Rejecting the patriarchal family
unit's commitment to male control, he adopts the alternative masculinities of
the feminist utopia, ideals of manhood that welcome new, egalitarian social
groupings, and recommends them to his audience.

The new conceptions of manhood this former patriarch offers value the
community and reject the isolating qualities of the nuclear family. In adopting Atan conceptions of maleness, he learns to recognize the importance of
the community to the lives of adults and the nourishment of children. He initially learns of the importance of community in a discussion with Augustine
concerning his decision to remain in Ata: " 'What made you decide to stay?'
asked Augustine. 'I don't know. Maybe it was you.' I had meant to please her,
but she only frowned. 'I hope not. One person is not enough' " (136). Bryant,
therefore, presents masculinities that are revolutionary in their commitment
to communities. Instead of small, patriarchal hierarchies, they are egalitarian,
extensive, nonnuclear, and open, which ensures the freedom of each family's
members. This freedom necessitates that children are free to associate with
members of the community and are not restricted to the control of their biological parents. They are instead raised by the society at large. As previously
described, the Atan people share each aspect of child upbringing outside of
birth. The narrator reflects this attitude toward children when he considers his
daughter: "She was truly, from the beginning, not our baby" (155). Instead of
being the property of her parents, this young female Atan behaves "as if every
adult were her parent and every child her brother or sister" (179) and this
social connection illustrates the communal qualities required of the new man
for the utopian polity to succeed. By replacing the traditionally masculine
interest in a nuclear, patriarchal family, Bryant, therefore, proposes through
her narrator that new ideals of manhood valuing community are required for
the development of a better, feminist society.

In addition to the protagonist's advocacy for equality across sex and gender
is his proposal, through his descriptions of Atan culture, of an egalitarian,
non-racist polity. As outlined by Edward Chan, Bryant imagines this utopian
treatment of race by disrupting the traditional racial semiotic in her novel

through both counter-signification and non-signification. This first method "actively calls into question the way race has traditionally signified" through "agglomeration in which the extremities of the physical markings of one race (blond hair) have not been erased, but instead remain, juxtaposed with markers that would 'normally' be associated with another race (oriental eyes)" (Chan 2006, 472). A young male Atan the protagonist meets, Chil-sing, for example, possesses such a combination of contrasting racial markers: "I looked into the face of a boy, a broad fair face with the slight down of a blonde beard. His hair was thick and long, curling down to his shoulders. His face was broad, with high cheek bones, and his eyes were wide and slanted with an oriental fold" (10). The second method Bryant utilizes "is a synthesis of phenotypical attributes such that the blend represents some arithmetical mean of various racial appearances" (Chan 2006, 471–472). As observed by the narrator, "most of the people" populating Ata are "of a racial blend I could not quite identify" since "their features formed a medium composite" (18) of races.

The problem Chan (2006) identifies in Bryant's approach to race and utopia is that her "disruption of the traditional racial semiotic suggests that identity is not in any intimate or significant way involved with how one exists as a social subject (i.e., how the subject is marked and consequently read as an object)" (478). Yet, as the observations of the narrator illustrate, Bryant's utopia is made up of people possessing unique bodily markers; the absence of violence according to these markers is due significantly to the new masculinities of this society. Noticing the amalgamated features of a subset of the Atan population, the protagonist marvels that he "saw no sign that these extreme types were in any way noticed or thought of as different by the others" (19). Through the presentation of a polity formed by and continuously forming healthy masculinities opposed to the subjugation of others according to markers such as race, Bryant offers to her audience, through her formerly misogynistic narrator, new ideals of manhood she identifies as fundamental to the development of a better, feminist society.

Central also to Ata's feminist utopia and the masculinities the narrator proposes is a lack of taboos on sex and sexuality. Upon touring Ata, the protagonist recognizes this openness to sexual practice, noting specifically the freedom of children to experiment: "Along the paths or in the fields, the naked children engaged in sex play the way animals do, touching and sniffing at one another, ignored by the adults" (51). The lack of taboos extends to sexualities; observing how "quite a lot of the sex play" among these children "was homosexual" (51), the narrator recognizes that queerness is not maligned in Ata as it is in the American patriarchy by traditional masculinities. The new performances of manhood Bryant presents in her novel as necessary for the improvement of society, therefore, reject sex as a social tool for distributing and curtailing power through control and subordination. In the traditionally masculine dystopia of the novel, the contemporary American capitalistic patriarchy, sex functions alongside popularity and wealth as rewards for the dominating self-made man. Bryant's utopia, on the other hand, favors a view of sex that removes from it traditionally masculine ideals of coercion, subordination, and power consolidation. Bryant presents new, utopian masculinities that view sex as an open, unrestricted instrument for connection and intimacy that, when correctly utilized, celebrates difference and equality over power and control. In this way, the utopian polity and its masculinities are mutually constitutive and produce, in contrast to the patriarchal economy, equality across sexes, gender, and races among other identity elements. As Bryant's narrator emphasizes, feminist-grounded masculinities are necessary for such socioeconomic improvements.

Moving from such commentary on socioeconomic alterations necessary at the intersection of masculinities and the nation, Bryant's narrator utilizes his position as a former patriarchal male to comment on the importance of emotional health to the project of transforming masculinities. As the protagonist explains, emotional self-care, enabled by the intuitive search for knowledge via dream analysis, mystical experience, and the development of a new consciousness, is a crucial step in adopting and maintaining alternative ideals of manhood.

As the narrator's transformation attests, alternatives to patriarchal conceptions of manhood must repair the emotional fracturing caused by its traditional counterpart. In *The Kin of Ata Are Waiting for You*, patriarchal subjects are damaged by hegemonic masculinities and this trauma is revealed in their dreams. The repercussions of murdering Connie, for example, manifest in those of the narrator as he is terrorized by unknown figures: "My eyes are shut. I am surrounded by shadowy shapes. They close in. I must fight them off. But I must not look at them. How can I fight if I can't see them? I must run, but they are all around me. I might run into the grasp of one. Don't look at them. They are closer. I feel their breath on me. I throw out my arms to hold them off. But they will swallow my hands" (5). In the text, the toxic effects of patriarchal masculinities manifest in the dreams of their adherents and, as exemplars of transformed, healthier masculinities, the Atan men populating the novel cherish their dreams as tools by which they may improve their emotional health. These utopian masculinities, therefore, embrace the emotional well-being of men, in contradiction of traditional scripts of manliness.

The tool utilized most effectively by these new men to better improve their emotional welfare is a type of dream hermeneutics in which subjects, moving beyond the mere analysis of dreams as signifiers of emotional health, interpret their dreams as sets of instruction that concern every aspect of life. In this polity, their language, consisting of few words, reflects the positioning of such a dream hermeneutics as the activity most prized by this community. The most frequently used words of their lexicon are "nagdeo" and "donagdeo" and each of these terms relates to these dreams. Making up an antonymic pair, the former term, "nagdeo," describes anything that cultivates dreaming while the latter term, "donagdeo," refers to anything preventing dreaming. In the pursuit of transcendent knowledge provided via dreams, these utopian subjects carefully consider methods of improving their dreams, focusing on their diets, workloads, relationships, and general and specific actions within the community.

As is demonstrated in the original perspective of the narrator, this focus on dreams is antithetical to hegemonic masculinities. Prior to his transformation, the protagonist expresses a traditionally rational position when discussing the use of dreams to make decisions with a male Atan, Sbgai: "'But what if a dream is followed and leads to trouble or hurt?' 'Why, then we see we misunderstood the message of the dream. Common sense! Reason.' 'You admit that common sense and reason are useful.' 'Indispensible! But they follow the dream.' 'In the world, we put them first'" (161). His initial opposition is grounded in hegemonic masculinities' valuation of reasoning above other methods for obtaining emotional and physical healing. During his incremental transformation that, as previously outlined, begins with his second homicidal act, the murder of Tran, and is completed with his trial confession at the conclusion of the novel, he learns to value and interpret dreams since "reality comes clothed in coverings we can recognize and describe" (168). His adoption of new, utopian masculinities, therefore, requires that he learn methods for interpreting his dreams and, through these strategies, become attuned to his state of emotional health. The narrator, therefore, calls for other men to practice self-care as an important tool of new masculinities.

Among the other methods Bryant's narrator presents as important to the transformation of men such as chanting, numerology, mythmaking, and dancing, isolation therapy provides a unique opportunity for him to engage with the contents of his dreams. In this novel, new masculinities require an openness to mystical methods of acquiring transcendent knowledge and a rejection of patriarchal masculinities' interest in strictly rational approaches to learning. As Lyman Tower Sargent (1983) outlines, this spiritual concern is one of "transcendence, a rejection . . . of the material" and an interest in "something beyond the rational" (32). The novel presents alternative masculinities that seek healing via new ways of knowing such as emotional experience, intuition, and the unconscious, all central to the narrator's experiences during isolation therapy. Utilizing the Atan isolation chambers, hol-kas, he experiences visions and confronts those shadow figures of his dreams representing the toxic qualities of his patriarchal self: "Without the strength or will to fight, I let go. I let go of something indefinable—my life, I suppose. Then

I opened my eyes to look at the shadow which moved in closest to me. It was me, of course. They were all me, in one rotten form after another. There were twelve of me and we did the dance of the numbers, in the empty la-ka which echoed with our yells and screams and stomps" (128). These dark shadow selves he faces represent those "rotten" aspects of his character directly traceable to hegemonic masculinities. Isolation therapy, therefore, is significant in the novel since it enables him to better understand his own emotional state and routes for healing.

Such healing comes from a final confrontation of two selves, one female and another male, and the defeat of long-held patriarchal ideals of manhood. His experience among these shadow selves continues until "after eons there were two of me left, facing each other across the fire pit. One of me was a woman, a hundred women, all the women, hurt, enraged, and furious, that I had ever known. One of me was a man, myself, every rotten, opportunistic, cruel, avaricious and vain self I had ever been" (129). Since there is a "relationship between the repression of parts of the self and the oppression of other people" (Pearson 1981, 68), the traditional man must liberate the feminine qualities of his identity to discontinue the subordination of others outside himself. These parts of his identity, male and female, confront each other in a combat of dance in which the victor becomes the leader of the ritual. After multiple failed attempts to destroy his female self, the narrator grows tired and ultimately follows her graceful movements, which replace his own aggressive approach. In this way, he finds healing through the acceptance of the feminine aspects of his own identity. As this passage demonstrates, the feminist goal of the novel—"the full and free attainment of the self" (Pearson 1981, 68)—positively impacts the men populating this new nation since they are able to accept both their feminine and masculine qualities. This focus on emotional well-being and nontraditional methods of healing signifies the adoption of healthier ideals of masculinity Bryant and her narrator present as necessary for the betterment of society.

As the text delineates, a significant problem plaguing the emotional well-being of patriarchal individuals such as the narrator is their "primitive, linear mode of consciousness, marked by internal repression and external oppression," which lacks any "integration of thought and feeling, ratiocination and intuition, conscious and unconscious minds" (Pearson 1981, 85). Carol Pearson (1981) in "Coming Home: Four Feminist Utopias and Patriarchal Experience" identifies how this ignoring of emotional health among traditionally masculine males strengthens patriarchy since there is a "relationship between the repression of parts of the self and the oppression of other people" (68). As Pearson outlines, though the narrator "is an extremely successful man in a patriarchal society, he is an alienated unhappy misogynist. When this man stops repressing the metaphorical women within himself, he is free from his need to dominate and conquer people in the outside world" (68). The protagonist and patriarchal males in general must, therefore, recognize the validity of their emotions and unconscious selves in order to heal emotionally and contribute to the development of a better society not predicated upon the oppression of others. As the narrator illuminates, the continual adherence to traditional masculinities and their neglect of their emotional statuses results in such nightmares becoming to a degree "the only real thing" (26) they experience. Central to the protagonist's tract on masculinity is the message that new conceptions of manhood are necessary that charge men with the responsibility of improving their emotional health.

While Bryant's novel possesses traditional traits such as its centering of heteronormative male experience, it is this framing of it as the nonfiction tract of a once hyperviolent patriarch that makes it a uniquely powerful work. Unlike other contemporary feminist utopias, *The Kin of Ata Are Waiting for You* is the conversion story of a murderer and rapist and Bryant, in crafting such a story, compels her audience to consider the most extreme implications of social constructionist gender theories. Bryant's novel, therefore, signifies a break from the essentialist gender ideologies common to radical feminism in the 1970s. In letting a former patriarch speak as it were, Bryant's utopia distinctly imagines the transformed, new man suitable for an ideal, egalitarian society and powerfully comments upon the difficulty with which traditional men may adopt alternative conceptions of manhood. Such a focus upon the malleability of masculinities and the centering of a male protagonist in *The Kin of Ata Are Waiting for You* illustrates a trend within early feminist utopian fiction that encompasses the novel upon which chapter 2 focuses, Ursula K. Le Guin's *The Dispossessed*.

NOTES

1. As Sam McBean (2014) outlines, feminist utopian novels such as Marge Piercy's *Woman on the Edge of Time* contrast with "over-arching theories of utopia as a distant or perfect world" since they utilize the genre as a sight for positing historically situated alternatives to current socioeconomic norms (42). Bryant's novel, like that of Piercy, which will be discussed in chapter 3, is dynamic in its connecting of the utopian polity to its dystopian alternative and the importance of dystopian citizens' actions to the development of the better society.

2. Carol Pearson (1981), for example, identifies as a trend within contemporary feminist utopias interests in "the low status and pay for 'women's work' " (63). In addition, she recognizes attempts to unite "the inhumane and marketplace and the humane hearth" (64) efforts to envision new types of families, the absence of coercion within polities, a lack of reliance upon abstract and objective ideals, interests in empathic and intuitive understanding, and the valuing of women's lived experiences

as central aspects of these utopian novels and the pragmatic political efforts espoused by their authors. Lucy Freibert (1983), on the other hand, locates trends such as the absence of private property, the offering of "food, clothing, education, medical care, travel, and recreation at common expense" (68) and the presence of organicist societies that advocate "the union of reason and nature, rather than the domination of nature practiced by the current male-oriented culture" (69) among these feminist works.

Chapter 2

Precarious Masculinities in Ursula K. Le Guin's *The Dispossessed*

The transformability of masculinities and the perspectives of male characters unite the focus of chapter 1, *The Kin of Ata Are Waiting for You*, and the novel this chapter concerns, Ursula K. Le Guin's *The Dispossessed*. There are, however, key distinctions between these feminist utopias. *The Kin of Ata Are Waiting for You* follows the gradual, positive transformation of a vile male protagonist who is both a murderer and a rapist. *The Dispossessed*, on the other hand, uniquely focuses upon the dynamic nature of masculinity through the experiences of a utopian, feminist-oriented male character. In contrast to *The Kin of Ata Are Waiting for You*, which presents the evils of traditional masculinities through its hyperviolent narrator and the possibility of him adopting a feminist-informed conception of manliness, *The Dispossessed* details through Le Guin's protagonist the precarious nature of alternative masculinities and the risk to women and society of men succumbing to patriarchal ideals of manhood. This analysis of *The Dispossessed* therefore contributes to ongoing discussions within masculinity studies of the socially situated and perilous nature of alternative masculinities.

Le Guin's representation of patriarchal and alternative masculinities is often overlooked; scholarship emphasizes her role as a writer who championed the feminine. Upon her death, obituaries hailed Le Guin as an "ambassador of the genres of the fantastic" (Clute 2018) who pushed for the recognition of science fiction as legitimate literature. Among her often-noted achievements is her inclusion of themes less prominent in science fiction prior to the 1970s such as gender fluidity, sexualities, and feminism. The *Washington Post* notes that Le Guin crafted "novels that grappled with issues of gender inequality, racism, and environmental destruction" (Smith 2018). Among her achievements, Le Guin is predominantly noted for the feminist content of her fiction and, more specifically, her inclusion of complex female characters. This inclusion of complex female characters coincided with her realistic, nuanced portrayals of masculinity that likewise challenged patriarchal ideologies. Alongside writers such as James Tiptree Jr., Zenna Henderson, Joanna Russ, Lee Killough, Pamela Sargent, and Octavia Butler, Le Guin "brought speculation about the future of sex roles to science fiction" (Smith 1986, viii–ix). Yet, the manner by which Le Guin utilized her writing to destabilize traditional masculinities is widely overlooked. Among the many tributes published after her death, only Gerald Jonas's article in the *New York Times* mentions her work in proposing alternative, nontoxic concepts of maleness. Her male protagonists, he only briefly notes, "avoid the macho posturing of so many science fiction and fantasy heroes" (Jonas 2018, B15). While it is widely accepted that Le Guin spearheaded a new era of science fiction that introduced revolutionary topics surrounding sexuality and gender roles, her unique, revolutionary treatments of traditional and nonnormative masculinities deserve greater critical attention.

The application of masculinities studies to a key novel of Le Guin's *Hainish Cycle*, *The Dispossessed*, allows us to see both masculinities studies and Le Guin's work in a new light. While Le Guin's novel, like *The Kin of Ata Are Waiting for You*, concerns the experiences of a male protagonist, its focus differs: *The Dispossessed* features a feminist-oriented man who must negotiate the temptations of the capitalistic patriarchy. This shift from conversion to backsliding necessitates a theoretical approach more significantly focused upon social formations of gender. Theoretical frameworks concerning ideologies of the nation and gender, for example, are particularly important in that they theorize how texts support or condemn masculinities through their imagined societies. David Buchbinder's *Studying Men and Masculinities* (2012) posits that gender is an instance of interpellation by which subjects and ideologies are constructed and reinforced. In this way, he posits that "the subject comes into existence through ideology" and "ideology is brought into being through the subject" (Buchbinder 2012, 36). This relationship between the subject and ideology hints upon the relationship between the subject's gender and society. Todd Reeser's aforementioned concept of the gendered nation emphasizes this relationship of the essence of a nation and its masculinities. In *Masculinities in Theory: An Introduction* (2010), he outlines the ways nationality and masculinity are elemental to and shape subjectivities. As Buchbinder and Reeser emphasize, masculinities involve the mutual construction of subjects and ideologies and such gender identities shape and are shaped by the essence of a nation. These theoretical conceptions of gender are relevant to *The Dispossessed* since Le Guin presents to her audience a male protagonist whose masculinities are dynamic and are shaped by the polities within which he lives and travels and the ideologies they espouse.

By illuminating this connection between masculinities and the nation, Le Guin links these traditional conceptions of manhood with, among other ideologies, nationalism. *The Dispossessed* represents an important warning concerning the conflation of nationalism and masculinities. Le Guin identifies in her work hierarchical social patterns—power consolidation, control, aggression, and domination—linking individual masculine performances to the macro-politics of the capitalistic patriarchy. *The Dispossessed* emphasizes connections between traditional masculinities that favor power and control and nationalistic policies manifesting these values on an international level.

Illustrating a significant trend among 1970s feminist utopian writers, Le Guin presents complex portrayals of masculinity in genre fiction. Le Guin creates protagonists compelled to negotiate masculine performances and the relationship of gender to social power. Her critiques of traditional masculinities therefore mark a significant departure from mainstream, male-dominated science fiction. Novels by noted authors such as the "Big Three," Robert Heinlein, Isaac Asimov, and Arthur C. Clarke, champion images of manhood characterized by heroic deeds, assertiveness, independence, strength, and power. Rico and his comrades in Heinlein's *Starship Troopers* (1959), for example, demonstrate a masculinity that is "something intensely physical, based on animal power, instinct, and aggression" and is "all body, so to speak, and no brain" (Hantke 1998, 498). Other male protagonists in Asimov and Clarke's works practice a masculinity that is hard science-oriented, wary of femininity as a threat to technological and social progress, and typically lacking any emotional complexity. These characters' positions as idealized figures of manhood are invariably portrayed as white, middle or upper class, and heterosexual. Writers such as Le Guin, in contrast, present invaluable portraits of masculinity qualified by varying sexualities, masculinities, races, and class positions heretofore absent from the genre.

Such nonnormative representations of manhood are notable since they replace the older, conservative masculinities of earlier speculative fiction. If women are traditionally portrayed in science fiction literature as complacent, passive objects of male desire lacking depth or complexity, men are depicted as ideally masculine, virile, and dominating—the super men outlined in my introduction. These idealized characters represent an impossible conception of masculinity, which male fans and writers may admire but fail to become. In contrast to this unrealistic, stereotypical image of manhood, Le Guin's novels, like *The Kin of Ata Are Waiting for You*, present characters performing nontraditional masculinities that, while ignored during the golden age of science fiction, are often central to feminist science fiction texts.

The Dispossessed is emblematic of this paradigm shift and centers the experiences of an alternatively masculine character, Shevek, as he experiences for the first time a capitalistic, patriarchal society. Like Le Guin's earlier work, *The Left Hand of Darkness* (1969), *The Dispossessed* involves interactions between an alien visitor and a host civilization whose gender order causes the protagonist and reader to rethink naturalized and marginalized conceptions of gender and sexuality. Importantly, while *The Left Hand of Darkness* focuses upon the exploration of two ungendered, ambisexual, physiologically fluid societies, *The Dispossessed* involves the exploration of a society not foreign to the reader but, instead, one that closely resembles that of the United States. Like Bryant, Le Guin presents contemporary American society, but in a defamiliarized way, meaning that she alters a conceptual form (contemporary American culture) while the nature of this concept (a patriarchal gender order) remains stable (Shklovsky 1965, 13). While the nation A-Io in the novel, for example, should not be analyzed as a simple, direct substitute for the United States, it is in part a significant allegory of contemporary American culture.

The nations of Urras, therefore, possess differences but also key similarities making such a comparison possible. As Keng, the Terran ambassador, identifies, these Urrasti nations differ from those of Earth in their restraint; while Terra is ecologically devastated as a result of corporate greed, Urras remains an ecologically functioning planet. Still, Keng's recognition of Urras as alive and in balance reveals the similarities she locates between those capitalistic patriarchies located on each planet. That she comments so positively about this planet in response to Shevek's observation that in Urrasti nations "there is nothing you can do that profit does not enter into, and fear of loss, and the wish for power" (345) reveals once more the incomplete but significant parallels Le Guin draws between the nations of each planet. In this way, A-Io in part signifies contemporary, capitalistic patriarchal systems and Le Guin, by centering non-hegemonic masculinities, engages her reader in a dialectic concerning manhood in, among other twentieth-century Western polities, contemporary America.

Central to the text's de-marginalization of alternative performances of manhood is its delineation of traditional masculinities. Three salient qualities specifically separate Le Guin's protagonist, Shevek, from his traditionally American masculine counterparts of the capitalist patriarchy he visits, A-Io: a disinterest in power and control, an absence of aggression, and an aversion to the domination of others. These qualities rejected by Shevek characterize capitalistic masculinities. The masculine script of the *self-made man*, for example, predicates a subject's value upon the accumulation of economic power and control via aggression and the domination of others. Deriving his self-worth not from financial or socioeconomic power but, instead, from community and connection, Shevek rejects these central tenets of contemporary American masculinities. Through these interactions of a feminist-oriented male protagonist with a patriarchal polity, Le

Guin emphasizes those elements of traditional masculinities that should be rejected.

The novel presents these traits as descriptive of both A-Io and, more specifically, five of its powerful citizens with whom Shevek comes in contact: Kimoe, Saio Pae, Chifoilisk, Oiie, and Atro. These characters resemble protagonists typical of golden age novels and are, therefore, the antagonists to the new masculinities to which Shevek subscribes. They are the self-made men of A-Io, concerned with the accumulation and maintenance of power. They are assertive, independent, and patriarchal, and possess immense social power, which they wield aggressively to subjugate and control others. In turn, this domination enables the refortification of their positions within the gender order. These physicists seek to gain political power over their global and interplanetary rivals through the development of temporal technologies for warfare and economic stability. This ambition leads to their unlikely partnership with Shevek, whom they desire to manipulate and control. Strategically, Le Guin places them on the periphery as problematic alternatives to the newly centered, egalitarian masculinity of Shevek. Throughout the novel, Le Guin places the protagonist in contrast with A-Io and these specific characters, inducing reconsiderations of traditional American masculinities in both her characters and audience.

Central to this destabilizing of normative masculinities is the way Le Guin, through these characters and Shevek, criticizes ideals of manhood found throughout science fiction predating *The Dispossessed*. Challenging historic trends of speculative fiction, Le Guin uncouples, through Shevek, traditional masculinities from the fields of science, technology, engineering, and mathematics that are widely portrayed by earlier writers as the domains of patriarchal men. Through Shevek, Le Guin presents a new man who, while participating in the scientific process, lacks the problematic characteristics of protagonists found in the fiction of Clarke and Asimov. Grounded in feminist conceptions of manhood, Shevek is not opposed to femininity and possesses an emotional complexity and acceptance of diversity and difference absent from earlier characters of speculative fiction. Though granted access to power due to his proficiency in scientific fields of research, he ultimately—after temporarily succumbing to the temptations of capitalism and the patriarchy— readopts his feminist conceptions of manhood and, as a result, works to make his technological breakthroughs universally available. Through Shevek, Le Guin disconnects masculinity from the fields of science, technology, engineering, and mathematics and offers an alternative both to traditional masculinities and those early speculative works supporting them.

The juxtaposition of masculinities Le Guin presents through Shevek and these patriarchal characters mirrors a contrast in the nations of which they are subjects. Le Guin utilizes these parallels in her novel to illuminate the relationship between national identity and masculinities. Specifically, the qualities of traditional masculinities are linked in the novel to the capital-istic polity of A-Io while those of feminist-oriented masculinities are tied to the anarchic society of Anarres. The nation of A-Io and its extratextual counterpart, the contemporary United States, produce and influence and are influenced by traditional masculinities. Le Guin highlights the need to trans-form both these gender scripts and the capitalistic economies and ideologies of exploitation that legitimize them and postulates an anarchic alternative to the capitalistic patriarchy that is "based on voluntary cooperation" instead of "competition and coercion" (Benfield 2006, 134). Informed by the teachings of the anarchist, Odo, these foundational principles of mutual agreement replace the traditionally masculine concepts of competition and intimidation, demonstrating the interconnected relationship of national socioeconomic sys-tems and gender. Central to Le Guin's interplanetary dialectic are the alterna-tive masculinities Shevek performs, which are necessary for the new, better social system she envisions. While she balks at labeling it a perfect, utopian system, she presents it as an ideal alternative to the capitalistic patriarchies of A-Io and the twentieth-century United States. Similarly, she presents non-exploitative masculinities as positive alternatives that reject the traditional masculine goals of accumulating power and control.

Le Guin introduces this contrast of subjectivities and their attending con-ceptions of nationality and gender at the onset of the novel. As a child in a history course, Shevek receives a visual lesson concerning A-Io, which introduces him to the intersecting forces of capitalism, masculinities, and heteronormativity and their relationship to power and control. Images such as the bodies of children stacked atop each other and lit on fire by men reveal the brutal, traditionally masculine response of those in power to control and destroy those situated near the bottom of the socioeconomic hierarchy and, therefore, forced into starvation. These lessons about the rival nation confuse and intrigue the young student who is unfamiliar with such concepts. This relationship of the empowered to the exploited, he learns, is predicated upon their position as self-made men privileged by their traditional masculinity, heterosexuality, and class position among other factors.

This lesson introduces the impact of traditional masculinities and their con-nection to power and control upon sexuality. The commodification of hetero-sexual intimacy and the female body is symbolized in the image of jeweled navels belonging to women subjugated and used by men of the upper class (42). These women sit idly and are served by those citizens lacking financial and, therefore, social capital. This passage outlines the patriarchal order of A-Io, beginning with the top echelon of propertied, heterosexual, traditionally masculine men and concluding with the nondescript servants populating the lowest socioeconomic stratum. In between these tiers are positioned "body profiteers" as Shevek's partner, Takver, calls women who weaponize their sexuality in the struggle against patriarchal men. These women are isolated from power and knowledge but valued and, therefore, compensated for their bodies, sexual favors, and performances of femininity, which, in turn, reinforce the masculinity of the propertied male. The oppressive nature of this patriarchal economy is outlined in grotesque detail as the visual lesson throws the privilege of these women in sharp relief against a backdrop of the starved and disenfranchised: "a close-up of dinnertime: soft mouths champing and smiling, smooth hands reaching out for delicacies wetly mounded in silver bowls. Then a switch back to the blind, blunt face of a dead child, mouth open, empty, black, dry. 'Side by side,' the quiet voice had said" (42). The socioeconomic position of these self-made men can never be secure and this, in turn, leads to the continued exploitation of others and the reinforcing of the capitalist-informed gender order (147). The traditional masculinities of A-Io and the contemporary United States create the masculine subjectivity of their citizens in a battle against femininity and fluidity. Representing an alternative, egalitarian masculinity relocated from the social margins, Shevek rejects the traditional American masculinities of the Urrasti with whom he comes in contact and also challenges their systems of power and control regarding sexuality.

The temptations of such patriarchal systems do temporarily sway Shevek, however, and Le Guin, in imagining her character's momentary but disastrous adoption of misogynistic attitudes toward women, emphasizes the precarious position of men performing alternative masculinities and the nations they represent. In a scene on Urras at a party held by Shevek's acquaintance, Vea, the protagonist, drunk and aroused, assaults his host, stopping only after he has ejaculated on her clothing. In his influential analysis of the novel, "To Read *The Dispossessed*," Samuel Delany finds fault with Le Guin's occasional essentialist presentations of conceptions of sexual attractiveness and her limited inclusion of female and queer characters in the foreground of the Anarresti sections of the text. While agreeing with Delany's criticism of the novel's limited inclusion of queer and female characters and essentialist portrayal of desire, I assert that this analysis of the novel overlooks the ways its portrayal of an imperfect utopia benefits ongoing discussions concerning American masculinities. Delany identifies in his analysis of this particular scene the essentialist nature of Shevek's reaction to the initial flirtatious behavior exhibited by Vea. According to Delany, since "men must learn to respond to" such performances "as erotic" (Delany 2009, 117) and Shevek, a man completely divorced from the local culture and norms, recognizes the intentions of Vea, this section of the text essentializes sexual attractiveness. Departing from Delany's analysis of this scene, I assert that Le Guin, while failing to note the ways this portrayal supports essentialist ideals of sexual attractiveness, attempts to display in this shocking scene the dangerous possibilities for the new man of speculative fiction to succumb to the temptations of the subjugating, traditional masculinities of an earlier era. Notwithstanding Delany's criticism, the scene highlights Le Guin's interest in the dynamic and, therefore, vulnerable state of utopian masculinities. In emphasizing the instability of masculinity, she illuminates the constant threat of feminist-oriented men succumbing to the temptations of patriarchy. In his analysis, Delany (2009) additionally criticizes the text's presentation of Anarres as a failed utopian polity with limited egalitarianism, illustrating the limitations of his reading of the novel "against its own ideal form" (107). A significant problem within Delany's assessment of *The Dispossessed* is his assertion that a utopian polity is necessary for the novel to reach its ideal form since Le Guin's depiction of imperfect, gendered nations and specifically the unstable nature of their national essences and masculinities enriches discussions surrounding the instability of alternative gender scripts. Like the feminist-oriented nation from which he originates, Shevek struggles to maintain alternative masculinities. He ultimately recognizes the dangers of misogyny, readopts a feminist-informed masculinity, and thereafter monitors himself, remaining steadfast against the influence of traditional gender ideologies. While Delany correctly observes how Anarres and its masculinities are not totally egalitarian, he is incorrect to assert that such an absence of a purely utopian polity weakens the novel since *The Dispossessed* is strengthened by its depiction of the instability and precarity of new masculinities.

The novel emphasizes such alternatives to traditional American masculinities through Shevek's recommitment to a conception of manhood that does not associate sexuality with power and control but, instead, with the mutual offering of the self between two partners. The extensive social freedoms allowed in Anarres result in Shevek only recommitting himself to feminist-oriented masculinities after many sexual experiences that, while not founded on power and control, view participants, like the body profiteers, as mere conduits for gratification. As a boy, he sleeps with many girls but eventually finds it to be a joyless endeavor marked by the use of another person as an object (157). These remembered experiences illustrate his initial similarities to Bryant's narrator, who, while reflecting upon his assault of Augustine, describes his ejaculation "like a sneeze without pleasure or relief" that caused him to feel he "had lost something again" (56). In stark contrast with those traditional ideals of manhood initially held by Bryant's protagonist and temporarily subscribed to by Shevek, the alternative masculinity to which he returns is qualified by the recognition of the subjectivity of sexual partners and the rejection of attempts to refigure sexual experience as an avenue for domination and the accumulation of social power.

This dissociation of sexuality from power and control is reflected not only in Anarresti subjectivities but also in the essence of the nation itself. Anarres, in opposition to A-Io, is a society in which gender and sexual fluidity are allowed to flourish. This societal norm, in turn, results in stark linguistic and cultural contrasts from its rival nation. The absence of patriarchal masculinities in Anarres, like Ata, results in sexuality and, in turn, language concerning it lacking themes of subjugation and coercion. Their language, for example, lacks "any proprietary idioms for the sexual act. In Pravic it made no sense for a man to say that he had 'had' a woman" (53). The only term possessing a similar meaning has the secondary usage as a curse and means "to rape." As a result, the Pravic word for sex is neutral and emphasizes that copulation involves the mutual participation of two people. Other sexualities, in addition, are not marginalized since patriarchal preoccupations with the gender order and its relationship to nonnormative sexual acts are absent. Shevek, as a typical child of Anarres, enjoys sexual experiences with boys and girls alike and this fact importantly does not affect his social standing. In the absence of traditional masculinities, power and control are dissociated from sexual experience and fluidity is welcomed as a normative, pleasurable subjective aspect.

Through his negative experiences on A-Io, Shevek also recognizes the negative impact of traditional masculinities and their emphases on power and control upon education. In conversations with the Urrasti scientists, the shoring up of knowledge is demonstrated to be key to the consolidation of power and control within a capitalistic market. When Shevek asks, for example, if all scientists in A-Io are men, Pae responds, "Scientists. Oh yes, certainly, they're all men. There are some female teachers in the girls' school, of course. But they never get past Certificate level" (73). Such a disparity among the sexes in the realm of education is considered a by-product of biological differences among men and women. To blur the proposed intellectual border separating the sexes risks biological abnormalities: "Of course, there's always a few exceptions, God-awful brainy women with vaginal atrophy" (73). Women are considered intellectually stunted members of society valued only in their use to reinforce the traditional masculinity of those self-made men whom they serve. In this way, Le Guin interrogates the archetypal scientists common to the novels of hard science fiction and their seemingly natural place at the pinnacles of power and knowledge. In highlighting the myriad women made invisible throughout the genre's history, Le Guin not only calls for new, complex portrayals of women but also nuanced explorations of masculinities invisible in much of science fiction.

Through these portrayals of the scientists of A-Io and Shevek and their contrasting views concerning biological sex and education, Le Guin illustrates the centrality of power and control to hegemonic masculine educational ideologies. Specifically, she depicts the tension and anxiety that result from interactions between alternative and traditional masculinities in academia. Continuing their discussion concerning sex and power, Shevek answers a question concerning the possibility of women being intellectually capable by listing female scientists who taught and mentored him. Recognizing one of these scholars, Gvarab, as a scientist with particularly significant influence, Oiie responds with offense, incredulity, and the reluctant recognition that his alternative, Shevek, has identified an error in Urrasti gender ideologies: "Can't tell from your names, of course . . . You make a point, I suppose of drawing no distinction between the sexes" (74).

Anxiety persists among these performers of traditional masculinities and they remain dubious of the merits of female education and academic achievements regardless of the demonstrated logic supporting Shevek's position. This apprehension illustrates the power of marginalized masculinities to disrupt hegemony and the fear such challenges produce among subscribers to traditional conceptions of manhood. In another interaction in which Shevek outlines the benefits of sexual equality on education, his interlocutors express incredulity and anxiety at the notion that women possess intellectual abilities on par with those of men. These views, expressed by Kimoe, are predicated upon the fear that the entry of women into scientific fields will destabilize current research and illustrate the nature of hegemonic masculine anxiety as fearful of gender order alterations. These apprehensions are presented as symptomatic of contemporary American masculinities and the anxieties they engender to maintain, at times violently, patriarchal hierarchies.

Such anxieties are produced in part by males who reject traditional masculinities and the gender order they seek to protect. The questioning of patriarchy by a male practicing an alternative, nonexploitative masculinity reveals the insecure position of these self-made men, seeking to maintain an unnatural social hierarchy. Like the unnamed narrator of *The Kin of Ata Are Waiting for You* prior to his conversion, these men harm themselves through the suppression of their own feminine qualities. They deny their own complex identities in favor of a gender binary, which compels them to adopt traditional performances of manhood so they may maintain socioeconomic power and control. In Shevek, the reader witnesses a new masculinity characterized by its rejection of these central aspects of its hegemonic counterpart.

Through this protagonist, Le Guin centers in the novel an alternative masculinity opposed to oppressive, hierarchical influences within education. Anarresti academics, reflective of the anarchic teachings of Odo upon which the nation was founded, must function as "a permanent revolution" whose origin is "a thinking mind" (10) and, therefore, oppose traditional, hierarchical systems of education. The organizing Odonian principle "that the dominant lifestyle is not permanently set but permits, indeed demands, personal choices to meet inevitable social and environmental changes" (Bierman 1975, 249) necessitates individualism and independence within education. In performing a masculinity that does not value power and control, Shevek identifies developing hierarchies within Anarresti education and vies for their removal.

Specifically, Shevek attacks figures within Anarresti education who accumulate power and control by minimizing the autonomy of students and scholars. "We don't educate for freedom. Education, the most important activity of the social organism, has become rigid, moralistic, authoritarian" (168). According to Shevek, instead of following the individualism of Odonian teachings, "kids learn to parrot Odo's words as if they were laws—the ultimate blasphemy!" (168). In direct opposition to the protagonist's egalitarian, pluralist stance is his mentor, Sabul, who uses educational hierarchies to commodify and, therefore, gain power from the appropriated intellectual work of others. As outlined by Takver, Sabul works tirelessly to subjugate Shevek and annex his advances in physics using his position of power. As a representative of traditional masculinities, Sabul labors to consolidate power and control within the Anarresti academy through the subjugation of others. Signifying a new, nonhierarchical masculine alternative, Shevek resists the allure of influence and authority made available to him as a result of his academic accomplishments and rejects traditional masculinities' emphases on power and control in education.

This attack upon coercive elements of education is part of Shevek's larger efforts to oppose the importation of traditionally masculine consolidations of power and control into Anarres. While this utopia, as Le Guin points out in the novel's subtitle, is ambiguous, it is rooted in positive alternative masculinities, resulting in its position as a constructive alternative to the polities of A-Io and the contemporary United States. In Anarres and A-Io, these elements, masculinities and nationality, shape each other and the nation. Like the national essence and traditional masculinities normalized in A-Io, the nationality and alternative concepts of maleness produced in Anarres are not permanent. Shevek's attacks upon developing hierarchical patterns reveal key characteristics of the gender-nation relationship unique to Anarres that cause it to be a positive alternative to that of A-Io, and, by extrapolation, to that of the United States.

Anarres is demonstrated to possess an improved gender-nation relationship through its encouragement of personal freedoms and individual activism. Shevek, for example, does not depart from Anarresti concepts of nation and gender through his rebellion but, instead, becomes an exemplary member of the Odonian society through his anarchic actions. In this way, Anarresti subjectivities—specifically their nationality and gender—function in opposition to the traditional masculinities and nationalism of A-Io. A-Io, like contemporary American culture, produces hierarchies as a result of the dialogue between its capitalistic and patriarchal national and gender ideologies.

Anarres, on the other hand, produces a distinctly different dialogue between its anarchic nationality and fluid genders. The result is a nation that, though at times influenced by outside oppressive ideologies, rejects consolidations of power and control. Shevek's attacks are made against subjugating, coercive masculinities taking hold in varying parts of Anarresti society.

Essential to Shevek's opposition to invasive, subjugating masculinities is the recognition that consolidations of control occur through myriad social institutions that, like education, buttress traditional masculinities. Through her dialectic of gendered nations, Le Guin identifies necessary ties between socioeconomic, governmental, and private institutions of a nation and its normalized masculinities. The social institutions of A-Io, for example, support traditional masculinities and this results in unequal distributions of power and efforts to control and disenfranchise within these societal bodies. Presenting her protagonist with signifiers of traditional masculinities' drive for power and control, Le Guin draws in Shevek's confusion a stark contrast in masculinities: "He had never seen a rat, or an army barracks, or an insane asylum, or a poorhouse, or a pawnshop, or an execution, or a thief, or a tenement, or a rent collector, or a man who wanted to work and could not find work to do, or a dead baby in a ditch" (283). These seemingly unrelated elements of A-Io society signify inequalities innate to traditional masculinities and supported by the institutions they produce. These oppressive realities of traditional masculine social networks are recognized by the protagonist as the fundamental human suffering in which the hierarchical ideologies governing this society are developed. Central to the ideals of Odonian society are new, nontraditional masculinities and the elimination of their attending oppressive social institutions.

Of the institutions considered in the novel, jail is critical to both the development of alternative, Odonian masculinities and the maturation of the protagonist. Two key texts of Odonian philosophy, *The Prison Letters* and *The Analogy*, were composed while Odo was imprisoned after an insurrection (87). During her nine years of captivity in a fort in Drio, the anarchic leader outlined her position against capitalistic, patriarchal polities and the coercive institutions they produce. Her radical theorizations of an anarchic society and non-subjugating masculinities form the philosophical foundation of Anarres and are in part the result of her experiences in A-Io and the prisons it utilizes to marginalize and silence.

Like Odo, Shevek is galvanized by his understanding of jail as an oppressive social establishment. As a young child, he leads his friends in an imaginative enactment of jail, leaning upon what they have learned in the classroom. Acting as guards, Shevek and Tirin lock their friend, Kadagv, under the west wing of the learning center they attend (35). While the experiment begins as an innocent exercise, the participants soon adopt their roles as oppressors and prisoner. Pushing Kadagv into his makeshift cell with considerable force, the boys quickly adopt their roles as members of a capitalistic patriarchy. They police Kadagy quietly, demonstrating no pity as their friend whimpers and nurses a scrape received in the altercation and therefore role-play the position of guards. Importantly, the boys find they are adopting these traditionally masculine ideals within a short period of time: "they were not playing the new role now, it was playing them" (37–38).

Le Guin connects this game with traditional masculinities and, more specifically, the precarious position of men performing alternative masculinities who must withstand the temptations of the capitalistic patriarchy. She chronicles the boys' expedient adoption of hierarchical masculinities and the trauma resulting from this temporary departure from egalitarian, alternative conceptions of manhood. As the young Anarresti boys begin their jail play-acting, they immediately adopt patriarchal attitudes toward women without being actively aware of their newly adopted sexism. Girls are automatically excluded from this game though the boys are not sure why this tendency to marginalize has taken root in their minds. While this conflict between masculinities and their treatments of women causes cognitive dissonance, the effects of their game on each member become profound during the imprisonment of their friend, Kadagv.

This overnight mock-incarceration grants to each boy newfound control over their comrade. Shevek feels this power when not disclosing the whereabouts of the boy. Yet, upon witnessing Tirin's more daring, exceedingly hierarchical action of lying to adult leaders in order to prevent the liberation of their confined friend, Shevek experiences discomfort because of the power he secretly possesses (39). Ultimately deciding to release his friend before the planned length of two days, Shevek suffers a traumatic response to the subjugation of Kadagv. He vomits and experiences spasms and exhaustion in reaction to the knowledge of his hierarchical actions. Traumatized by his experience with traditional, masculine social institutions, the protagonist ceases to find such play-acting an interesting exercise. Recognizing the impact of such an experiment upon their identities and performances of gender, the boys shrink away from the enactment of patriarchal masculinities and none ever return to their mock prison (40). Le Guin, therefore, illustrates in this passage both the connections between the social institutions and masculinities of the contemporary United States and the constant temptations the capitalistic patriarchy presents to alternative, feminist-oriented men.

Shevek's understanding of traditional masculinities' buttressing of social institutions ventures beyond jail to other organizations, including the military and the free market. He, for example, in understanding the organizational logic of the army, identifies the influence of traditional masculinities upon the armed forces and questions this conception of manhood. Such a system of power and control, he recognizes, is necessary for convincing soldiers to commit acts of violence, but he fails to "see where courage, or manliness, or fitness entered in" (304). As an Odonian, he performs a masculinity that values freedom and rejects the subjugating trends of masculinities normalized in A-Io and, therefore, the contemporary United States.

Shevek traces connections between such trends and the capitalistic free market. Although he does not fully comprehend the banking industry as a result of his background, he recognizes capitalistic markets as exploitative. The gendered nation produces an economic hierarchy similar to and influenced by its gender order. Those occupying the lower economic echelons are marginalized by those in power to the point of invisibility. Identifying and condemning capitalistic institutions that exploit and marginalize, Shevek asks, "where were the hands, the people who made? Out of sight, somewhere else. Behind walls. All the people in all the shops were either buyers or sellers. They had no relation to the things but that of possession" (132). In this way, the nation's economic system echoes its gender order, possessing at its core principles of consumption and ownership. The radical masculinity Shevek presents destabilizes consumerist behaviors encouraged by a ruling class that believes "if people can possess enough things they will be content to live in prison" (138). His revolution seeks to overturn traditional masculinities and the institutions they produce.

This work of undermining traditional masculinities and their attending institutions is necessary not only in A-Io but also the ambiguous utopia of Anarres. Given the aforementioned mutually constitutive relationship between gender and the nation and the previously outlined danger that men performing alternative masculinities may adopt traditional gender scripts, there exists also the danger that a feminist-oriented society may be infiltrated by patriarchal ideologies and transformed. Portraying the anarchic nation as a positive but imperfect alternative to its patriarchal, capitalistic rival, Le Guin explores how the mutability of the two aforementioned concepts of subjectivity, nationality and gender, reveal the dynamic nature of the nation and, more specifically, its institutions. As such organizations grow, they provide greater opportunities for power and control to be possessed by a few subjects and may cultivate, therefore, patriarchal atmospheres. Shevek's opposition to traditional masculinities involves the recognition of such gender ideologies as invasive and capable of, in addition to altering his own gender, infiltrating egalitarian societies.

This infiltration by traditional masculinities involves the introduction of hierarchical attitudes valuing power and control to Anarresti socioeconomic institutions. Importantly, this infiltration does not require the overt restructuring of social institutions but, instead, the subtle control of public opinion. Members of the "social organism," as the protagonist describes Anarres, are coerced by prevailing moral notions, meaning that "the social conscience completely dominates the individual conscience, instead of striking a balance with it" (329). Institutions pressure the individual to conform. Subjects deemed morally upright and invaluable members of these organizations may consolidate power and insure the complicity of others through the implied threat of social marginalization.

As this demonstrates, what endangers this feminist nation is the introduction of masculine consolidations of power via the control of public opinion, a method best exemplified by the aforementioned control of Shevek by Sabul early in the novel. As previously demonstrated, Sabul coerces Shevek and his student only later recognizes the subjugation and complicity that transpired. This complicity is significantly produced by Anarresti fears of public opinion. An individual's fears of being ostracized or labeled egocentric or lazy (329) may be manipulated by those wishing to accumulate power and control. Bedap explains to Shevek that Sabul receives his power from public opinion and the reluctance of individuals to challenge his authority and this accumulated power therefore stifles individual liberties. What threatens this feminist society is the introduction of traditional, masculine quests for power and control made possible by such manipulations of and complicity to public opinion.

Le Guin provides in the character, Tirin, the clearest example of the danger of Anarresti society. A childhood friend who later pursues a career as a playwright, Tirin is described as an artist who constantly challenges the status quo and calls for societal improvement through satire. Socially marginalized in reaction to a play he wrote interpreted as departing from Anarresti ideals, Tirin eventually suffers a mental breakdown. When hearing that he has been institutionalized, Shevek reasons that Tirin likely requested treatment. In response, Bedap explains that Tirin's breakdown is in reaction to the ostracization he suffers for producing his controversial play. The pressure to comply to desires of the social organism, as Shevek labels the nation, leads to mental anguish. As Le Guin illustrates in this passage, societal emphases upon normalizing mechanisms such as public opinion can lead to the introduction of traditional, masculine hierarchies. The citizens of Anarres, through their focus upon public opinion, have created networks of power predicated upon the exclusion of those who rebel and the inclusion of conforming citizens. (329). It is for this reason that Tirin suffers a mental breakdown. He refuses to comply within a system of power and control and suffers for this rebellion. "He never did it, he never could build walls. He was a natural rebel. He was a natural Odonian—a real one! He was a free man, and the rest of us, his brothers, drove him insane in punishment for his first free act" (329). Shevek must fight against these traditional masculine systems of power and control so Anarres and the Odonion alternative masculinities it produces may survive. Le Guin suggests that tendencies to abuse or dominate are not purely the results of capitalism but are symptomatic also of the traditional American masculinities supporting this economic system. The Anarresti must, therefore, safeguard against the importation of exploitative A-Io economic and gender hierarchies.

Shevek's opposition to governmental foreign policies favoring aggression and domination points to these features as destructive. These qualities of traditional masculinities are demonstrated in the novel to be key to the international policies of A-Io and antithetical to those of Anarres. Like the hegemonic, masculine traits of power and control, aggressive and dominating attitudes toward others reflect ideologies of manhood within A-Io society and pose a similar risk of importation to the Anarresti people. Such aggression and domination are the negative manifestations of traditional masculinities on a macro, international level as a result of the interactions between these differently gendered nations. Specifically, the traditionally masculine desire to aggressively dominate others is manifested in two key elements of American and A-Io foreign policy: nationalism and cultural hegemony. Representative of an alternative masculinity, Shevek destabilizes nationalistic and imperialistic policies of aggression and domination and the gender ideologies informing them.

Nationalism is a predominant characteristic of A-Io foreign policy. As a tool for stabilizing internal power structures, it enables the capitalistic patriarchy to attack and dominate other polities with limited domestic criticism. This tendency toward internal unification is a result of the fear nationalism induces in its subscribers toward other nations and people groups. Fear induces the subjects of A-Io to unite in opposition to perceived external threats and, importantly, such fearful allegiance is a product of the traditionally masculine gendered nation. Atro explains this relationship between nationalism, aggression, domination, and national masculinities to Shevek, describing the foundational ideology of Annaresti culture, Odoniasm, as feminine and therefore unable to instill in its followers a loyalty to the nation. In the traditionally masculinized nation, A-Io, on the other hand, citizens performing patriarchal masculinities predicated upon aggression and domination favor nationalism and enjoy privileged social positions within a hierarchy fortified by nationalism and traditional ideals of manhood. A performer of Anarresti masculinities, Shevek rejects such aggressive, dominating attitudes toward others and the nationalistic policies they promote.

Shevek's aforementioned opposition to the importing of traditional masculinities into Anarres means that he works also to destabilize developing nationalism within the anarchic nation. In a conversation with a friend, Kvetur, for example, he criticizes the growing belief among Anarresti that they should violently oppose Urras. Instead, he suggests that they reject such nationalistic tendencies to place Anarres in opposition to the nations of Urras. These attempts, though, are not successful and Shevek's reminder that the Urrasti are in part responsible for the development of their nation is met with derision. Shevek actively opposes nationalistic ideals with which he comes into contact in his daily life and highlights the threat of traditional masculinities' dominating policies to Anarres.

Recognizing the connection between gender and the nation, he rejects the ethical validity of the founders of Anarres who, due to nationalistic ideals, isolated themselves and their invaluable societal improvements from the nations of Urras: "The explorer who will not come back or send back his ships to tell his tale is not an explorer, only an adventurer, and his sons are born in exile" (89). Identifying isolationist policies as ill-disguised manifestations of nationalism and the will to possess advantages and power over other nations, Shevek labors to bridge the neighboring planets through communication. "The Settlers had taken one step away. He had taken two. He stood by himself, because he had taken the metaphysical risk. And he had been fool enough to think that he might serve to bring together two worlds to which he did not belong" (89). Such attempts illustrate his understanding that the importation of traditional masculinities entails the introduction of nationalism to Anarresti foreign policy.

These criticisms of Anarresti culture demonstrate the protagonist's commitment to alternative masculinities and his recognition that such gender scripts, like the nation, are permeable and, therefore, unstable. Standing in dramatic contrast to those problematic masculine characters of both A-Io and Anarres, Shevek is presented to the reader as an imperfect but positive alternative to traditional conceptions of manhood who learns to monitor himself after succumbing to the temptations of the capitalistic patriarchy. Opposing nationalistic policies of aggression and domination, he interacts with the people of A-Io in a productive, egalitarian manner. Recognizing the people of both Anarres and A-Io as equal regardless of nationality, gender, sexuality, or class position, for example, he refuses the titles of respect placed upon him by the Urrasti. The citizens of A-Io who believe in a natural hierarchy based upon identity markers such as gender, nationality, and class rank are, in response, unable to accept the egalitarian views espoused by the protagonist. Only those Urrasti citizens isolated from power and subjugated by their own gendered nations are willing to accept new, alternative masculinities not predicated upon nationalism and opposed to aggression and domination.

The willingness of the marginalized subjects of A-Io to revolt against the capitalist patriarchy leads those in power to prevent communication between Shevek and these rebel groups. In this way, they attempt to limit the effectiveness of a new, nonaggressive foreign policy produced by the anarchic nation and its masculinities that value open communication between citizens of all

nations. Realizing only after significant time has passed that he has allowed
the self-made men of A-Io to isolate him, Shevek repents of his inaction and
seeks to join the rebellion. He is initially made aware of these revolutionaries through an unsigned letter he receives. This correspondence galvanizes
within him a desire to free the people of A-Io. His acceptance of Urrasti
hospitality, he realizes, demonstrates the seductive dangers of propertar-
ian philosophy. "He had been co-opted—just as Chifoilisk had said" (192).
Recognizing his shortcomings, Shevek again recommits himself to the egalitarian, non-nationalistic policy of meeting and seeking to aid the subjects of
other nations, regardless of their social position.

Such a nonexploitative approach to foreign policy contrasts starkly with
that of A-Io, which adopts imperialistic attitudes toward international relations. As a distorted portrayal of the United States, A-Io engages in a proxy
war against Thu, a nation acting as a defamiliarized representative of the
Soviet Union. Taking place in the less powerful nation of Benbili, the conflict echoes the Vietnam War and illustrates the imperialistic, dominating,
and aggressive foreign policies of both a totalitarian socialist regime and a
capitalistic republic. The Benbili revolution and imperialistic intervention
of A-Io, like the nation's domestic policies of subjugation, cause an initially
reluctant Shevek to reconsider his inaction and silence. As an ambassador of
an anarchic nation favoring nontraditional masculinities, he recognizes his
responsibility to take part in revolutionary Urrasti efforts to actively counter
aggressive, dominating attacks upon other polities and oppose the military of
A-Io, which are informed by patriarchal masculinities. The military industry
represents the salient effects of traditional masculinities upon the nation: it
consolidates power and control through its subjugation of enlisted men and
women and wins the support of the citizenry through nationalistic policies of
aggressively dominating other nations.

Presenting such connections between masculinities and social institutions
such as the military, Le Guin emphasizes the mutually constitutive relationship of gender and the nation. She reveals in her novel the necessary ties
between socioeconomic, military, and governmental structures constituting
a society and its hegemonic masculinity. A-Io seeks not only to control its
subjects but also to continuously broaden the borders of its power and this
is what Shevek identifies as the cause of human suffering and hierarchies of
power in the nation. Anarres, as a gendered, feminist nation, originates in
rebellion toward A-Io and, therefore, rejects the interconnected hegemonic
masculinity, socioeconomic systems, and private structures making up the
capitalistic patriarchy. As outlined by the protagonist, this rebellion produces
some key differences between the two nations. While Anarres lacks beauty
except in the faces of its citizens, A-Io is visually stunning but the faces of
its subjects hint at the oppression they suffer (229). Symbolizing the peace

and tranquility brought about through the anarchic, alternatively masculine nation, these faces belong to those who contentedly lack property and value diverse sexualities, races, and genders among other identity elements. This acceptance of nontoxic, alternative masculinities brings about true freedom and its signifier, the eyes, replaces the old symbol of the commodified sexuality of Urrasti women, the jeweled navel: "Here you see the jewels, there you see the eyes. And in the eyes you see the splendor, the splendor of the human spirit. Because our men and women are free" (229). Challenges to patriarchal efforts to consolidate power and control domestically and aggressively dominate internationally produce freedom to perform varying masculinities opposing hegemony. Importantly, the challenge Shevek mounts frees access to information in order to prevent the aggressive domination of other nations by patriarchies such as A-Io.

Shevek releases information because he understands Odonian anarchism and its attending masculinities to be representative of "a permanent revolution" that "begins in the thinking mind" (333). Believing that his scientific work may be responsible for greater communication and understanding among nations, Shevek continues it in defiance of public opinion and opposes A-Io efforts to gain exclusive information about his developing tool for intergalactic communication. These actions illustrate his opposition to domestic consolidations of power and control and foreign policies supporting the aggression and domination of other nations. Accordingly, he and Takver decide they must relocate and start a printing syndicate via which they may produce and circulate formerly censored texts including Tirin's play. In doing so, he risks "the self for the sake of" (271) Anarres, Urras, and other nations and is marginalized by those in growing power and others complacent to this developing masculine hierarchy. He and Takver are labeled traitors and Sadik, their child, is branded an egoizer, an Anarresti term for a hierarchal, myopic individual. Odonian rhetoric is deployed to manipulate him and his partner, individualists truly following the teachings of Odo. Shevek labors in the novel to defend the ambiguously utopian, impermanent but positive nationality and masculinities of Anarres. He does this by disrupting emerging traditional masculinities and their attending hierarchies of power and control.

The unsettling of traditional masculinities by the protagonist represents a significant moment within speculative fiction. Like Bryant, Le Guin centers in her novel the experiences of a male character negotiating patriarchal and alternative masculinities. Unlike *The Kin of Ata Are Waiting for You*, which focuses upon the recovery and conversion of a patriarch, *The Dispossessed* traces the struggles of an alternative, feminist-oriented man to withstand the temptations of capitalism and misogyny. Le Guin presents in her novel a male character who, after succumbing to traditional ideals of manhood, subscribes ultimately to a masculine script not predicated upon "animal power, instinct, and aggression" (Hantke 1998, 498) but, instead, opposing consolidations of power and control over others. Speaking to the rebels gathered on the streets of A-Io, he calls for a new brotherhood among men rejecting traditional masculinities of subjugation, violence, and the consolidation of power. The new masculinity Shevek proposes, like the one adopted by Bryant's unnamed protagonist, rejects capitalistic, patriarchal gender orders and favors nonhierarchical social systems opposing control, aggression, and domination. Unlike Bryant's narrator, who values dreams as a source of transcendent knowledge and utilizes writing as a method for disseminating information concerning alternative masculinities, Shevek is inspired directly by the feminist and anarchic political theory of Odo. Similarly interested in the spreading of invaluable information, he opts not to compose a tract but, instead, to make available the data related to his new communication invention. His actions at least temporarily prevent the consolidation of power by nations hording such important breakthroughs and are therefore grounded in his alternative masculinity.

Shevek represents a new type of male character that, like Bryant's unnamed narrator, values feminist principles and rejects the desires for power and subordination endemic to the capitalistic patriarchy. Through this character and his experiences in A-Io, a defamiliarized portrait of American society, Le Guin is able to engage her audience in a dialectic concerning manhood in the contemporary United States. Applying masculinities studies' theoretical tools to science fiction, therefore, allows for a better understanding of how writers such as Le Guin circumvent or directly challenge normalized conceptions of manhood. Moving beyond Bryant's interest in the possibility of transforming patriarchal men, Le Guin considers the feminist-oriented, new man and illuminates the unstable qualities of such new masculinities and the nations cultivating them. Choosing not to present an idealized, protected utopia, Le Guin, by emphasizing like Bryant the instability of gender roles, adds considerable complexity to discussions concerning the better society and its corresponding masculinities. Such interests in the precarious nature of the feminist utopia and its alternative masculinities are further developed in Marge Piercy's *Woman on the Edge of Time*, the focus of chapter 3. By focusing on male protagonists as they encounter feminist-oriented nations and masculinities and their patriarchal counterparts, Le Guin, like Bryant, illuminates how ideals of manhood are constructed and the methods by which improved alternative masculinities may be developed.

Chapter 3

Complicating Manhood in Marge Piercy's *Woman on the Edge of Time*

Marge Piercy's *Woman on the Edge of Time*, and the subjects of chapters 4 and 5, Octavia Butler's *Lilith's Brood* trilogy and N.K. Jemisin's *Broken Earth* series, respectively, share an interest in widening and complicating the sociopolitical focuses of the feminist utopian genre. While representing a shift in feminist speculative fiction toward centralizing traditionally marginalized characters such as women of color, these novels are customarily analyzed for their portrayals of women. Scholars of *Woman on the Edge of Time* have considered its vital role in introducing to science fiction new, complex female characters and feminist societies, and its centering of characters traditionally placed on the margins due to their race and gender. The novel is significant in its depiction of the experiences of a woman of color. Characters like Connie from *The Kin of Ata* move from the margin of the narrative to its center. Focused upon the experiences of a Latinx Mexican American female whose name, Consuelo or Connie, harkens back to this early character in Bryant's novel *Woman on the Edge of Time* considers how misogynist and utopian male characters impact her. Though men exist as complementary characters, their influence and the impact of their masculinities upon the experiences of the protagonist and the possibility of a feminist utopia are significant. Piercy's novel uses its male characters in ways similar to earlier feminist texts such as *The Kin of Ata Are Waiting for You* and *The Dispossessed*. This analysis uniquely contributes to ongoing discussions of American masculinity by tracing Piercy's emphases upon complex, intersectional identities, the functioning of masculine and feminist societies, and the necessity of reshaping society in order for improved masculinities to be realized.

Often cited alongside Joanna Russ, Ursula K. Le Guin, James Tiptree Jr., and others as a central voice in 1970s feminist science fiction, Marge Piercy is a feminist poet, novelist, and recipient of the Arthur C. Clarke Award for science fiction. Her critiques of traditional masculinities and femininities exemplify Brian Attebery's description of a radical change in science fiction, making it "virtually impossible for an SF writer to take gender for granted any more" (Attebery 2002, 6). Piercy's novels such as *Woman on the Edge of Time* and *He, She and It* (1991) highlight the socially constructed and subjugating natures of gender roles, making them essential works at the intersection of masculinity studies and contemporary American science fiction. Her characters rebel against intersecting systems of oppression and, as a result, disrupt normative ideologies, especially those concerning gender. *Woman on the Edge of Time*, therefore, literally embodies "every ideal of the counterculture/Movement: ecological wisdom, community, androgyny, ritual, respect for madness, propertylessness, etc." ("Woman on the Edge of Time" 2019). Among these revolutionary ideals is Piercy's presentation of new, egalitarian conceptions of masculinity. What she contributes to conversations at the intersection of gender and society, therefore, is a new conception of manhood based upon connection, vulnerability, and equality that, as she illustrates, is germane to the utopian project and the betterment of contemporary American society.

Piercy creates in her novels women's utopias, places "where what women do not have can exist—i.e., a sense of community, since many women are isolated while raising their children. A place where women are not punished for their sexuality, a place where raising children is communal or quasi-communal, a place where in old age people are respected and taken care of" (Furlanetto 2014, 421). Piercy imagines a society in *Woman on the Edge of Time* in which women are afforded power and opportunities denied them by patriarchal social systems. Since patriarchal societies are predicated upon the conscription of men into traditional conceptions of manhood, the feminist environment Piercy develops allows alternative masculinities to flourish. Unlike their traditionally masculine counterparts, the new men populating Piercy's utopia value their feminine qualities and seek to eliminate the patriarchal order. *Woman on the Edge of Time* presents male and female characters who are characterized by and perform social functions traditionally deemed both masculine and feminine and are, therefore, androgynous. This aspect of the novel places it in contrast with Ursula K. Le Guin's *The Left Hand of Darkness* (1969), which, as previously discussed, is criticized for its presentation of biologically androgynous characters marked as men linguistically through the use of masculine pronouns and socially via their "roles which we are culturally conditioned to perceive as 'male'" (Anna 1978, 151). Piercy's male characters break from traditional gender scripts, offering alternative performances of manhood. In place of traditionally masculine desires for power and control, Piercy presents male characters focused on community, healing, connection, and fraternity.

Such new conceptions of manhood are positioned against those afore-mentioned traditional masculinities of genre fiction: the so-called super-men. Donna Fancourt's (2002) identification of a "movement away from an emphasis on sexual difference, and towards a society that promotes connection with others" (109) as central to feminist utopias hints at the necessity for men to undergo a paradigm shift in consciousness—a new masculinity—for society to be improved. Such a change in consciousness rejects the values of the traditional supermen of science fiction. Piercy, like Dorothy Bryant and Ursula K. Le Guin,[1] rejects the traditional masculinities of earlier speculative fiction and replaces them with male characters performing new, utopian interpretations of manhood.

Such a presentation of new masculinities as central to the utopian project unites *Woman on the Edge of Time*, Piercy's first speculative work, *Dance the Eagle to Sleep* (1970), and her later novel, *He, She and It*. A precursor to works such as *Woman on the Edge of Time* and *He, She and It* that likewise explores dystopian and utopian possibilities, *Dance the Eagle to Sleep* concerns the attempts of four teenagers to build a visionary society in opposition to the capitalistic, patriarchal system of the United States. Piercy identifies in this early work a connection further elaborated upon in *Woman on the Edge of Time*: a better society requires improved, feminist-informed masculinities. Building on the alternative vision in *Dance the Eagle to Sleep*, *Woman on the Edge of Time* comments critically on contemporary American society and contains "a conglomeration of the various utopian aspirations of the '60s and '70s" in that "it strives to bring together the concepts of racial, cultural and sexual liberation in a vision predicated on economic transformation, particularly in regard to property and production" (Somay and RMP 1984, 30).

Such connections similarly bind *Woman on the Edge of Time* to *He, She and It*. Both novels, for example, focus on the possibility of reconceptualizing masculinity through, among other tools, the utilization of new technologies. In *Woman on the Edge of Time*, the reproductive division of labor is blurred through the use of technologies enabling men to breast feed. The cyborg, Yod, in *He, She and It* likewise learns to perform new, nurturing masculinities, leading him to be "in some respects . . . more 'human' than other human beings, notably the masculine figures who are inhumanly mechanical, unemotional, unloving" (Deery 1994, 39). Each of these novels includes positive, alternative masculinities as central to utopian societies and traditional masculinities as normalized within their patriarchal counterparts. These utopias reveal Piercy's consistent interest in the better society and its attending masculinities. In this endeavor to present the improved, feminist polity, Piercy proved groundbreaking in her presentation of complex male characters and societies that enable the flourishing of new, positive masculinities.

Crucial to Piercy's depiction of these alternative masculinities and nonnormative gender scripts more broadly is the way she imagines in each of
her characters—both male and female—a combination of traits traditionally
identified as feminine and masculine. In this way, she breaks from the trend
among male writers to present visions of the androgyne in which a "masculine
personality" is "fulfilled and completed by the feminine" (Annas 1978, 147).
Pamela Annas groups "together loosely under the concept of androgyny" a
range of examples "from visions of worlds which have entirely eliminated
men and therefore sexual polarization, through visions of worlds which are
biologically androgynous, to visions of worlds in which male and female
functions and roles simply are not sharply differentiated" (146). Central to
Woman on the Edge of Time is a vision of androgyny encapsulating these last
two examples; in Piercy's novel, social and biological roles do not belong
strictly to the categories of traditional masculinity or femininity. Instead,
male characters balance traditionally masculine goals such as military service
with their desires to raise and nurture a child. Female characters meanwhile
occupy positions of social power and these roles showcase personality
qualities traditionally labeled as masculine. Critics of androgyny as a tool in
speculative fiction such as Jean Elshtain (1981) posit that "the full achievement of an androgynous world is possible only with the total elimination of
sex roles" and the elimination of connections between biological sex and
procreation (7). Piercy's presentation of androgyny and its attending gender-
queer, alternative ideals of manhood is made possible through the utilization
of technologies, such as the brooder and those developments allowing men
to breastfeed, to differentiate reproductive roles. Piercy's vision of alternative
masculinities, with its emphasis on technology and a more complex gender
dynamic, is, therefore, radical among feminist utopias.

The structure of Piercy's novel adds considerable strength to this utopian
message. Like *The Kin of Ata Are Waiting for You* and *The Dispossessed*,
Woman on the Edge of Time follows a protagonist who travels between utopian and dystopian societies. Unlike these texts, which follow male citizens
of dystopia and utopia, respectively, Piercy's novel centers the experiences
of a disempowered female citizen of dystopia—the contemporary United
States—as she experiences life within a drastically improved, feminist polity. Confined to a mental institution early in the narrative, Consuelo Ramos
discovers she can communicate with people of the future and even travel
mentally across space and time to explore their utopian community. The
novel, like the novels of Bryant and Le Guin, interweaves utopian and dystopian passages in order to dramatically demarcate the differences separating
patriarchal and feminist societies and the masculinities each nation normalizes. Central to this functioning of the novel and its presentation of contrasting utopian and dystopian performances of manhood is Piercy's use of time

travel as a powerful literary device. Able to travel across time and therefore visit a future feminist utopia and patriarchal dystopia, the novel's protagonist, Connie, and the reader through her are prompted to compare three possible societies. The connections Piercy draws between the contemporary American dystopia and these two possible futures, a feminist utopia and a nightmarish patriarchal alternative, illustrate the binary struggle between two societies with antithetical feminine and masculine gender scripts.

The dystopian societies of the text, the United States in the present and a future version of the society in which the ideals of capitalistic patriarchy are taken to their extreme, are presented in tandem with those passages located in the future utopia. Piercy compels her reader to note the differences separating these polities by alternating, through the protagonist's ability to time travel, the setting of her novel from the dystopian to the utopian nation and vice versa. The qualities of this utopia, a future, collectivist anarchical community located in present-day Mattapoisett, Massachusetts, are, therefore, contrasted strikingly with those of these patriarchal alternatives. In this way, the structure of the novel and its intermingling of utopian and dystopian passages add considerable power to Piercy's gender analysis. This juxtaposition of nations parallels a contrast in traditional and new conceptions of manhood that produces the dialectic of masculinities central to Piercy's novel. Building upon "Mikhail Bakhtin's emphasis on the importance of generic heterogeneity as a source of dialogic" power, Keith Booker (1994) identifies as "an important source of energy for" *Woman on the Edge of Time* "the resultant dialogue between" (340) these imagined utopian and dystopian nations visited by Connie. Just as the novel's contrast between these dystopian and utopian visions increases its power, its inclusion of traditional and alternative masculinities in opposition to one another intensifies the dialectic of the utopian text concerning gender.

The feminist qualities of this utopia reveal the significance of masculinities to Mattapoisett. Requiring of its citizens a balanced focus on community, interdependence, responsibilities, and an interest in equality, this idealized society compels attitudes absent from traditional masculinities and implies, therefore, a need for alternative conceptions of manhood. Karen Stein's (2013) claim that in the novel "it is necessary 'to make men over' as more sensitive and nurturing people so that they fit into the communal society" (129) reiterates this common understanding of the way the text connects to issues of masculinity.[2] As Stein's analysis reveals, the remaking of masculinities is pivotal to the positive transformation of patriarchal societies.

Piercy's presentation of disruptive, future masculinities is unique in its "emphasis upon purposeful human action in bringing about utopia" (Somay 1984, 30). In the text, the direct tracing of the impact of present actions upon the future is made possible by Connie's time-traveling abilities. When the future is altered and Connie arrives not in Mattapoisett but instead in a patriarchal, dystopian New York, she and her utopian allies recognize a causative event in her own time: the development of a cognitive biotechnology enabling control of the mind and emotions. A wrongfully confined patient of the mental institution at which this tool is developed, Connie resolves to halt the research project. Concluding with Connie fatally poisoning the doctors spearheading this work, the novel offers to the reader as apparent the assurance that the utopian future is at least temporarily protected and that actions today will lead either to alternative masculinities and utopia or dystopia. Piercy presents her utopia as vulnerable to present actions and the influence of capitalism and the patriarchy and her novel, therefore, shares similarities with *The Kin of Ata Are Waiting for You* and *The Dispossessed.* Bryant's unnamed narrator, for example, writes a didactic tract concerning traditional masculinities and Le Guin's protagonist opposes capitalistic patriarchal attempts to control technology and information. In *Woman on the Edge of Time,* however, this connection between present actions and the future development of patriarchal or feminist polities is more strikingly emphasized through Piercy's use of time travel.

This depiction of both future utopian and dystopian polities and their dependence upon events and characters in the present enables the novel to escape what is often considered a fatal flaw of utopian writing, its tendency toward the ahistorical and static.[3] In the novel, Connie must choose between two possible futures, a feminist utopia and patriarchal dystopia. Prodding the reader to consider possible configurations of gendered societies and the possibility of influencing the development of such a future society in the present, Piercy radically reenvisions the utopian genre. Avoiding the tendency among traditional utopian writers to favor "over-arching theories of utopia as a distant or perfect world" and to thus fail to present "historically specific and situated alternatives" (McBean 2014, 42) to socioeconomic ideologies, she presents a dynamic utopia connected to the historical setting of its audience. The power of the text is derived significantly from its inclusion of time travel as a means of critiquing masculinities and considering future dystopian and utopian societies alongside the society in which Connie resides, the contemporary United States.

Central to this presentation of the twentieth-century United States is its tracing of the impact of intersectionality upon marginalized subjects such as Connie. In this way, the novel outlines those gendered networks of power that must be disrupted for new masculinities to be normalized. Through Connie's experiences, we see how interconnecting systems of sexism and racism work to marginalize and disempower the protagonist and others. The men with whom Connie comes into contact are either medical professionals or part of her social network. The men are positioned at varying distances from power and their contrasts reveal connections existing between intersectionality and masculinities. The doctors populating the novel in the twentieth-century time frame, Redding, Morgan, and Acker, maintain powerful social and economic positions as educated, white, heterosexual performers of traditional masculinity. The men with whom Connie comes in contact outside the medical institution, mostly working-class men of color, on the other hand, wield less masculine authority due to their race and class positions.

The traditional masculinities of these men marginalized by class and race are informed by the concept of *machismo*. As demonstrated by Alfredo Mirandé in *Hombres y Machos: Masculinity and Latino Culture* (1997), the understanding of this term and its performance is heavily influenced not "by region but by socioeconomic status" and therefore varies according to the social and economic positioning of its subscriber. As Piercy illustrates in the novel, a man such as Geraldo, Dolly's pimp, who possesses little socioeconomic power, conceives of machismo "as exaggerated masculinity predicated on male dominance and authoritarianism, violence, aggressiveness, drunkenness, dumb, irresponsibleness, selfishness, stubbornness, and the unwillingness to back down for even the most trivial matter" (Mirandé 1997, 77). In contrast, other men of color, such as Connie's brother Luis, who possess socioeconomic power and seek to pass as white in order to increase this amount of control, limit their public demonstrations of machismo since the application of this term "to Mexicans or Latino" by white men is "imbued with such negative attributes as male dominance, patriarchy, authoritarianism, and spousal abuse" (66). Machismo, therefore, is a type of hypermasculinity demonstrated by those men of color with whom Connie comes into contact in her personal life that, like its white masculine counterpart, exploits those marginalized further from power according to the logic of sexism, racism, and homophobia.

While prevented from fully accessing the power granted to his white counterparts due to his ethnicity, Luis, for example, exercises complete control over women in his life such as Connie. He experiences intersectionality as a financially successful, heterosexual man hindered by discrimination according to his race. He wields the power he has by subjugating those situated further from power. While he channels his anger into efforts to accumulate economic power, he also directs this resentment toward those few people whom he is able to control, his family. Preoccupied, for example, with the appearances of his children and wife, Luis orders his son, Mark, to eat more in order to develop a masculine physique and baselessly accuses the women of the family, his daughter, Dolly, and wife, Adele, of being overweight. Besides these harsh, demeaning criticisms, the interactions between Luis and his family are controlled by him as a means of exercising that power denied to him in contemporary American society. Luis dominates his family, releasing upon them the anger he accumulates from his experiences in a systemically racist society.

This brutality is utilized by Piercy to reveal connections between traditional gender roles and intersectionality. Able to have his sister freed or confined indefinitely, Luis leverages this power, demanding that Connie perform traditionally feminine roles during a visit home he authorizes. Specifically, he demands that she perform domestic duties and refrain from offering her own opinion on matters during her stay. In this way, Luis takes advantage of a system that disenfranchises women and provides men power over them. Within patriarchy, male subjects who are not able to maintain the privileged hegemonic position are compelled to remain complicit to patriarchy, thereby benefiting "from the patriarchal dividend, the advantage men in general gain from the overall subordination of women" (Connell 1995, 79). Interlocking systems of oppression such as racism, sexism, and homophobia, therefore, affect both Connie and those men such as Luis whose identity markers distance them from hegemony but grant them power for their complicity to patriarchy.

The traditional masculinities of these marginalized men are characterized by desires to consolidate power and control over others and are informed by capitalistic, patriarchal socioeconomic systems and a sexist paradigm of consciousness. As outlined in the introduction, Shulamith Firestone's materialist critique of inequality among the sexes further illuminates the ways Piercy presents class, race, and gender as connected systems of oppression. Writing during the height of second-wave feminism, Firestone provided in *The Dialectic of Sex: The Case for Feminist Revolution* (1970) an influential map for bridging Marxist and psychoanalytic theories of inequality. The importance of this theory of sex and class in developing the utopian society is outlined in the novel by Bolivar, a male inhabitant of Mattapoisett: "I guess I see the original division of labor, that first dichotomy, as enabling later divvies into haves and have-nots, powerful and powerless, enjoyers and workers, rapists and victims. The patriarchal mind/body split turned the body to machine and the rest of the universe into booty on which the will could run rampant, using, discarding, destroying" (229).

The male characters populating the contemporary United States of the text illustrate these connections and act as representatives of traditional masculinity, focused upon exercising power over others and attaining higher positions within socioeconomic hierarchies. The role of economic gains in validating the masculine identities of these characters is illustrated in Connie's recounting of the murder of her lover, Martín, who died senselessly because "men without jobs proved they were still men on the bodies of other men, on the bodies of women" (232–233). As this passage reveals, capitalism and patriarchy work in concert to reinforce exploitative networks of power. Violence such as the knife fight that results in the death of Martín results from a need among economically disadvantaged men to have their masculinity recognized through other means. The desire of traditionally masculine characters to consolidate power and control over *the other*, identified by markers such as race, sexuality, and gender, are symptomatic of capitalistic, patriarchal masculinities and are trenchantly exposed in the novel.

The patriarchal, capitalistic men with whom Connie comes into contact throughout her personal life desire to have power and control over her. These traditionally masculine men meet the criteria for what Connie describes to the citizens of Mattapoisett as a *real* man: He "is supposed to be . . . strong, hold his liquor, attractive to women, able to beat out other men, lucky, hard, tough, macho we call it, muy hombre . . . not to be a fool . . . not to get too involved . . . to look out for number one . . . to make good money," to acquiesce to those possessing power, and to subjugate individuals lower in the power hierarchy (127). As Piercy notes in this passage, a man is identified by his ability to dominate and subjugate others according to the logic of capitalism, sexism, racism, and homophobia.

These marginalized men seek through complicity to consolidate control over women as a means of validating their manhood, which is threatened by the racist ideologies of white patriarchal hegemony. The manner in which Connie is registered as a patient reveals, for example, the collaboration of a complicit, traditionally masculine character, Dolly's pimp, referred to in the novel as Geraldo, and a similar male doctor powerfully positioned due to his class and race. In his approach to gain power through an alliance with a hegemonic male, the doctor, Geraldo communicates respect for the position of his hegemonic counterpart and compliance to patriarchal networks of power. He is demure and understands how to communicate with those possessing power in the white patriarchy. As a result, Geraldo gains access to greater power and control over Connie, demonstrated by the silencing of the protagonist as these men decide her fate. Ultimately, through his recognition of and cooperation with masculine social patterns, Geraldo succeeds in isolating Connie who, under temporary observation, becomes from the perspectives of the doctor and medical staff a lifeless corpse to be measured and weighed (14). This collaboration between complicit and hegemonic masculinities is later reiterated by Piercy when Luis requests that Connie be committed instead of temporarily observed. A compromise is struck between these men who, while occupying disparate socioeconomic positions, are united by their mutual control over the woman whose fate they negotiate. The manner by which Connie is systemically dominated and controlled is the product of men marginalized according to race and class who gain control through their complicity to patriarchal networks of power.

Through Dolly's pimps Geraldo and Vic, Piercy highlights how the efforts of complicit men to consolidate power and control affect two generations of women. Each violently dominates Dolly and gains social power and economic profit from her subjugation. Connie outlines this exploitation, identifying Geraldo as the man who pimps, beats, robs, and sells Dolly, hits her daughter, Nita, and takes the money gained through the exploitation of Dolly's body (9). Commodifying Dolly's body and sexuality and forcing her to have an abortion in order to continue her work as a prostitute, Geraldo partakes in the capitalistic patriarchy, accumulating profit through the domination of *the other*, marginalized due to her class position, biological sex, and race. Commenting on the continual, cross-generational nature of this exploitative trend among men complicit to patriarchy, Connie identifies her niece's pimp as one of countless men who seek to control her. He represents every abusive man with whom she has come into contact, including her father and second husband. Geraldo, through his traditional performance of manhood, represents a larger, toxic trend among men of color to remain complicit to patriarchy through the domination of others. Piercy presents as central to her utopian vision the challenging of patriarchal concepts of manhood and the complicity of men marginalized according to racist ideologies.

The relationship of class and ethnicity to traditional masculinities is further delineated by Piercy in the early experiences of Connie with a white man, Chuck. Prior to the events of the novel, Connie attempts to gain power through education. She attends a community college in Chicago to become a teacher but, due to a lack of funds, is obliged to type papers for a fellow student, a young white man named Chuck, in order to gain access to his typewriter for her own work. Piercy provides few details concerning their relationship, but it is disclosed that they date until, due to her eventual pregnancy, Connie is deserted by Chuck. As a result, Connie finds herself void of both hope and confidence and unable to complete her education. In reflecting upon the events that followed in which she was further disempowered as a result of not performing ideal femininity, Connie identifies the intersectional nature of her subjugation. Due to her unique identity as a female and member of the Latinx community, she is labeled a "woman spoiled" or "chingada," (264) and is financially devastated by an expensive and dangerous abortion, the ostracization of her by her family and Chuck, and her inability to complete her education. The traditionally American masculine value of walking over others (127) is, therefore, exemplified both by Chuck and the varying socioeconomic systems—the nuclear family, capitalistic healthcare, and gender ideologies—that distance Connie further from power. Piercy specifically presents the nuclear family as a microcosm of socioeconomic inequality; the mother, she demonstrates through Connie, is exploited and subordinated while the father, as exemplified by Chuck, is able to ignore his responsibilities to her and the child. In this way, Chuck exemplifies the complicit pattern of masculinity and, through his exploitation and abandonment of Connie, shirks responsibilities that would restrict his capacity for upward socioeconomic movement.

The relationship of the traditionally masculine exploitation of *the other* to race and the commodification of the female body is further highlighted by Piercy through the relationship of Dolly and her second pimp and boyfriend, Vic. A white male possessing significant power, Vic pressures Dolly to pass as white and maintain an unhealthy weight in order to attract wealthier clients. Dolly additionally dyes her hair red and tells her clients that she is of Spanish and Irish descent since she earns the most from white Americans who value bodily markers associated with whiteness (236–237). Seeking greater socioeconomic power, Vic consolidates control over Dolly, whom he considers a valuable object for economic exploitation. He compels Dolly to alter her body through cosmetics and to take speed in order to achieve this desired appearance. Through Vic, Piercy emphasizes how the contemporary United States compels women to present themselves in a way favoring traditionally masculine valuations of whiteness and misogynistic beauty standards.

Piercy further outlines the ways the capitalistic patriarchy pressures men of color to pass as white in order to gain socioeconomic power through the actions of another complicit, traditionally masculine character, Luis. A Mexican American businessman who owns and manages a successful plant nursery, Luis epitomizes the self-made man, though he is hindered from fully realizing this identity due to his race. As previously outlined, this masculine model involves the deriving of a man's identity from his "activities in the public sphere, measured by accumulated wealth and status, by geographic and social mobility." Since his status is dependent upon the market and his own socioeconomic successes and failures, the self-made man is "mobile, competitive, aggressive in business . . . temperamentally restless, chronically insecure, and desperate to achieve a solid grounding for a masculine identity" (Kimmel 2006, 137). Luis, as a Mexican American, is offered limited opportunities for upward mobility. In response, he remains complicit to traditional patterns of masculinity and seeks to pass as white in order to accumulate further socioeconomic power.

As Piercy demonstrates, race, ethnicity, and complicity to patriarchy are linked and Luis seeks to alleviate his own intersectional disadvantage by appearing to be a hegemonic, white male. Connie recognizes this desire on the part of her brother when she recounts his return from military service prior to the events of the novel: "When he had come back, he had contempt for the rest of them. His anger and unruly pride had been channeled into a desire to get ahead, to grab money, to succeed like an Anglo . . . Jesús had been scared he would go bad, they would lose him to the streets. None of them had guessed they would lose him to the Anglos, entirely" (397). Desiring to pass as a hegemonic male—white, upper class, straight—he dominates those around him who are identified as *other*, prefers the Americanized pronunciation of his name, and conforms to the dressing norms of middle-class white America. As evidenced by notes attributed to the New York Neuro-Psychiatric Institute included at the end of the text, Luis at least partially succeeds in these efforts to pass and this success grants him considerable power over his sister: "Mr. Camacho is a well-dressed man (gray business suit) who appears to be in his 40s. He operates a wholesale-retail nursery and has a confident, expansive manner. I would consider him to be a reliable informant who expresses genuine concern for his sister" (416). Signaling through his middle-class attire a complicity to capitalistic, patriarchal networks of power, Luis consolidates control over women such as Connie through this loyalty to current socioeconomic systems. Through the personal relationships of Connie to Luis as well as Vic and Geraldo, Piercy charts the negative impact of traditional masculinities upon a Mexican American woman and the centrality of race as a factor of complicity and subordination. Tracing intersectionality and the specific ways traditional masculinities connect with the logic of racism to marginalize others, Piercy illustrates the dystopian qualities of patriarchy in the contemporary United States and the importance of class and ethnicity in the shaping of patriarchal ideals of manhood.

These dystopian patriarchal qualities permeate the institutions of the gendered nation and, more specifically, the medical establishment. In the novel, the nature of diagnosis and "how mental illness gets constructed—frequently based on stereotypical readings of surface characteristics such as behavior, age, poverty, body odors, or ethnicity—and is used as a form of social control" are implicated as forces of intersectionality (Martinson 2003, 53). The text illustrates, therefore, how traditional masculinities possess a mutually constitutive relationship not only with the nation but those institutions contained within its networks of power. As a result of prior experiences with hospitals, including the hysterectomy to which she was subjected, Connie recognizes this relationship between patriarchy and healthcare. The presence of intersectionality within contemporary American healthcare is most clearly illuminated by Piercy in her depiction of the rules governing the behavior of Connie and her fellow patients in these institutions and the treatments to which she is subjected.

Through the guidelines and treatments to which Connie is compelled to submit within these hospitals, Piercy outlines the toxic influence of traditional masculinities in health care. Female patients, for example, are expected to perform traditional femininities and are "punished for unladylike behavior" (156). While the use of explicit language is a punishable offense, volunteering to complete tasks associated with femininity such as cleaning, aiding the nurses, and assisting with the laundry (369) is rewarded with the allowance of greater personal liberties. Central to the treatment plans developed by these male doctors is the adoption by female patients of traditional gender roles and those unwilling to adopt these feminine roles are subjected to further domination and control. The increased severity of these treatments and their relationship to patriarchy are exemplified by the use of shock therapy. The female recipients of this treatment either forget about their fear and oppression or become "more scared of being burned in the head again" than of patriarchal control and return home to their subjugated roles and responsibilities (83). As Connie states, these shock treatments are repeated each time a female patient departs from the gender role assigned to her by the ideologies of traditional masculinity. Repeat offenders, or "shock zombies" as Connie calls them, are relocated to the back wards where they sit idly and giggling, unable to fully function due to the scarring of their brains (83). In this way, medicine as a traditionally male-dominated arena acts as a form of gender control and subjugation reinforcing patriarchy and centralizing control among traditionally masculine males.

Traditional masculinities seek to reinforce heteronormativity, exemplified in the hospitals' homophobic policies that harm queer patients. Connie's fellow patient and friend, Skip, for example, is identified as pathological due to his identification as a gay man. As Skip outlines, the harmful treatments imposed on these patients are the products of patriarchal desires to enforce heteronormativity: "They don't like us, you know. We're lepers . . . You know what the last experiment was they pulled on me? They stuck electrodes on my prick and showed me dirty pictures, and when I got a hard-on about men, they shocked me" (177). Subjected to a newly developed brain implant through which his desires and actions are manipulated, Skip eventually commits suicide in order to escape the control of this dystopian mental health institution. The patients Piercy presents are, therefore, imprisoned and subjugated in order to force upon them the logic of patriarchy and traditional conceptions of manhood.

A new neuroscientific and cognitive treatment plan makes possible the complete consolidation of power and control by these physicians over the minds and bodies of their patients. By implanting a new technological device in the brains of patients, these doctors are able to control their actions and emotional states, thereby imposing upon the minds and bodies of patients their own wills. These men seek to control and subjugate marginalized subjects such as Connie, desiring ultimately to place inside her a mechanism via which they may dominate her will. In contrast to the technologies of Mattapoisett, which are marked by their egalitarian effects and valuation of embodiment and emotional knowledge, this device empowers traditionally masculine men in places of power to control female bodies, restrict emotional experiences, and enforce the sanitized rationality they sanction as superior to the knowledges derived from embodied experience. As outlined by Connie, they "believed feeling itself a disease, something to be cut out like a rotten appendix. Cold, calculating, ambitious, believing themselves rational and superior, they chased the crouching female animal through the brain with a scalpel" (308). As Connie recognizes, these men develop a tool enabling them to have complete control over the minds of women and to, therefore, enforce patriarchal values such as the distrust of disembodied knowledge upon them.

When she is eventually subjected to this treatment, Connie transforms into an image of traditional, hyperfeminine qualities, an object acted upon by outside, patriarchal forces. Piercy reveals in such a treatment plan how the interests of traditional masculinities are served by major institutions within the gendered nation, the contemporary United States. Pushed to the margins of power due to her sex, race, and class position, Connie faces the prospect of losing her very mind and body to those subscribing to traditional masculinities. Piercy, therefore, highlights in the novel those toxic elements of patriarchal visions of manhood that must be confronted for a new, egalitarian future to be possible. As she demonstrates, such a possibility is predicated upon the present. Failure to realize this ideal polity through activism in the present increases the likelihood of another, dystopian future characterized by traditional masculinities.

As Piercy reveals through Connie's visit to a hypermasculine, dystopian New York of a possible future, the toxic elements of the contemporary American capitalistic patriarchy led to greater inequalities along the lines of class and sex among other identity elements. The hypermasculine nation Connie visits represents a possible future for societies increasingly predicated upon the domination and control of women. An unbridled patriarchy, the nation is a hyper-capitalistic society stratified according to race, class, and biological sex and controlled by an upper class living in isolation from the devastated and polluted ecologies of the Earth. As a dystopian possibility, it refracts those aspects Peter Fitting (1985) identifies as central to the utopian society of Mattapoisett: "(1) the basic living units developed as alternatives to the nuclear family; (2) the question of gender and the division of labor; (3) sexuality itself, both as an index to human fulfillment and in opposition to heterosexism and/or attempts to limit it to procreation" (165). In presenting a dystopian future that, in contrast, allows for familial and communal bonding only for the elite class, divides labor according to strict gender and class lines, and exploits working-class women for their sexualities and reproductive functions within a heterosexist paradigm, Piercy intensifies the dialectic of masculinities central to this feminist utopia. The performances of manhood presented in this dystopian setting, therefore, are positioned in direct opposition to those alternative masculinities of Mattapoisett and this contrast induces in the reader a reconsideration of traditional gender ideologies.

These dystopian masculinities reject embodied knowledge and seek to consolidate power and control over the other. The two male characters described during Connie's visit, Cash and an unnamed guard, demonstrate such desires informed by patriarchal and capitalistic ideologies. Cash is the boyfriend and client of Gildina, a "contract girl" paid on retainer for sex. A type of substitute for the nuclear family, their relationship involves the contractual exploitation of Gildina. The dystopian performance of masculinity to which Cash subscribes is predicated upon the treatment of Gildina as a product to be purchased typically for the length of a month, consumed at his leisure, and discarded when these sexual experiences grow stale, at which point, she must locate a new partner at the risk of being identified as no longer desirable and, as a result, harvested for organs. While Gildina may sue if he breaks his contract, Cash and other men of his class position exercise almost complete control over such contracted women, placing them in isolation and under constant monitoring. Perhaps most conspicuously, this level of patriarchal control is reflected in the bodily alterations and appearances of these women. As Connie reflects, Gildina has "a tiny waist, enormous sharp breasts . . . Her stomach was flat but her hips and buttocks were oversized and audaciously curved. She looked as if she could hardly walk for the extravagance of her breasts and buttocks, her thighs that collided as she shuffled a few steps" (313). This role as a disempowered and enslaved sex worker and the other position available to women of Gildina's socioeconomic position, that of a mother who, as she explains, are designed or "cored" to reproduce constantly (316), reflect the centrality of traditional masculinities in feminist dystopias. Besides this focus on controlling and subjugating women, such conceptions of manhood are predicated upon the elimination of emotions and the rejection of embodied knowledge.

The performative nature of masculinities results in the necessity for these men to silence emotional responses that could prevent them from fully adopting their hypermasculine social role. Gildina explains how Cash, whose name hints at the connection binding capitalism and patriarchy, underwent surgical alterations for this purpose: "He's had SC . . . Sharpened control, real-like. He's been through mind control. He turns off fear and pain and fatigue and sleep, like he's got a switch. He's like a Cybo, almost! He can control the fibers in his spinal cord, control his body temperature. He's a fighting machine, like they say" (324). As Vara Neverow outlines, *embodiment* "honors the unique subjectivity, physicality and agency of the individual in community" and is "linked to personal identity, to responsibility, to emotional health, to sensuality, to choice." *Incorporation*, on the other hand, "is linked to the annihilation of the individual, to the hierarchical subordination of the subject to a conglomerate, to the obliteration of uniqueness, to the tyranny of uniformity" (Neverow 1994, 22). In this dystopian future, the traditionally masculine project of incorporation results in the annihilation of individuals complicit to it such as Cash. Able to submit the body to the control of the mind and eliminate embodied experience, Cash signifies toxic masculinity and is therefore positioned by Piercy against the utopian performances of manhood found in Mattapoisett. While the new masculinities of the utopian polity value communal self-reflection and "worming" as a method for analyzing subconscious biases, these dystopian conceptions of manhood value the cutting off of such reflections as the irrational, emotive products of the body over which the mind must triumph.

Through her sympathetic portrayal of a protagonist who seeks to disrupt the progress of mind-control experiments in the present to protect a future utopian society, Piercy emphasizes the importance of current actions to insure an ideal, feminist future. In highlighting the significance of traditional masculinities in both the dystopian future and present, she more specifically identifies the necessity of embracing alternative conceptions of manhood to impact the future. Foundational to Piercy's novel is the understanding that the imagining of masculine alternatives has an important part to play in the societal transformation required to liberate humankind from patriarchy. The outlining of these new ideals of manliness is central, therefore, to the project of imagining a new, egalitarian nation.

A central message of Piercy's novel is that such improved polities are characterized by alternative performances of manhood that reject ideologies of power and control. In the preface to the 2016 edition of the novel, Piercy identifies utopia as "born of the hunger for something better" and relying "on hope as the engine for imagining such a future" (xi). The utopian image of manhood she provides offers hope that such transformations of society and gender are possible. This new image of masculinity is inseparable from the utopian nation in which it is situated and, therefore, bears qualities that parallel this society, "an ideal 22nd-century utopia based on tolerance, nurturing, communality, ecological responsibility, and the complete effacement of conventional gender differences" (Booker 1994, 339).

Piercy presents in her male utopian characters new masculinities that, like the feminist utopia, value community and embodied knowledge. Bolivar, a utopian male, departs from traditional masculinities by seeking connection in order to heal emotionally. When his close friend, Jackrabbit, dies in battle, he initially suppresses his emotions in a typically traditional masculine style. Yet, during the funeral, he participates in a ritualistic dance with the healer, Erzulia, that releases his grief. Allowing herself to be possessed by the memory of Jackrabbit, Erzulia introduces through her body his presence and this experience causes Bolivar's grief to surface. Welcoming the embrace of

Erzulia and others, Bolivar weeps for Jackrabbit. This scene presents aspects of new masculinities, specifically their interest in community and rituals of grieving and their acceptance of embodied knowledge, that contrast dramatically with the traditional ideals of manhood possessed by the male characters of the present and future dystopias. Cash, for example, represents later stages of patriarchal masculinities that seek increasingly more extreme methods, enabled by technology, for divorcing the mind from the body and the male from community. Similarly, men in the twentieth-century United States such as Luis separate themselves from others and neglect social connections in order to avoid vulnerability and increase feelings of control and power. In contrast to these negative, traditionally masculine perceptions of embodied knowledge and community, the new men Piercy presents recognize the importance of such experiences and seek to cultivate meaningful connections with others.

These new gender conceptions replace isolation and the suppression of emotions with social connection and the expression of feelings. Central to this disruption of normative masculinities is community and vulnerability as tools for mourning and healing from a loss. Unlike the traditionally masculine desire to seek out isolation during times of grief, Bolivar and other utopian male subjects connect with others and strengthen community. Their openness to embodied knowledge and a new, community-oriented consciousness enables them to properly face their grief and express deeply felt emotions rejected by traditional masculinities. In this way, they contrast strikingly with the masculinities of the twentieth-century United States, which are characterized by a need among men to suppress emotion and seek separation from others during traumatic experiences. The new masculinities Piercy presents in Mattapoisett are marked by such interests in embodied knowledge and communal connection as well as the rejection of traditional desires to consolidate power and control.

A society seeking to eliminate hierarchical networks of power, Mattapoisett develops alternative masculinities. Contradicting the sociopolitical logic of the dystopian capitalistic patriarchies presented in the novel, the United States in both the present and possible future, it rejects capitalism and other interconnected rationales of subjugation such as sexism, homophobia, and racism. The new masculinities Piercy presents in Mattapoisett are posited as ideal yet imperfect performances of manhood that embrace a new paradigm of consciousness in which embodied knowledge and communal connection are valued while traditional desires to consolidate power and control are rejected.

The new masculinities of Mattapoisett are presented via those male characters with whom Connie comes into contact—Bee, Jackrabbit, Barbarossa, and Bolivar. Each of these characters demonstrates an openness to gender roles and sexualities absent from traditional masculinities. Barbarossa and Bee, for example, illustrate the influence of such new conceptions of manhood upon parenting. Bee is a "com" or co-mother to Innocente and shares these responsibilities with two partners, Otter and Luxembourg. A caring and involved parent, Bee shocks Connie with his open expression of emotions, crying during the opening "naming" ritual in which children are recognized as adults and choose new names for themselves after proving their ability to survive in the wild. The very name he chooses, "Innocente," illustrates his hope that in the future power structures valuing control and domination will be completely removed. As Bee explains, while traveling in Latin America, he contemplated the centuries of colonization and environmental exploitation and looks forward to "that day when all trace of that pillaging will be healed" (121). He selects the name "Innocente" out of a hope for eliminating the remnants of racism and patriarchy. By allowing alternatively masculine interests in the elimination of power and control to influence the name he initially chose for the child and later recognizing that same child as an adult free to adopt a new name, Bee is disinterested in familial control and is representative of the new masculinities Piercy presents as central to the feminist utopia.

Barbarossa, who attends the "brooder" via which babies are born without the need for biological parents, is similarly positioned as an alternative to traditional masculinities. During their first encounter, Connie is disturbed by the technological advancements that have enabled men such as Barbarossa to take on one of the most significant roles of motherhood, nursing. A middle-aged man with a red beard, Barbarossa additionally possesses small breasts that enable him to fulfill his role as caregiver. Focused upon the sustenance of these children and the "serene enjoyment" (142) of such an intimate form of nurturing, Barbarossa, like Bee, illustrates the enriching capabilities of new masculinities.

An openness to diverse sexualities is another core principle of these alternative performances of manhood. Jackrabbit, a nineteen-year-old artist, illustrates this acceptance of and interest in alternative sexualities. Jackrabbit is a queer character who performs a new masculinity in which other sexualities are accepted and respected. Involved with Luciente and Bolivar, he enjoys multiple relationships simultaneously and a range of sexual experiences. While Skip, a fellow patient of Connie's committed by his family because he is homosexual, is hospitalized, experimented upon, and eventually driven to suicide by his marginalization within a heteronormative patriarchy, Jackrabbit stands as an example of how such queer men may flourish within a new society in which alternative masculinities are valued.

Another fundamental alteration to masculinities focuses on community and how communal connections allow for healing. The work of incorporating into masculinities a new, communal consciousness is informed by the teachings of earlier cultures that valued conflict resolution, community, and the acceptance of each passage of life including development, physical and mental illness, and death (132). Mattapoisett has over time moved "towards a society that promotes connection with others," signaling "the necessary shift in consciousness that is intrinsic to" the feminist utopia (Fancourt 2002, 109). The power of this new, community-oriented consciousness is specifically presented by Piercy in Bolivar and his openness to communal forms of therapy. Such an openness is demonstrated when the community seeks to end a rivalry between Bolivar and Luciente over Jackrabbit. A small group is initially formed to "worm" or identify through meditation, contemplation, and discussion those drives or issues preventing harmony between them. These communal efforts and Bolivar's willingness to connect with others in order to solve relational problems mark a significant departure from traditional masculinities.

As an anarchist society, Mattapoisett's aim is of "integrating people back into the natural world and eliminating power relationships" (ix). Such feminist interests are evidenced by its approach to medicine, education, agriculture, and government. In place of a medical establishment that exploits patients according to the logic of capitalism, patriarchy, and attending ideologies of subjugation, Mattapoisett possesses healers who practice naturalistic treatment approaches. Such healers do not resort to the removing of bodily organs but, instead, utilize their knowledge of the natural as well as technologies to treat the patient. They remove organs or smaller body parts only rarely and instead program local cells to regrow or heal (170). In addition, they do not seek above all to extend life but teach instead to be accepting of death. Informed by the beliefs of societies that were previously and erroneously deemed inferior, they reject traditionally patriarchal and coldly rational ideals in which life is prolonged and, instead, seek to comfort and enrich the experiences of each patient. This alteration is another product of the feminist paradigm shift in consciousness Piercy imagines. In presenting a "glimpse of the possibilities for social consciousness and community life" as the product of "a willingness to look at death more openly" (Matarese 1991, 109), Piercy includes as central to this social progress the advent of new, heathier masculinities opposed to patriarchal networks of power.

The mental health institutions of Mattapoisett, in contrast to their dystopian counterparts of the present and future United States, value the autonomy and individuality of the patient and this also signals a departure from patriarchal societies marked by traditional masculinities. These institutions position patients within natural, pleasant landscapes. They exist in this utopia as havens for people regardless of their reasons for seeking such asylum. As the text delineates, citizens visit such places to heal, escape, gain strength, seek spiritual enlightenment, or release anger among other reasons (67). In the utopia, subjects such as Jackrabbit, who seeks such mental healing and sanctuary often, are not stigmatized for their needs and do so according to their own free will. In this way, the mental health institutions Piercy imagines in this utopia lack those interconnecting forces of subjugation typical of such organizations in the contemporary United States.

The absence of hierarchical perspectives in these alternative masculinities results in significant departures from the educational and governmental practices of the contemporary United States. Specifically, these institutions do not reinforce networks of power through the awarding of degrees or the granting of significant governing powers. Influenced significantly by a paradigm of masculinities not predicated upon domination and control, these institutions imprint upon the student and civil servant the meaningfulness of learning and community. Students, for example, are educated in their village prior to their naming ceremony. After this point, they contact teachers in their fields and begin to learn under their mentorship once a position is available. Depending upon the chosen field of study, these students may relocate to another location in the utopia. Informed significantly by new, egalitarian masculinities, this utopian educational system replaces patriarchal approaches to learning— focused upon profit, social mobility, and competition—with one focused exclusively upon community, education, and the natural world.

Such alternative masculinities influence the governmental practices of Mattapoisett, which lack those capitalistic, patriarchal aspects of civil service common to the United States. The planning council for this township is made up of citizens chosen not by election but by lot, thereby preventing the development of a political class. In addition, the temporary nature of these positions, typically one year in length, and the absence of any social or economic promotion as a product of this role eliminate the possibility of hierarchical systems of power developing. In the next level of government, regional planning, representatives are chosen by lot and meet to discuss problems and recommend actions. Such recommendations are made public and citizens in disagreement may express their concerns. Compromise is also often reached outside of this formal system with groups and individuals bartering over necessary resources (162–163). Central to the governing practices of Mattapoisett is the voice of each citizen. The manner in which this polity removes socioeconomic influences protects it from the corrupting elements of capitalistic patriarchies. In place of such ideologies foundational to systems of power and control, Piercy imagines a utopian anarchy whose egalitarian system of government, predicated upon the elimination of power consolidation and subjugation, reflects those alternative masculinities central to this society.

Such new male gender scripts are reflected in the utopian community's non-exploitative approach to the environment. Demonstrating a non-patriarchal, dominating relationship to nature, Mattapoisett possesses several key qualities of an ecofeminist society: "nonhierarchical forms of organization, recycling of wastes, simpler living styles involving less-polluting 'soft' technologies, and labor-intensive rather than capital-intensive economic methods" (Merchant 1989, 295). In contrast to this feminist utopia are both the capitalistic patriarchy of Connie's present, the contemporary United States, and the dystopian vision of a future New York in which "multis" or multinational corporations have consolidated such power that the Earth has been stripped of its resources and is no longer inhabitable for life. By limiting the use of technologies to those dangerous or mundane tasks requiring completion, centering as the primary purpose of labor the enrichment of human lives in relationship both to each other and nature, and removing from agricultural industries the possibility to accumulate capital and market power, the citizens of Mattapoisett work to maintain a nation whose treatment of nature reflects its nonhierarchical conceptions of masculinity.

The key social organizations of Mattapoisett including its medical, educational, agricultural, and governmental institutions highlight the influence of masculinities upon national identity and the mutually constitutive relationship existing between *gender* and *nation*. The connections Piercy locates "among issues of racism, classism, sexism, and environmental abuse" (Stratton 2001, 306) strengthen both her critiques of contemporary American culture and the possibility she posits of moving toward a better society through the elimination of hierarchical perspectives central to traditional masculinities. Presenting to her reader individual characters performing new, egalitarian masculinities, Piercy illustrates the methods by which men may work toward a better future through the introduction of new forms of manhood in the present.

The dialectic of masculinities Piercy provides and the manner in which the text prompts readers to consider the benefit of alternative ideals of manliness demonstrate Piercy's concern "with the liberatory dimension of the choices which people make in the present" (King 1991, 77). Explaining the necessity for contacting Connie, Luciente states, "We must fight to come to exist, to remain in existence, to be the future that happens. That's why we reached you" (213). In this feminist utopian novel, Piercy similarly outlines for her audience the necessity to adopt new masculinities qualified by a feminist paradigm of consciousness and a rejection of traditional desires to dominate and control. By presenting the possibility of such utopian masculinities as predicated upon the outcome of present discussions concerning gender and manhood, she calls for her male readers to recognize the urgent need to depart from traditional, patriarchal ideologies of masculinity.

As this chapter illustrates, feminist utopian fiction enables the decentering of white, heteronormative, male perspectives and the altering of masculinity.

Woman on the Edge of Time represents a key development in the feminist utopian genre in that it signals a widening focus among such writers to incorporate and center the experiences of women of color and illuminate how traditional masculinities subjugate such subjects through racism and classism. *The Kin of Ata Are Waiting for You* is significant in its framing as the retrospective analysis of misogynistic masculinities by a converted patriarch. *The Dispossessed* further complicates narratives surrounding gender by presenting the failures and successes of an initially feminist-oriented male protagonist. Departing from these focuses upon male characters negotiating masculinities, *Woman on the Edge of Time* relocates patriarchal and utopian men to the narrative margins. By replacing such characters with a woman of color who must navigate patriarchal dystopias to ensure the future development of a feminist society, Piercy illuminates the impact of masculinities upon such marginalized women. In its focus on the importance of ethnicity and intersectionality, *Woman on the Edge of Time* foreshadows the works of other feminist writers such as Octavia Butler, discussed in the next chapter.

NOTES

1. Though Le Guin's presentation of the androgyne in *The Left Hand of Darkness* is problematic, as previously outlined, her later work *The Dispossessed* successfully imagines new masculinities possessing qualities traditionally labeled both feminine and masculine. It is this later novel, the focus of my analysis in chapter 2, that serves as an example of Le Guin's depiction of new, transformed masculinities.

2. Erin McKenna (2001) locates a similar message in the novel, positing that "*Woman on the Edge of Time* not only presents a vision of an anarchistic society of the future, but . . . also focuses on the dangers of and need to get beyond violence, especially male violence" (69).

3. Alice Waters (2009) locates this dynamic aspect in both *Woman on the Edge of Time* and Moore's "Greater Than Gods" (1939). *Woman on the Edge of Time*, therefore, is situated within a tradition of feminist speculative writing in which utopian and dystopian narrative elements are utilized to express anxieties surrounding current, traditionally masculine, patriarchal networks of power and the possibility in the present of developing egalitarian gender ideologies and socioeconomic systems.

Chapter 4

Masculinity Crossing Borders in Octavia Butler's *Lilith's Brood*

The fiction works of Octavia Butler, especially her *Lilith's Brood* trilogy, act as successors to the feminist speculative novels discussed in previous chapters. Like Bryant's *The Kin of Ata Are Waiting for You* and Le Guin's *The Dispossessed, Lilith's Brood* emphasizes the possibility of transforming patriarchal masculinities and highlights the need to eliminate current hierarchical socioeconomic systems for alternative ideals of manhood to flourish. The first novel of Butler's trilogy, *Dawn*, centers the experiences of a woman of color negotiating societal systems of power that uniquely marginalize her based upon her identity. The protagonists of *Adulthood Rites* and *Imago*, the second and third novels in Butler's trilogy, are subjugated due to their non-normative racial, gender, and sexual identities. The alternative masculinities Butler posits as necessary for eliminating the oppression of such subjects are not unique to or unattainable by individuals belonging to particular biological sexes, genders, or races (represented by species in her trilogy).

Utilizing the speculative genre to imagine the crossing of both gender and biological barriers, Butler presents a human population as it joins and procreates with an alien species but does not assert that humankind must become something else to adopt feminist-oriented masculinities. She presents "porosity in apparently commonsensical and unbridgeable biological barriers" (Kilgore and Samantrai 2010, 357) and the gender scripts associated with them and both her alien and human characters prove capable of adopting patriarchal and alternative masculinities. As this chapter illustrates, in developing a feminist utopia predicated upon the transformation of traditional masculinities and emphasizing the socially constructed nature of these gender scripts, Butler dramatically illustrates the power of science fiction in discussing the future of masculinity.

Butler's radical materialist presentation of masculinity is an overlooked element of her fiction, which is predominantly valued for its use of the speculative genre to center the experiences of women and people of color in contemporary American culture. In the years since her death, Butler has received considerable attention for her work at the intersection of speculative fiction, race, and feminism. Her fiction is often noted as invaluable due its inclusion of revolutionary topics within science fiction literature, typified by its pushing of "the genre to speak to our deepest, culturally burdened horrors as well as to our transcendent hopes" (Kilgore and Samantrai 2010, 355). Viewing herself as responsible to three central constituencies, "the science-fiction audience, the black audience and the feminist audience" (Potts 1996, 336), Butler rejected the character types and themes common to genre fiction in favor of complexity that spoke to diverse experiences. Her works mark a significant recalibration in feminist science fiction in that they center characters historically marginalized due to their races, sexualities, and genders and illuminate the ways traditional masculinities are socially constructed and may therefore be adopted across these identity markers.

This focus on traditionally marginalized characters, fundamental to *Lilith's Brood*, appears in the time period between *Woman on the Edge of Time* in 1976 and the publication of *Dawn* in 1987 in Butler's short story "Bloodchild" (1984) and novel *Wild Seed*. The Nebula and Hugo Award-winning short story "Bloodchild" is told from the traditional perspective of a male character who experiences the feminine by being impregnated by an alien. The story follows the experiences of Gan, a male human who is coerced into acting as a host for the eggs of T'Gatoi, a female member of the alien Tlic species. Through these experiences, Gan better understands and accepts his own fluidity regarding his physiological makeup and masculinity. In this way, the experiences of male humans such as Gan mirror those of women whose reproductive functions are monitored and controlled by others in power. In chronicling Gan's move toward adaptation and viewing his body as not essentially, traditionally masculine, "Bloodchild" illuminates the socially constructed nature of gender. Moving beyond this positive vision of deconstructed masculinity, however, Butler subverts utopian conceptions of gender in "Bloodchild" through the possession among the Tlic species of masculine traits. Since Tlic males are violent and live for a limited amount of time, the Tlic characters present in the novel are female and their possession of traits traditionally classified as masculine complicates utopian conceptions of alternative masculinities. Dependent upon humans to host their eggs for reproduction to occur, the Tlic females consolidate power and control over their human counterparts to insure the continuation of their species. The story acts as an early signifier of Butler's interests in centering the experiences of formally marginalized characters (in this case, women, but imposed onto a male character) and complicating utopian conceptions of transformed masculinities. It bridges the gap separating earlier works such as *The Kin of Ata Are Waiting for You* that focus on traditional men encountering new societies and masculinities and later texts such as *Dawn* that decenter male experience and problematize the utopian resolutions of these earlier feminist novels.

Wild Seed more clearly bridges the gap between *Woman on the Edge of Time* and the first entry in Butler's trilogy, *Dawn*. Specifically, *Wild Seed* brings from the margins characters marked as other according to their identities and focuses upon the compromises they must consider within a decidedly nonutopian world. Focused upon the experiences of Anyanwu, an African woman of color gifted with supernatural healing powers and the ability to transform herself into any animal or human, Butler's novel is driven by Anyanwu's conflict with a hypermasculine adversary, Doro, an ancient African male. Like Anyanwu, Doro is immortal, but his immortality is dependent upon the complete consolidation of power and control over others. Killing others in order to subsume their physical bodies, he is a dominating, traditionally masculine entity desiring above all else to breed a nation of superhumans through which he may enhance his power. The novel offers a revolutionary focus upon a character whose experiences are shaped by both her race and biological sex. It is also significant, however, in that it signals a move within feminist speculative fiction toward complex stories reflecting the lived experiences of women of color.

This complexity manifests most trenchantly in the resolution of conflict between two societies Butler presents near the end of *Wild Seed*, one led by Anyanwu and another by Doro. After the accidental death of Doro's son, Isaac, compels Anyanwu to flee from Doro's seed village, Doro searches for Anyanwu for a century, finally locating her in Louisiana where she has developed her own colony. In stark contrast to Doro's seed villages in which he maintains complete control of the occupants' reproductive practices, Anyanwu's colony, informed by feminist ideals, allows for reproductive freedom. Presenting Doro's villages as the logical product of his hypermasculinity and Anyanwu's community as reflective of her aversion to such patriarchal conceptions of manhood, Butler tacitly comments on the connections existing between the nation and gender. It is this issue of control and power over reproductive rights that Butler presents as central to the conflict between Doro and Anyanwu.

Taking control over Anyanwu's Louisiana community, Doro introduces his breeding program to its inhabitants, stipulating sexual partners and monitoring procreation. As a result of the violence and subjugation that results, Anyanwu chooses to commit suicide but is stopped by Doro, who offers a compromise to prevent her death. This agreement stipulates that Doro may no longer kill carelessly and his victims may not be members of the community.

In return, Anyanwu must act as an ally to Doro, assisting him in his project of locating promising, powerful individuals. By concluding *Wild Seed* not with the victory of Anyanwu over Doro but with this problematic compromise, Butler centers the experiences of women of color and the complex choices they must negotiate in a decidedly nonutopian world. *Wild Seed* links earlier feminist novels such as *Woman on the Edge of Time* to *Dawn* in that it, like Piercy's novel, relocates female characters of color from the textual margins to its center and it, like the first novel of *Lilith's Brood*, introduces complexity and compromise to imagined utopian and dystopian polities.

Though Butler, through this final conflict between Doro and Anyanwu, comments in *Wild Seed* on the mutually constitutive relationship of the nation and gender, it is in *Lilith's Brood* that she most clearly draws connections between power structures and masculinities and presents utopian and dystopian visions of manhood as the necessary products of competing nations. *Lilith's Brood* presents Butler's most trenchant critique of gender, the possibility she imagines of men adopting healthier gender roles and supplanting traditional, heteronormative masculinities, and the positive impact the adoption of such alternative masculinities has in combating intersectional forces of oppression. Through its inclusion of protagonists differentiated by race, sexuality, and gender and its interest in the compromises necessary for a better nation to be realized, this trilogy culminates key changes within contemporary feminist utopian fiction.

This chapter traces the connections Butler locates in her *Lilith's Brood* trilogy between traditional masculinities and the will to dominate and subjugate others according to contrasting sexualities, genders, and races. The novels making up this trilogy, *Dawn, Adulthood Rites*, and *Imago*, portray a continuing conflict between the human survivors of a nuclear war that nearly destroyed the Earth and the Oankali, an alien species that, while rescuing these humans and restoring the ecologies of the planet, demonstrate a similar, traditionally masculine will to subjugate and control. Butler introduces the conflict in *Dawn*, as the human survivors negotiate the Oankali requirement that they reproduce with the aliens, which will bring about the end of humanity as a distinct species. Set decades after the events of *Dawn, Adulthood Rites* focuses on Akin, the first human-born Oankali-human male construct, who recognizes the problematic hierarchical behaviors of both the Oankali society and the human separatists' communities seeking a return to patriarchal capitalistic rule. At the conclusion of this second text, Akin successfully negotiates the creation of a human separatist colony on Mars for those desiring an autonomous human society. This second novel in the trilogy concludes without a complete resolution to the conflict. *Imago*, the final entry in the series, follows Jodahs, the first human-born ooloi construct, who, as a member of this third Oankali gender, campaigns for and ultimately is granted the ability to develop a new Oankali-human town that rejects the traditionally masculine hierarchies of both the human separatist and Oankali polities. Across this trilogy, Butler charts the conflicts arising between traditional masculinities and imagines their ending as the result of new, egalitarian ideals of manhood that reject desires to dominate and control those considered *other* according to their race, gender, and sexuality. Butler's trilogy explores the elements of these masculinities that are central to the creation of a society that, while imperfect, possesses key utopian features.

A close analysis of *Lilith's Brood* reveals key connections Butler emphasizes between patriarchy and other oppressive ideologies such as racism. Race, for example, is central to the American conceptions of manhood Butler presents in this trilogy. If, as Kimmel (2006) observes, "American men try to *control themselves*" and as a result "project their fears onto *others*" (6) before escaping as a last resort in dealing with difference, the *others* onto which they project their fears are marked significantly by their race. In seeking to perform an impossible conception of masculinity requiring self-sufficiency through the accumulation of power and control and the subjugation of others, these adherents to traditional masculinities dominate others identified as outside favored racial categories. In these texts, Butler presents this connection between traditional masculinities and racism both among her human characters according to traditional racial categories and, to a greater extent, in encounters between her Oankali and human characters in which *species* acts as a distortion of *race*. In addition, she highlights the way in which these hierarchical views of race, informed by traditional masculinities, are empowered by the master narratives valued by the gendered nation.

The specific metanarrative Butler identifies as central to the ideologies of the human separatists, for example, is the biblical creation myth and, more specifically, the account of Lilith, the first woman. While the cyborg, as described by Donna Haraway (1991), is powerful in its disconnection from traditional Western ideologies and, therefore, "would not recognize the Garden of Eden" (151), the human separatists in Butler's novels identify this paradisiacal location of biblical origins as a site of great power in justifying racial and gender ideologies. Their hatred for Lilith, for example, is informed by a patriarchal will to subjugate women illustrated in the biblical story of Lilith, the first wife of Adam, who was removed from Eden "because she refused to submit to his rule (in particular, would not lie beneath him in sex)." Accepting this narrative as universally true and illustrative of the ideal, unequal relationship between the sexes, these men rationalize traditional masculinities' efforts to dominate as natural. The punishment of the biblical Lilith for challenging such patriarchal rule "was to couple with 'demons' and give birth to a monstrous brood of children" (Peppers 1995, 49). The development of Oankali-human construct children is seen by these separatists through this biblical lens and they reject such miscegenation as unholy.

These separatists likewise rely upon the biblical account of creation to justify their traditionally masculine attitudes toward race. Drawing from a Western religious iconography that portrays "the black woman . . . as Lilith," whose evil acts are "responsible for sin" (O'Neale 1986, 142) entering the world, these human men valuing patriarchal masculinities return to the origin myths unrecognized by the cyborg in order to naturalize their desires to subjugate those considered *other* according to their gender and race among other factors. They utilize the biblical origin myth to condemn those rejecting their traditionally masculine appeals to patriarchal and racist rule. Drawing from master narratives in stark contrast to this Western myth, the Oankali likewise justify their hierarchical behavior according to cultural narratives used to naturalize the subjugation of others. Relying upon a master narrative of progress and evolutionary change, they subjugate humans according to both their sexualities, genders, and racial differences. As organic beings with a history that, while demonstrably more egalitarian than their human counterparts, remains problematic, the Oankali introduce their own traditional ideologies concerning family, distributions of power, sexualities, and gender to the human survivors. Butler's trilogy reveals parallels existing between the ideologies of the humans and Oankali regarding social systems of power and specifically masculinities.

In opposition to such hierarchical perspectives, *Lilith's Brood* presents new masculinities that, while imperfect, are significantly more egalitarian than their patriarchal alternatives. While Butler denied the presence of utopian themes within her own works, there are glimpses of such alternatives to toxic masculinity in her texts, most notably among the aliens and human-alien hybrids. She rejected the possibility that "imperfect humans can form a perfect society" (Beal 1986, 14) and her presentation of the ideal polity as not solely human informed her belief that she was not a utopian writer. I contend, though, that *Lilith's Brood* contains dystopian and utopian elements working in concert to present new, ideal masculinities and social orders. Though her Oankali-human hybrid characters perform the most positive alternative masculinities in these texts, she imagines in both her Oankali and human characters positive alternatives to hegemonic masculinities. In this fashion, the *Lilith's Brood* series continues the work of the aforementioned feminist fiction predating it and may be accurately described—like Le Guin's *The Dispossessed*—as ambiguously utopian.

The positive effects of the trilogy's undermining of heteronormativity may seemingly belie Butler's views concerning human nature and masculinity. Throughout her novels, Butler appears to present essentialist views of gender and, more specifically, masculinity. According to Hoda M. Zaki (1990),

Butler does not adopt a materialist form of feminism, which considers the social and historical construction of gender and subjectivity in analyses of patriarchy (240). In Zaki's analysis, Butler is essentialist, asserting a natural connection between the genetic makeup of men and the aggressive will to dominate characterizing traditional conceptions of manhood. This will to dominate—paired with intelligence—is dubbed the "human contradiction" by the Oankali species in *Lilith's Brood* and men accordingly possess more of this contradiction than women. If the logic of her novels is understood to be that, "abandoning the human body is a necessary prerequisite for real human alteration" (Zaki 1990, 242), the efficacy of prodding her readers to critique traditional conceptions of maleness may seem futile.

A materialist analysis of Butler's works, however, reveals positive changes among her characters' performances of maleness, providing at least the hope of some alteration in toxic masculinity. This critique contends that Butler's characters, both Oankali and human, prove capable of adopting healthy conceptions of manhood and developing social orders or, to return to Reeser, *gendered nations* reflective of these views. The utopian elements Zaki identifies in these texts illustrate this point. The ability of "individuals occasionally to escape the grip of instinct and genetic structure on human behavior" and the presentation of "alien societies" that "stand in the sort of political comparison to existing human social arrangements" (243) illustrate how Butler identifies a key relationship between the nation and its normalized genders and, therefore, the possibility for change. Specifically, normative masculine qualities such as the desire for power and control via aggression and domination are possessed by both human and alien characters to varying degrees and are informed by their specific societies. In addition, these Oankali and human characters demonstrate an ability to adopt new, egalitarian masculinities and social orders in direct opposition to these negative, traditional traits and patterns.

Butler critiques traditional American masculinities as represented by her human characters and their Oankali counterparts, the latter of which act as defamiliarized representatives of these masculinities. As previously outlined, to *defamiliarize*, according to Victor Shklovsky (1965), means to alter conceptual forms while the nature of such concepts remains stable (13). This distortion of forms brings attention to the natural qualities of the concept and requires the observer to consider it outside its usual cultural environment. Such a theorization may be applied to studies of gender since traditional masculinities, for example, may be defamiliarized through their performance by an unfamiliar, or, in the case of these novels, inhuman, subject. In this way, their unaltered, problematic nature is thrown into sharp relief. Challenging "the automatism or perception" of the reader, Butler creates "a vision which results from" an engaged or "deautomized perception"

(Shklovksy 1965, 22). In making the familiar strange, Butler calls for her audience to consider this vision, which involves the rethinking of gender norms and the rejection of hegemonic masculinities. With this theoretical tool in tow, we may consider Butler's presentation of power and control, aggression, and domination as products of normalized American masculinities. A materialist analysis of these texts, therefore, reveals the possibilities for these human, alien, and hybrid characters to both adopt and reject the traditionally masculine desire to consolidate power and control through aggression and domination.

The radical masculinities imagined by Butler and other feminist science fiction writers such as Le Guin, Piercy, and Russ is necessarily tied to that of their pulp speculative fiction forbearers. These writers—like a select few of their pulp predecessors—"retain the depiction of female strength" and reject the patriarchal and "pessimistic ending of" the typical pulp texts that often find the female "put back into her place, subordinate to the male characters" (Roberts 1993, 64). An attending result of this more egalitarian presentation of femininity, I argue, is the production of new male characters whose admirable qualities such as strength, honor, and loyalty remain intact while their traditional, patriarchal attitudes toward women are replaced by a new masculinity that values equality. If fantasy, as Delaney (2009) asserts, considers what is impossible while science fiction concerns itself with what has not happened, speculative fiction is fertile ground for new conceptions of femininity and masculinity that may influence future configurations of gender (61).

The inclusion of new, egalitarian masculinities found in the works of these authors echoes Le Guin's (1975) call for new visions in speculative fiction, namely the replacement of Victorian, imperialist fantasies with "such deeply radical, futuristic concepts as Liberty, Equality, and Fraternity" (210). According to Le Guin (1975), male elitism in science fiction is importantly a "symptom of a whole which is authoritarian, power-worshiping, and intensely parochial" (208). Challenging sexism in genre fiction necessarily entails opposition to larger aggressive and dominating attitudes toward *the other*. A central aspect of the aforementioned superman of golden age science fiction, for example, is his race. The patriarchal ideologies informing the superman influence both his racial makeup—he is always white—and his subjugating, racist attitude toward those identified as other according to this category of identity. Sexism must be understood, therefore, as connected to other related forms of aggression directed at a host of others categorized as such by their class position, race, language, and sexuality among other elements. The new man of science fiction is the product of feminist speculative writers such as Bryant, Le Guin, Piercy, Butler, and Jemisin who imagine new worlds in which both sexes benefit from the desire to promote liberty, equality, and fraternity instead of the aggressive values found in the majority of the pulp texts.

This new man, like the revolutionary, complex female characters presented in feminist science fiction, replaces older conceptions of gender informed by "present-day, white, middle-class suburbia" (Russ 2007, 206). While the technological tools and settings of these texts are typically distinct from those of the twentieth-century United States, the conservative social values of contemporary American culture remain intact. Joanna Russ (2007), for example, locates several key traditional values in science fiction and specifically the space opera subgenre; such stories, she observes, often include "a feudal economic and social structure" in which "women are important as prizes or motives," "active or ambitious women are evil," "women are supernaturally beautiful," "women are weak and/or kept off stage," "women's powers are passive and involuntary," and "the real focus of interest is not on women at all" (208–209) but on the traditionally masculine protagonists populating these works. Such traditional images of women and men are necessarily tied to each other; the undermining of patriarchal images of women in science fiction, therefore, produces healthier, alternative portrayals of men in opposition to heteronormative, middle-class gender scripts.

Butler destabilizes the legitimizing powers of essentialist gender theories by presenting conflicts between masculinities and aligning her audience not with performers of problematic scripts of manhood but, instead, her female protagonist. Set 250 years after the conclusion of a nuclear war that devastated most of the Earth's surface and ozone layer, the novel chronicles the experiences of Lilith Iyapo, a black human female enlisted by her alien captors to act as a leader of her fellow human survivors. During her first experiences with the alien colonizers aboard their ship, Lilith witnesses a divergence among the Oankali concerning the desire for power and control in her assigned ooloi, Nikanj and its parent, Kahguyaht. Nikanj, an adolescent novice learning the art of genetic alterations, explains to her the nature of her subjugation and its own complicity to the wishes of its parent ooloi, Kahguyaht. This parent, referred to by Nikanj by the familial title "Ooan," requires that Nikanj make prescribed genetic alterations to Lilith, whether through consensual or violent means: "Ooan wanted me to act and say nothing . . . to . . . surprise you. I won't do that." Elaborating further, the young ooloi outlines its need to complete this task as a sign of maturation and that, as an adolescent, it will not yet be able to provide the pleasure usually produced in such intimate encounters: "I would like to wait, do it when I'm mature. I could make it pleasurable for you then. It should be pleasurable. But Ooan . . . I understand what it feels. It says I have to change you now" (Butler 2000, 75). The options presented to Lilith are to succumb to the pressures impressed upon her by Nikanj to allow it to penetrate and alter her mind or to be altered by force at the hands of Kahguyaht. This ultimatum illustrates both the problematic masculinities common to the Oankali and their human counterparts and the choices available to both species to challenge or submit to the hegemonic gender order. Aligning the reader with Lilith, Butler calls for her audience to consider the value of new, utopian masculinities based on fraternity, equality, and liberty.

Butler's call for new masculinities—supported by a materialist conception of gender—involves the distorted presentation of the aforementioned four patterns of masculinity identified by Connell. These patterns—hegemony, complicity, subordination, and marginalization—represent the narrow options available to male subjects within the patriarchal gender order. Of these patterns, Nikanj chooses to remain complicit to the hegemonic, traditionally masculine desires for power and control possessed by Kahguyaht. Ultimately, Lilith is coerced into a mind-altering form of assault at the behest of Kahguyaht and the complicity of Nikanj. Her dissent is clearly outlined: "'What's frightening is the idea of being tampered with.' She drew a deep breath. 'Listen, no part of me is more definitive of who I am than my brain. I don't want—'" (Butler 2000, 76). Such pleas highlight the nature of this assault; this act represents the violent penetration and subjugation of Lilith's mind and body. Having intoxicated Lilith into a sleep-like state through the use of substances produced by its body, Nikanj enters her via its node-like appendages and alters her mind so she may retrieve heretofore inaccessible memories. The description Butler provides of Lilith's emotional state upon awakening from this induced sleep echoes accounts of sexual assault: "When she awoke, at ease and only mildly confused, she found herself fully clothed and alone. She lay still, wondering what Nikanj had done to her" (Butler 2000, 80). A materialist reading of this section reveals the connections Butler identifies between national attitudes toward *the other* and masculinities. Both Nikanj and Kahguyaht demonstrate an ability to adopt or reject masculinities, though they risk subordination and marginalization. This possibility of adopting alternative, egalitarian masculinities defines Butler's inclusion of new performances of manhood as central to a comparatively utopian society. Her adoption of a materialist conception of gender and her call for new, healthier masculinities within both science fiction and society can be seen more clearly through the examination of these male characters.

The social constructionist attributes of the masculinity to which Nikanj subscribes are revealed, for example, by a key ethical dilemma it experiences. Though Nikanj remains complicit, it recognizes the unethical qualities of its actions and the system of power and subjugation these actions serve; this in turn reveals Butler's presentation of traditional masculinities as not essentially human. In its conversation with Lilith, Nikanj recognizes the unethical qualities of its parent's actions: "Ooan says humans—any new trade partner

species—can't be treated the way we must treat each other. It's right up to
a point. I just think it goes too far. We were bred to work with you" (Butler
2000, 81). This passage reveals Nikanj's acceptance of human subordination to the Oankali to an unspecified degree, its disagreement with its parent
concerning the degree of subordination acceptable, and its unwillingness to
challenge Kahguyaht, fearing marginalization, a key pattern of masculinity.
Still, its desire to negotiate peacefully with humans illustrates its support
for alternative masculinities opposed to power and control: "We should be
able to find ways through most of our differences" (Butler 2000, 81). As
a subject complicit to hegemonic masculinity but in disagreement with it,
Nikanj represents the possibility for positive change and the adoption of new
performances of masculinity. While Nikanj hardly represents an ideal alternative to traditional masculinities, its approach to this situation reveals a divide
within Oankali culture that echoes human disputes over gender. Through
such disagreements, Butler illustrates the materialist qualities of masculinity
and, specifically, the ability for participants to question normalized desires
to consolidate power and gain control over others. Butler presents in *Dawn*
problematic ideals of manhood possessed by Oankali characters that will later
be challenged by Oankali, human, and hybrid revolutionaries in *Adulthood
Rites* and *Imago*. Her work represents in this way a non-essentialist critique of
traditional masculinities and the proposal of ambiguously utopian alternatives
to these gender scripts.

Butler's critique of masculinities involves the inclusion of human characters whose phallocentric attitudes illustrate the connections Le Guin locates
between imperialist fantasies of the subjugation of *the other* and patriarchy.
The human males populating these works violently react in opposition to the
other, in this case, the Oankali colonizers. In her position as leader, Lilith
must convince her fellow human beings to adopt the Oankali way of life
and mate with them in order to create a stronger, hybrid species. This task
proves dangerous as those humans she awakens from hypersleep maintain
the traditionally masculine conception of the other as a dangerous entity
to be combated and subjugated. This friction eventually erupts into armed
conflict. Lilith's human partner, Joseph, a Chinese-Canadian survivor, is
murdered and the group of survivors is sent to Earth without their leader.
In *Adulthood Rites*, separatist camps are formed by those human survivors
favoring patriarchal systems of power and conceptions of masculinity remi-
niscent of Earth before the war and Oankali colonization. These attempts to
reintroduce human normative masculinities involve the deployment of traditional tools of gender conscription—hegemony, subordination, complicity,
and marginalization—and the resurrection of capitalist conceptions of maleness. In this way, the separatists seek to create a new gendered nation based
largely upon traditional American masculinities of the twentieth century.

Their ultimate failure to achieve this goal is due to the absence of the nation and economy in which such traditional American masculinities flourished, the United States during the second half of the twentieth century. As Michael Kimmel (2006) points out, the self-made man representative of American traditional masculinities requires a capitalistic, patriarchal system in order to flourish (147). Butler illustrates through the human separatists of her series, therefore, a historically situated, materialist understanding of masculinities.

By revealing the central reasons for these separatists' opposition to Oankali socioeconomic systems, Butler emphasizes connections between industry, social systems of power, and gender. The concept of the gendered society "is an important aspect of gender studies since those cultural codings affect everyone in a nationally based context" (Reeser 2010, 171). Male power, "a subjectivity linked to power," "can be thought of both as created by institutions and as creating them." In this way, "the process of the construction of masculinity" is "a constant back-and-forth movement between masculinity and institutions" (Reeser 2010, 20). Discontent with the prospects of an agrarian life, a system espoused by the Oankali, the separatists seek to reconstruct their precolonial systems of commerce and industry, networks that facilitate constructions of traditional American gender scripts. In working toward this goal, they fight to re-gender their civilization, so it conforms to traditional American conceptions of masculinity in opposition to normative Oankali genders. This gendering of the nation often involves its leader, as her or his gender, for better or worse, is taken as analogous of the society. Lacking advanced order or leadership hierarchies, the separatists of this trilogy seek to gender their nascent civilization by drawing such an analogy between it and a more nebulous ideological figure, the aforementioned self-made man.

The societies Butler imagines are not able, however, to provide a social or economic environment necessary for the self-made man to flourish. The absence of those societal systems that once allowed men to divorce themselves from physical labor and ground their senses of manhood in economic gain produces a heightened anxiety among those subscribing to traditional American conceptions of manhood. The self-made man acts as an absent, illusive idea influencing male resistors in these novels. Though they subscribe to traditional masculinities, their new material conditions do not allow for such a reawakening of contemporary American gender norms. Butler imagines a future in which the historical context for current American masculinities no longer exists and human males must adapt to a new gender order or challenge such hierarchies altogether. While it remains ambiguous, there are important utopian themes at play concerning new images of manhood in the series.

The new images of maleness Butler produces are linked to the rejection of the accumulation of power and control through aggression. Importantly, the characters most exemplifying these radical, egalitarian masculinities are neither human nor Oankali; they are the hybrid descendants of Lilith and her mates, both human and *other*. In this way, Butler illustrates the nature of traditional masculinities as not essential to humanity but, instead, situated within specific societies whose distributions of power favor authoritarian ideals of manhood and subjugate those labeled *other* according to their gender, race, sexuality, ability, and nationality among other factors. The new, ideal masculinities Butler proposes in the remaining installments of this trilogy incorporate diversity and the three elements Le Guin calls for: liberty, equality, and fraternity.

In developing human male characters and Oankali-human hybrids who oppose aggression, subjugation, and domination and, instead, support liberty, equality, and fraternity, Butler challenges the masculinities of the supermen populating the so-called golden age of science fiction. Like Haraway's (1991) cyborg that rejects Western origin myths and their "dream of community on the model of the organic family" (151), Butler's characters—specifically her hybrid children, Akin and Jodahs—reject the social Darwinian metanarratives justifying the masculinities of the supermen and replace them with new, egalitarian conceptions of manhood. Informed significantly by their experiences as racial hybrids, these characters reject both racist ideologies and the traditional masculinities supporting oppositions to the other according to race, sexuality, and gender.

By aligning her audience with these characters and in opposition to traditional masculinities, Butler rejects these earlier writers' speculations of evolutionary progress as predicated upon aggression and subjugation. Texts concerning such supermen typically involve an optimistic prediction of the future in which humankind progresses onto the next stage of evolutionary development. The utopian aspects of these works, however, are belied by the violence attending such advancements. John W. Campbell Jr. and the authors he influenced conceived of the superman as a figure whose leadership role is justified by his advanced physical, intellectual, and sexual abilities. His pushing of humankind toward progress, often violently, is therefore considered a form of "long-term benevolence" that "often involves short-term cruelties" ranging "from the withholding of technology to selective executions of dangerous individuals" (Attebery 2002, 67). Butler includes early in *Dawn* an example of such short-term cruelties when Lilith finds upon awakening that her body has been altered without her consent; her immune system has been strengthened and her cells have been modified to prevent the growth of cancer. In this way, the Oankali have forcefully made Lilith a superwoman. Butler (2000) highlights the unethical nature of such long-term benevolence through the thoughts of her protagonist: "This was one more thing they had done to her body without her consent and supposedly for her own good" (32). This concern with such short-term cruelties justified by their end result remains with Lilith throughout her interactions with the Oankali: "Was that what she was headed for? Forced artificial insemination. Surrogate motherhood? Fertility drugs and forced 'donations' of eggs? Implantation of unrelated fertilized eggs. Removal of children from mothers at birth . . . Humans had done these things to captive breeders—all for a higher good, of course" (Butler 2000, 60).

Butler connects in this passage the traditionally masculine will to dominate to racist ideologies, highlighting the similarities between the Oankali subjugation of human survivors and historical human accounts of slavery, both of which are informed by similarly patriarchal and racist ideologies. At the conclusion of *Dawn*, Lilith's fears are realized when she is notified that she has been impregnated by her ooloi partner without her consent. The traditional masculinities Butler defamiliarizes in these texts, therefore, are characterized by a will to dominate the other in order to reach a new level of evolutionary development. The adoption or rejection of this approach to evolutionary progress demarcates the opposing masculinities of Butler's trilogy.

Such a positivist conception of social Darwinian progress and the short-term cruelties it justifies are rejected by the new men of Butler's texts. In the second novel of her trilogy, *Adulthood Rites*, she presents, for example, an activist for new masculinities who seeks to undermine the short-term cruelties justified by the Oankali and human separatists and, therefore, acts as an ideal replacement for the supermen of earlier science fiction. Lilith's son, Akin, is a human-born male hybrid whose experiences as a hostage of the human resistor camp, Phoenix, and as a member of the Oankali-human camps reveal to him problematic aspects of both human and Oankali polities. He challenges each society's practices of subjugating the other based upon certain attributes: nonnormative sexualities, genders, class positions, and races (defamiliarized by Butler as *species*). He, like Haraway's cyborg, rejects the dualisms of Western civilization such as human/animal that have "been systematic to the logics and practices of domination of women, people of color, nature, workers, animals-in short, domination of all constituted as others" (Haraway 1991, 177). He is an activist for new masculinities who rejects traditional Western myths and teleology and the products of this tradition that are presented among the human survivors and defamiliarized by those Oankali characters favoring traditional gender scripts.

One such product of Western ideologies Akin challenges is the domination and subjugation of those marginalized according to their nonnormative sexualities. During his time in Phoenix, he learns of the separatist commitment to heteronormative sexualities. Troubled by their aversion to homosexuality and understanding of sexual experience as hierarchical, he introduces to them new, egalitarian understandings of sexualities. Pivotal to Butler's critique of traditional masculinities and their marginalizing of other sexualities are Akin's critiques of the Oankali intolerance of sexualities not normalized in their culture. In challenging the normalization of select sexualities, Akin disrupts traditional American masculinities defamiliarized by Butler within Oankali society. Specifically, he considers the criticisms levied by these separatists at the Oankali and their intolerance of human sexualities as a result of their quest for the next step of evolutionary progress. Central to this complaint is the human-to-human intimacy denied these survivors during and after their first sexual encounters with the Oankali: "Human beings liked to touch one another—needed to. But once they mated through an ooloi, they could not mate with each other in the Human way—could not even stroke and handle one another in the Human way. Akin did not understand why they needed this, but he knew they did, knew it frustrated and embittered them that they could not" (Butler 2000, 305). While he is ultimately unable to aid his partners in achieving this goal of direct intimacy, his attitude toward this need demonstrates a new, egalitarian approach to other sexualities. Butler provides in Akin a new masculinity within speculative fiction that rejects social Darwinian justifications of domination and instead seeks to introduce new, nonhierarchical, alternative masculinities.

Butler's aligning of her audience with these human-Oankali constructs is strengthened by their similarities to humans as subjects capable of adopting both toxic and egalitarian masculinities. Instead of presenting in these Oankali and hybrid characters utopian exemplars of new masculinities that possess perspectives as morally simplistic as their golden age supermen predecessors, Butler depicts their struggles and occasional failures to actualize egalitarian concepts of manhood. While Akin, for example, does not deny information to human survivors in order to subjugate their wills to a greater evolutionary goal, Jodahs withholds information from its human partners, Tomás and Jesusa, concerning the ramifications of intimacy with an ooloi in order to develop a relationship with them. Informing them only much later of the permanent biological dependency each participant will experience on the other members forming the relationship, Jodahs recognizes the unethical qualities of its actions and seeks to ease the suffering produced. It attempts to correct its mistake by providing that which its actions denied its human partners: intimacy without the necessity of its presence. After linking with the nervous systems of Tomás and Jesusa, Jodahs connects their neural networks directly, providing the direct, intimate contact they desire: "It was not illusion. They were in contact through me. Then I gave them a bit of illusion. I 'vanished' for them. For a moment, they were together, holding one another. There was no one between them. By the time Jesusa finished her scream of surprise, I was 'back,' and more exhausted than ever. I let them go and lay down" (Butler 2000, 646).

Butler illustrates in this passage the performative qualities of masculinities and the imperfect qualities of these new men of speculative fiction who must recognize and combat their own culturally informed biases toward marginalized groups. In addition, Butler depicts the importance of oppressed groups gaining access to those tools denied them according to the subjugating logic of traditional masculinities. As the first hybrid ooloi whose power granted the construct generation power only heretofore possessed by the Oankali and whose existence caused great uproar among the Oankali, Jodahs is uniquely equipped to challenge human and Oankali hierarchies of power. As an ooloi, it possesses a more advanced, powerful version of the Oankali organelle that allows for genetic manipulation, the yashi. It, therefore, actualizes new, egalitarian masculinities in its battle to provide humans and constructs access to this powerful biotechnology, its ownership of traditionally masculine mistakes, and its acceptance of sexual needs and preferences not normalized by hegemony.

The power of this new conception of masculinity is most trenchantly manifested in these hybrids' fights for the rights of human and Oankali subjects to live, govern, and reproduce with complete autonomy and to not, therefore, be required to engage in each society's system of trade. Rejecting overtly the "short-term cruelties" thought to be justified by the achievement of long-term evolutionary goals, Lilith's children challenge the normative, hierarchical attitudes of both the Oankali and human species according to species/race. While living in Phoenix, Akin, for example, learns to condemn conceptions of the *other* as valuable merely for trade after noticing such racist attitudes among the human separatists. Neci, a female survivor, wishes to forcefully remove the sensory organs of kidnapped hybrid children in order to increase the profit earned from their sale. In Neci's actions Akin recognizes the final product of traditional masculinities' attitudes toward the other according to race/species and the justification for harming such marginalized subjects as a side effect of free market trade. Butler illustrates the materialist nature of masculinities through this inclusion of a gendered society whose desires to revive traditional Western ideologies results in the subjugation of others according to the logic of capitalistic patriarchy and racism.

Maintaining this materialist portrait of traditional masculinities as the products of specific polities, Butler includes images of similar inequalities in Oankali society. Upon talking with a female human ally, Tate, Akin learns that the Oankali similarly subjugate others in order to benefit from trade, though these transactions involve strictly genetic profiteering. Considering those past species coerced into such biological exchanges, he asserts they were merely "consumed" by the Oankali and posits that such enforced trades with species are "wrong and unnecessary" (Butler 2000, 443). In opposition, he proposes that the human separatists be granted their own Akjai, a segment of a population allowed to continue without modification: "There should be Humans who don't change or die—Humans to go on if the Dinso and Toaht unions fail" (Butler 2000, 378). Rejecting the notion that the supermen—the Oankali in this case—are justified in forcing their seemingly less advanced counterparts to follow their directives for the sake of evolutionary progress, Butler provides in Akin a new image of manhood that seeks to eliminate oppressive social hierarchies. Recognizing key connections between the nation and the masculinities it normalizes, she incorporates characters that reject the gendered systems of power unique to each society.

The nature of Lilith's two hybrid children, Akin and Jodahs, as nonhierarchical revolutionaries fighting aggression and domination is not due solely to their genetic information. While biological makeup influences the actions of subjects, their adoptions of particular masculinities are influenced by other elements, as Akin points out: "Chance exists. Mutation. Unexpected effects of the new environment. Things no one has thought of" (Butler 2000, 501). Instead, their egalitarian perspectives are informed by their exposure—rare among members of the trader villages—to both polities, those of the partnered Oankali and humans and those of the human separatists. Butler centralizes in her narrative characters who, like Haraway's cyborg, lack a rigid commitment to the metanarratives of either society. Their egalitarian perspectives and the new masculinities they adopt are shaped by the diverse milieus in which they developed. In this way, Butler proposes new masculinities within speculative fiction and society that are only possible through a materialist understanding of gender.

While Butler identified herself as an essentialist, there is ample evidence from her texts to demonstrate an understanding of hegemonic masculinities as significantly socially produced. As Nancy Jesser (2002) outlines, "a biological humanity is not, it seems Butler is saying, a 'fixed' humanity. Butler acknowledges the force of biology and environment/history/learning" (43). She presents power and control, aggression, and domination as aspects of traditional masculinities uniquely influenced by societal factors. The balance she strikes between biological and societal aspects of masculinities involves the interaction she portrays between biology and performativity. During a conversation with two female construct children, Shkaht and Amma, Akin delineates the similarities between the Oankali and humankind, highlighting the possibility of significant improvements within human culture if such truths could be recognized: "We are them! And we are the Oankali. You know. If they could perceive, they would know!" In response, Shkaht presents a biologically essentialist case for the continued hierarchical behavior of humankind: "If they could perceive, they would be us. They can't and they aren't." Tellingly, Akin retorts in support of the materialist case for humankind and, therefore, its ability to adopt new, healthier masculinities: "I can see the conflict in their genes—the new intelligence put at the service of ancient hierarchical tendencies. But . . . they didn't have to destroy themselves. They certainly don't have to do it again" (Butler 2000, 377). Analyzing these texts through a materialist lens, therefore, reveals the possibilities for these human, alien, and hybrid characters to both adopt and reject the traditionally masculine desire to consolidate power and control through aggression and domination.

Through her development of human, Oankali and Oankali-human construct characters that oppose aggression, subjugation, and domination, Butler presents a new man of speculative fiction. Due to the nature of masculinities, which must be negotiated and performed daily through a series of decisions and actions, these characters are not idealized, perfect exemplars of healthier conceptions of manhood. Unlike the supermen they replace, they are not simplified heroes but, instead, falter in their efforts to challenge the gender scripts of their nations. They are united by the utopian qualities of their masculinities, specifically, their dedication to overthrowing oppressive systems of power that consolidate control through aggression and domination. Like those characters produced by other feminist science fiction authors such as Bryant, Le Guin, and Piercy, Butler's hybrids represent a distinct, new image of manhood in contemporary speculative fiction. As is further demonstrated by N.K. Jemisin's *Broken Earth* series, the focus of chapter 5, this new man is a unique product of feminist utopian writing and its imagining of ideal polities in which all subjects, and not just supermen, enjoy the "deeply radical, futuristic concepts" (210) Le Guin (1975) identifies as needed in speculative fiction: liberty, equality, and fraternity.

Chapter 5

"This Is the Way a New World Begins"

Revolutionary Masculinities in N.K. Jemisin's Broken Earth *Trilogy*

As Marge Piercy's *Woman on the Edge of Time* and Octavia Butler's *Lilith's Brood* series brought from the margins protagonists traditionally overlooked in science fiction due to their identity markers, N.K. Jemisin's *Broken Earth* trilogy further widens the sociopolitical range of the feminist utopia. As successors to Piercy's feminist fiction, Jemisin's novels, for example, similarly focus upon complex female characters traditionally placed on the margins due to their biological sex and race and consider the ways individuals may influence the future of a society. Like *Woman on the Edge of Time*, Jemisin's *Broken Earth* series traces how patriarchal male characters and their feminist-oriented counterparts impact women of color and society more broadly. Departing from the work of Piercy, however, Jemisin's trilogy expands the focus of feminist utopias to consider the negative effects of traditional masculinities upon subjects possessing nonnormative racial, sexual, and gender identities; it is this development of the genre that connects Jemisin's fiction to that of Butler. Like Butler, Jemisin stresses the centrality of compromise to the utopian endeavors of marginalized individuals. Through the *Broken Earth* trilogy, Jemisin continues Butler's recalibration of feminist science fiction to center characters historically marginalized due to their races, sexualities, and genders and emphasize the ways patriarchal masculinities are socially constructed and may therefore be performed by individuals possessing diverse combinations of these identity markers. A successor of the feminist utopian fiction of Piercy and Butler, Jemisin's trilogy adds considerable complexity to discussions surrounding science fiction and masculinities, emphasizing the patriarchal gendering of contemporary societies, the imperfect attributes of feminist-oriented utopian nations and their conceptions of manhood, and the importance of historically contextualizing patriarchal masculinities in order to fundamentally reshape societies and the masculinities it normalizes.

Recognized within both academic and popular circles for her contributions to fantasy and science fiction, N.K. Jemisin demonstrates the continuing suitability of genre fiction to imagine improved societies and the possible future of gender, race, environmentalism, and sex among other topics. The recipient of two Locus awards, the first African American to receive a Hugo award, and the first writer to receive this latter prize for three consecutive years, Jemisin is lauded for her incorporation into science fiction of radically new perspectives and her challenging of the norms of the genre. She, like other black writers casually referred to as "Octavia's Brood" such as Nalo Hopkinson, Nisi Shawl, Nnedi Okorafor, and Andrea Hairston, reveals in her writing an indebtedness to Octavia Butler and her exemplary incorporation of intersectionality and racial, cultural, and ethnic differences into feminist utopian texts. Though limited academic work has yet been generated concerning such elements of the *Broken Earth* trilogy, the series has prompted initial, promising scholarship and Jemisin herself has been celebrated by popular periodicals such as *Entertainment Weekly* as "Fantasy's New Queen" (Canfield 2018, 65). As Jemisin and her groundbreaking series illustrate, there continues a trend within feminist utopian texts from the margins to the mainstream and from the centering of white, heteronormative perspectives to that of diverse viewpoints influenced by intersectionality.

This chapter illuminates the relationships Jemisin presents between traditional masculinities and the desire to accumulate power and control over those marked by nonnormative identity markers and the necessity she stresses of comprehensively transforming contemporary American society to positively alter its masculine gender scripts. Presenting a radical, materialist account of masculinity similar to that of Butler, Jemisin illustrates the socially situated nature of patriarchal masculinities and their mutually constitutive relationship to the nation. Transforming masculinities requires, as Jemisin emphasizes, a thorough understanding of the societal context in which these concepts of manhood are cultivated. Published nearly thirty years after Butler's *Lilith's Brood* trilogy, the *Broken Earth* series focuses upon a post-apocalyptic world whose ecological instabilities, which include earthquakes, acidic rains, and famines, are traceable to an earlier, traditionally gendered nation. This earlier society, Syl Anagist, was marked by inequality among its human subjects and its exploitative attitude to the natural world. Like this earlier nation, the present-day polity—a system of city-states making up the supercontinent of the Stillness and united by older, imperial ideologies from a former nation, the Sanzed Empire—seeks power over the Earth through the subordination of it and members of the orogenic race who are marked by the ability to manipulate thermal and kinetic energy to influence seismic events. In contrast to this patriarchal nation and its traditional masculinities, feminist utopias are presented in the trilogy that value alternative ideals of manliness and oppose efforts to control others based upon identity markers such as race. Like Bryant, Le Guin, Piercy, and Butler, Jemisin emphasizes the instability and imperfection of these utopias. Marking an optimistic departure from Butler's *Wild Seed* and *Dawn*, Jemisin concludes her trilogy with a devastated world and the possibility that the survivors upon which the texts focus will develop a new, critical utopia based upon feminist values, marked by alternative conceptions of manhood, and characterized in opposition to the nation its predecessor represents, the contemporary United States.

The *Broken Earth* trilogy emphasizes the patriarchal gendering of contemporary American society and the necessity of transforming traditional masculinities through its presentation of a similarly racist patriarchy, the city-states or *comms* of the Stillness. In these novels, Jemisin traces the ways patriarchal masculinities are normalized and impact subjects possessing nonnormative identity markers. Jemisin's portrait of the dystopian patriarchy emphasizes the way such societies revise or fabricate historical documents and manufacture lore and metanarratives meant to justify patriarchal masculinities. In addition, Jemisin illustrates through her portrayal of this dystopia the way patriarchal masculinities and the nations they influence cultivate racist ideologies and practices. Finally, Jemisin's presentation of this nightmarish patriarchy emphasizes the manner by which two patterns of masculinity, hegemony, and complicity, negatively impact the lives of those distanced from power according to their unfavored identity markers. Through her presentation of this racist patriarchy, Jemisin, then, outlines the ways such societies legitimize their power structure, fortify racist policies, and, through the patterns of masculinity, ensure a patriarchal distribution of power.

A key way this hierarchical society normalizes its patriarchal and racist masculinities is by ignoring or manipulating historical documents that challenge traditional masculinities. Additionally, the racist patriarchy replaces such radical, accurate, and complete historical accounts with altered or fabricated documents meant to normalize racist, patriarchal masculinities. Existing approximately 40,000 years after the destruction of an earlier, similarly patriarchal nation, Syl Anagist, the inhabitants of the Stillness, though belonging to decentralized, independent city-states, adhere to stonelore attributed to historical lorists that normalizes patriarchal, racist policies across the continent; notably absent from these accounts are those that challenge traditional masculinities and the patriarchy. A central method by which Yumenes, the seat of power in the present setting of the novels, has undermined such radical lorist accounts is through the delegitimizing of such information by its patriarchal government and educational system. Dating back to "twenty-five thousand years ago . . . when" the role of lorists "became distorted into near–uselessness," such attempts to discredit accounts from the margins involved government propaganda and "the First through Seventh Universities disavowing their

work as apocryphal and probably inaccurate" (Jemisin 2016, 2). Undermining
the role of lorists, the Yumenescene leadership preserve only those fragments
of stonelore that do not challenge current patriarchal networks of power and
supplement these accounts with their own legends.

As Jemisin illuminates in her trilogy, racist patriarchies stabilize traditional
masculinities and the patriarchal nation through the manufacturing of such
new legends and the fabrication or manipulation of historical accounts. As
outlined by Essun's travel partner and childhood friend, Tonkee, who challenges this system of leadership and its control over historical information,
such "Leadership legends have the air of a myth concocted to justify their
place in society" (Jemisin 2016, 91). The metanarratives derived from incomplete lorist accounts and these legends passed down by those in power justify,
like their Sylanagistine predecessors, patriarchal interests in power and control over those possessing nonnormative identity markers. The Yumenescene
metanarratives discourage "reconsideration, reorientation. Wisdom is set in
stone" (Jemisin 2016, 204). These metanarratives support patriarchal sociopolitical polities, instructing subjects enduring a fifth season to follow strategies such as "building a wall, taking in the useful and excluding the useless,
arming and storing and hoping for luck" that reinforce oppressive, patriarchal
attitudes toward others (Jemisin 2015, 409). The Yumenescene metanarratives similarly justify racist attitudes toward others such as orogenes: "They
kill us because they've got stonelore telling them at every turn that we're
born evil—some kind of agents of Father Earth, monsters that barely qualify
as human" (Jemisin 2015, 124). The Second Yumenescene Lore Council's
Declaration on the Rights of the Orogenically Afflicted is, for example, utilized to dehumanize orogenes and justify their subjugation: "We rule, therefore, that though they bear some resemblance to we of good and wholesome
lineage, and though they must be managed with kind hand to the benefit of
both bond and free, any degree of orogenic ability must be assumed to negate
its corresponding personhood. They are rightfully to be held and regarded
as an inferior and dependent species" (Jemisin 2016, 258). Such historical
declarations, taught to children in school or *creche*, promulgate racist metanarratives that support traditional, racist masculinities.

These Yumenescene historical documents are supplemented with fragments of stonelore tablets utilized to justify racist policies, resulting in the
rejection of those tablets undermining patriarchal ideologies. Tablet Two,
for example, was presumably damaged at some point in the past due to its
controversial content. Other tablets found "in one of the dead cities on Tapita
Plateau" contained lore so distinctly different from the patriarchal mainstream that its finding hints at the possibility that, after such radical accounts
were edited and altered in suspiciously similar ways, there transpired a new
"admonition against changing the lore" (Jemisin 2015, 125). In contrast to

such controversial, rejected lore are stories such as those of Shemshena, that are utilized to justify the subjugation of the orogenes. Utilized to justify the current Yumenescene power network, the story focuses upon a supposed attack upon Yumenes orchestrated by an evil orogene, Misalem. Such actions, according to the tale presented as fact, terrorize the people of Yumenes who know of no way to defeat such a powerful orogene. In response, a hero, Shemshena, emerges whose racial and class background make her ideally suited to defend this racist patriarchy: "she was—a renowned fighter of the finest Sanzed lineages. Moreover, she was an Innovator in use-caste, and thus she had studied orogenes and understood something of how their power worked" (Jemisin 2015, 90). Focused upon Shemshena and the defeat of Misalem, the legend reinforces racist and patriarchal conceptions of those possessing nonnormative identity elements. Other accounts, which agree that Misalem was the sole survive of a cannibalistic Sanze raid, are dismissed and their records are destroyed so the patriarchal ideologies of the nation may be preserved. The metanarratives supporting these hierarchical, oppressive perspectives result in a gendered nation that values the subjugation of others according to race, class, and gender among other identity markers. A pivotal message of the *Broken Earth* trilogy concerns, therefore, the ways racist patriarchies replace radical, authentic records with fabricated historical accounts and new metanarratives that serve this network of power and the masculinities it favors.

Pivotal also to Jemisin's novels are the connections they emphasize between the patriarchal masculinities such biased accounts and metanarratives normalize and racist social policies endemic to the nation. In these novels, Jemisin traces the ways racist, patriarchal masculinities are normalized and impact subjects possessing nonnormative identity markers. As a network of small communities that formerly belonged to the patriarchal Sanzed Empire, the city-states of the Stillness connect patriarchy with race. Individuals most valued in this network of comms possess traits associated with the Sanzed Empire since "everyone is measured by their standard deviations from the Sanzed mean" (Jemisin 2015, 112). Populating the affluent, stable central region of the supercontinent, the Sanzed people of both sexes are physically imposing and tall and possess bronze-brown skin and ashblow hair, which is described as "coarse and thick, generally growing in an upward flare; at length, it falls around the face and shoulders. It is acid-resistant and retains little water after immersion, and has been proven effective as an ash filter in extreme circumstances" (Jemisin 2015, 457). The Sanzed Equatorial Affiliation, casually referred to as the Old Sanze Empire, which maintains cultural and economic influence though it no longer officially exists, and the racist policies it favors originated in the so-called Madness Season. As Alabaster, the former mentor of the protagonist, Essun, explains, in order to survive, the Sanzed groups united and attacked other communities they dehumanized according to race. Resulting in the cannibalization of these other races deemed inferior during this fifth season, the racist policies enacted by the Sanzed people continue to shape the socioeconomic systems of the Stillness in the present-day setting of the series. These patriarchal nations cultivate traditional masculinities that reinforce racist public policies.

While Jemisin presents connections binding such racist and patriarchal policies through characters possessing identity markers associated with non-Sanzed geographical locations such as those of the midlats, somidlats, and arctics, her presentation of the orogene racial group and its extensive subjuga-tion most trenchantly emphasizes her interest in tracing connections between patriarchal and racist ideologies. Though Essun, who is grouped with what Yumenescenes consider "mongrel midlatters" possessing "enough Sanzed in them to show, not enough to tell," experiences discrimination for her lim-ited possession of Sanzed qualities, she endures substantial subjugation due to her racial identity as an orogene (Jemisin 2015, 10). The Yumenescene racist patriarchy influencing if not officially governing the Stillness does not recognize orogenes as humans, but instead values them merely as tools used to fortify and protect this polity and fears them as significant threats to society. Valuing traditionally masculine interests in consolidating power and control over the orogenes, the Yumenescene leadership fortifies patriarchal networks of power that reinforce the four patterns of masculinity. Focusing upon characters located in positions of hegemony, complicity, subjugation, and marginalization, Jemisin emphasizes how patriarchal nations such as the Old Sanze Empire and the traditional masculinities it normalizes support rac-ist, oppressive social policies.

The *Broken Earth* trilogy further illuminates through its portrayal of the racist patriarchy connections between traditional masculinities and racism and the dependence of the first pattern of masculinity, hegemony, upon the subjugation of others according to their racial identity markers. Though nominally an empire, the government of the Stillness is in fact led by a race of individuals, the Guardians, who seek to control and stabilize the nation through the subjugation of the orogenes, derisively referred to by the pejora-tive "roggas" to emphasize their perceived racial degeneracy. As Alabaster explains, the Guardians subjugate the orogenes so they may, through the power of the enslaved, better control the Earth and weather events: they want "roggas made safe and useful, stills doing all the work and thinking they run the place, Guardians *actually* in charge of everything. Controlling the people who can control natural disasters" (Jemisin 2016, 205). Jemisin, therefore, outlines in her novels how the hegemonic position of traditional masculini-ties necessitates the subjugation of those marked as other due to, among other identity elements, their race.

Pivotal to Jemisin's portrayal of the dystopian patriarchy is her outlining of how racist, patriarchal masculinities subjugate through coercive, violent behavior those marked as other. A notable example of such racist and patriarchal interests in distancing from power those possessing nonnormative racial identities occurs when a young Essun, initially named Damaya, is taken under the custody of a Guardian, Schaffa. Representing the Fulcrum to which he intends to take Essun, Schaffa removes the child from the abusive atmosphere of her homes, but Essun quickly learns that her new paternal figure signals an escalation of her disempowerment and subjugation. During their trip to the Fulcrum, Schaffa calmly presents Essun with an initial test that will determine, based upon her willingness and ability to be subordinated, her survival or death: "Schaffa sighs and folds his free arm around her waist. 'Be still, and be brave. I'm going to break your hand now'" (Jemisin 2015, 97). In reaction to Essun, who pleads for the test to end, Schaffa outlines the complete subjugation of her and other orogenes to Schaffa and the Guardians as required for their survival: "Never say no to me . . . Orogenes have no right to say no. I am your Guardian. I will break every bone in your hand, every bone in your body, if I deem it necessary to make the world safe from you" (Jemisin 2015, 99). Representative of hegemony within this traditionally masculine patriarchy, Schaffa demands the complete subordination of those belonging to the unfavored, orogenic race. As a Guardian, Schaffa abuses Essun and other orogenes and therefore embodies the subjugating, patriarchal masculinities of this gendered dystopia. As Essun explains, "the whole damned world is Schaffa" (Jemisin 2016, 328–329). Jemisin illustrates through Schaffa's consistent, violent actions, including the abuse of Essun and other orogenes, how men occupying the hegemonic pattern of masculinity uniquely impact and disempower nonnormative subjects according to the racist logic endemic to traditional masculinities within the contemporary United States.

Unique to Jemisin's novels and their presentation of the dystopian patriarchy is their emphasis upon the social conditioning and programming of such subjects embodying the hegemonic pattern of masculinity. Building upon the radical materialist framework present in Butler's *Lilith's Brood* trilogy, Jemisin outlines how men occupying positions of power within the racist patriarchy are trained mentally to accept societal inequalities. As a child, Guardians such as Schaffa are forcibly altered and a corestone, taken from the center of the Earth, is embedded in the left lobe of their sessapinae. This alteration repurposes the sessapinae, making it sensitive to orogenic activity instead of to the inner movements of the earth. In addition, this change causes prolonged life with the negative effect of consistent pain, which the Guardians fight off with the release of endorphins through actions such as smiling. Throughout his abuse of orogenes and stills, those individuals possessing no orogenic power, Schaffa maintains, as a result of this training, a belief that his actions serve the greater needs of this polity. In the same scene in which Schaffa breaks Essun's arm, Schaffa expresses his love for the young girl and seeks to justify his violent subordination of her: "I have hurt you so that you will hurt no one else" (Jemisin 2015, 99). As Schaffa further explains, "it's about control. Give me no reason to doubt yours, and I will never hurt you again" (Jemisin 2015, 102). As a result of the reprogramming of Schaffa's body, which allows him to maintain complete control over orogenes such as Damaya, and the retraining of his mind so that he accepts patriarchal views of those he disempowers, Schaffa is rendered an ideal, hegemonic performer of traditional masculinities who embodies and serves the patriarchy. By tracing the social conditioning involved in the promulgation of traditional masculinities, Jemisin therefore illuminates the mechanisms by which the racist patriarchy fortifies and consolidates power.

Central to Jemisin's portrayal of the racist patriarchy is her emphasis on how the violence endemic to the society is frequently both an effort to consolidate power over others and a response by hegemonic men to the temporary disruption of their social conditioning. Upon meeting a woman at an inn, Schaffa hesitates but eventually allows her to seduce him since he is aware that such pleasure will temporarily minimize the pain of his programming. When he journeys through this same area months later, Schaffa finds the woman visibly pregnant. Fearful that the child she carries possesses his powerful abilities, Schaffa reacts violently and embodies the terrorizing qualities of patriarchal masculinities. Using a poniard, he stabs her, hoping to kill the child and spare her life. Justifying the patriarchal control of this woman's body through his quest as a hegemonic male to protect the polity he embodies, Schaffa seeks to forcefully terminate the pregnancy and, as a result of the defense mounted by this woman, her family, and others, murders half of the town before departing. The manner by which Schaffa swiftly pivots from his romantic feelings toward this woman to a violent, murderous desire to control her body and the life it nurtures illustrates the connections Jemisin traces between the socially situated and conditioned nature of patriarchal masculinities and the subjugation of those classified as others according to their racial makeup.

Jemisin traces in her presentation of the dystopian patriarchy the manner by which men occupying another pattern of masculinity, complicity, harm women and people possessing nonnormative racial identities. Jija, Essun's husband with whom she has a daughter, Nassun, accepts his complicity to patriarchal, racist networks of power and exemplifies the racist attitudes of this dystopian, traditionally masculine nation. Staunchly oppressive toward orogenes, Jija, like Schaffa, murders his and Essun's second child, Uche, when he discovers the boy possesses orogenic powers. Due to Uche's abilities, this murder is normalized by Old Sanze imperial metanarratives and

Jija's traditionally masculine attitude toward others distanced from power according to their racial identity is validated. In diagnosing Jija's actions, Essun therefore connects his murderous violence to the patriarchal masculinities favored by this gendered nation: "The kind of hate that can make a man murder his own son? It came from everyone around you" (Jemisin 2015, 57). As Nassun later recognizes, Jija fears orogenic power and attempts to disguise such fears through his adoption of patriarchal masculinities: "She understands that he is fragile, despite his outward strength and stolidity. The cracks in him are new but dangerous, like the edges of tectonic plates" (Jemisin 2016, 112–113). This pent-up energy and hatred, fueled by racist conceptions of manliness and fear, erupts a final time when Jija attempts to murder Nassun and is killed as a result. Throughout these texts, Essun and Nassun are subjected to traumatizing violence through Jija. As Jemisin diagnoses through this father and husband, traditional masculinities fortifying the racist patriarchy demand the subjugation of those possessing non-favored identity markers and the complicity of men distanced from hegemony. Nassun and Essun, like Connie in *Woman on the Edge of Time*, experience considerable harm through their personal relationships to a man who adopts a pattern of complicity to patriarchal masculinities. In presenting a dystopian patriarchy characterized by these patriarchal patterns, Jemisin emphasizes the mechanisms by which traditional men consolidate power and control.

The *Broken Earth* trilogy links patriarchy and racism and illustrates connections between the patterns of masculinity—hegemony, complicity, subordination, and marginalization—and racist ideologies. Jemisin highlights through Jija the murderous, coercive, and controlling aspects of men complicit to racist patriarchies and the unique ways women of color are harmed by men performing traditional masculinities. Through her presentation of Schaffa as a violent, hegemonic male who, motivated by patriarchal and racist ideologies in which he trusts, subjugates and murders others to fortify and protect the nation, Jemisin highlights the toxic, socially situated qualities of masculinity. Focusing upon characters located in positions of hegemony, complicity, subjugation, and marginalization, Jemisin underscores how patriarchal nations such as the Old Sanze Empire support racist, oppressive social policies. She additionally notes how such racist policies are justified through appeals to altered historical documents and manufactured lore and metanarratives. As the *Broken Earth* trilogy emphasizes, the destabilization of the racist, patriarchal nation requires the transformation of its traditional masculinities, the challenging of its historical justification, and the disruption of its networks of power based upon racism and the patterns of masculinity.

The societal alternatives Jemisin presents in her trilogy are, like those of earlier feminist writers, precariously positioned and marked by compromise. Like the utopia, Mattapoisett, in Piercy's *Woman on the Edge of Time*, the ideal, feminist-oriented polities Jemisin imagines are not determined to exist; they depend upon women and men performing alternative, non-patriarchal masculinities to ensure their existence and continuation. Jemisin similarly builds upon Butler's presentation in *Wild Seed* and the *Lilith's Brood* series of utopian societies that are imperfect. The *Broken Earth* trilogy continues a trend within feminist speculative fiction of narratives concerned with improved masculinities and polities informed by the lived experiences of women of color. The improved, imperfect polities of the text, Meov and Castrima-under, are represented and substantially shaped by their male citizens who model new, egalitarian masculinities that oppose interests in power and control.

Jemisin presents in the first and least compromised utopia of the trilogy, Meov, a nation ideally marked by a stark opposition to power consolidation and patriarchy. In this island utopia, people possessing non-patriarchal sexualities, for example, are not relocated to the societal margins. Reflecting upon her sexual experiences with a male who embodies the masculinities of Meov, Innon, and Alabaster, Essun, who is referred to as "Syenite" in this passage of her life, recognizes the value of a society that does not stigmatize queer sexualities: "no one in Meov will care, no matter what. That's another turn-on, probably: the utter lack of fear. Imagine that" (Jemisin 2015, 372). A nation that normalizes and finds pleasure in nonnormative sexualities, Meov opposes traditionally masculine interests in stigmatizing queer sexualities. Jemisin therefore presents through Meov a pivotal quality of alternative masculinities located similarly in the works of Bryant, Le Guin, Piercy, and Butler: an openness to other sexualities.

Similarly, Jemisin presents through Meov utopian masculinities that do not disempower subjects according to their biological sex or race. A feminist-oriented nation, Meov possibly predates the Sanzed racist patriarchy it opposes and exists outside this oppressive polity's scope of notice and influence, robbing from coastal towns periodically to sustain itself. Desiring only to "die free" of "Sanze," the Meovites cultivate a utopia that ensures the freedom of its citizens regardless of their biological sex or race (Jemisin 2015, 294). After giving birth to her and Alabaster's son, Corundum, Syenite is astonished to find how Meovites share childcare responsibilities regardless of their sex. Nursing, like all parental work, for example, is done communally and men care equally for children. Similar to earlier feminist writers, Jemisin imagines an egalitarian society that eliminates traditional gender roles and favors new masculinities that reject patriarchal interests in consolidating power and control over others.

The utopian masculinities Jemisin presents through Meov value non-patriarchal treatments of citizens regardless of their racial makeup. Unlike the Sanzed patriarchy that marginalizes orogenes such as Syenite, Meov consistently reminds her that she is a valued societal member regardless of her race. This acceptance of subjects possessing nonnormative racial identities permeates the nation's system of power. As Alabaster explains, the nation has survived longer than any other non-Sanzed polity because, instead of killing their orogene subjects, they allow them to thrive and even occupy positions of power (Jemisin 2015, 296). The utopia Jemisin imagines directly opposes control and power gathered and utilized to send to the margins citizens possessing nonnormative sexualities, biological sexes, and races, among other identity markers. The feminist utopia Jemisin imagines is characterized by freedom and opposition to patriarchal attempts to consolidate power and control. Such interests in freedom and the elimination of patriarchal power networks are shaped by and in turn shape the alternative masculinities of this feminist nation.

The new conceptions of manhood cultivated by Jemisin's feminist utopia are marked by an openness to queer sexualities, blurred gender roles, intimacy, and community. A representative of Meovite masculinities, Innon models both for Alabaster and the male audience of the novel new masculinities that value connection. A man marked by his orogenic racial identity, queer sexuality, and traditionally masculine traits such as courage and leadership qualities, Innon performs alternative masculinities and values intimacy and community with men such as Alabaster who have been harmed by traditional conceptions of manhood and the societies they engender. Traumatized by his experiences within a racist patriarchy that enslaved him, forced him to have sexual intercourse with female partners, and likely subjugated his offspring as node maintainers, Alabaster heals through his relationship with Innon. When Alabaster cries throughout the night, Innon remains by his side and comforts him. Illustrating the alternatively masculine commitment to emotional healing and intimacy, Innon diagnoses the harmful effects of patriarchal masculinities upon Alabaster: "Many things have broken him. He holds himself together with spit and endless smiling, but all can see the cracks" (Jemisin 2015, 357). Seeking to comfort and provide strength to Alabaster, Innon represents an amalgamation of the alternatively masculine traits Jemisin posits: an interest in the traditional qualities of bravery and steadfastness and new interests in community and the dispelling of power hierarchies that subjugate sexual, biological, and racial qualities marked other. Syenite's description of Innon taking a traditional leadership position while holding her child, Corundum, hints at this combination of traditional and alternative masculine qualities: Innon, she observes, is "on the upper deck, one hand on the pilot's wheel and the other holding Coru against his hip" (Jemisin 2015, 435). As Jemisin illustrates through Innon, a model of new masculinities for both Alabaster and the novel's audience, and the utopia he embodies, central to the feminist-oriented conceptions of masculinity in the *Broken Earth* trilogy is an openness to intimacy, social connection, queer sexualities, and blurred gender roles.

The fragility and liminality of this feminist utopia illustrate the continuation of important trends established by earlier writers such as Piercy and Butler. Drawing from traditional utopian trends dating back to Thomas More's *Utopia* in which the ideal society exists in isolation, Jemisin presents Meov as an ideal, island nation uncorrupted by the racist patriarchy governing the mainland. Drawing also from feminist utopian trends, Jemisin imagines Meov to be like those improved nations populating *Woman on the Edge of Time*, *Wild Seed*, and *Lilith's Brood*. As a feminist-oriented utopia, Meov is, for example, dependent upon the actions of those populating and surrounding it and is therefore in consistent danger of alteration. Looking back at the time they spent in this feminist utopia, Alabaster and Essun recognize both the possible threat and hopeful promise of this polity: " 'They would've turned on us, too, one day. You know they would have.' When Corundum proved too powerful, or if they'd managed to drive off the Guardians only to have to leave Meov and move elsewhere. It was inevitable. He makes an affirmative sound. 'Then why?' He lets out a long, slow sigh. 'There was a chance they wouldn't' " (Jemisin 2016, 319). By highlighting these threats to and hopes of the utopia and Essun's family, Jemisin emphasizes the fragility and liminality of feminist utopias isolated from and not engaging with a patriarchal world.

The *Broken Earth* series presents in contrast to Meov another, more realistic feminist utopia, Castrima-under, that likewise values feminist-oriented conceptions of masculinity characterized by an openness to intimacy, social connection, queer sexualities, and blurred gender roles. Like those utopias populating Butler's *Wild Seed* and *Lilith's Brood*, Castrima-under is pragmatic and marked by compromise. In opposition to the Sanze-influenced city-states making up the Stillness, Castrima-under rejects patriarchal and racist hierarchies of power and desires for control over others. Complex and imperfect, the polity is governed by a female leader, Ykka, who relies upon a team of advisors representing diverse socioeconomic groups to enrich her perspective. The nation equally values orogenes and stills and operates as a commune in which all able-bodied citizens are expected to contribute their labor to the nation's functioning. All societal roles are assigned without the alignment of such positions to race and gender lines among other patriarchal rationales. Marked by compromise and imperfection, the nation acts as a realistic, utopian alternative to Meov and the perfect, isolated nations of traditional utopian fiction. Through Castrima-under, Jemisin presents a pragmatic, feminist-oriented utopia that values alternative masculinities that reject power and control and favor instead otherness and community.

This complex utopia and the masculinities it normalizes are embodied by its leader, Ykka, a woman who possesses traditionally masculine qualities such as bravery and strength but condemns patriarchal ideologies that distance those possessing nonnormative identity elements from power. As a female orogene, Ykka is marked both by her nonnormative racial identity and biological sex and her position of power therefore emphasizes the anti-patriarchal nature of this nation. Her role as a leader embodying a radical, anti-patriarchal nation is emphasized by her materialist conception of gender and recognition that the patriarchal nation may be transformed through the positive alteration of its masculinities. In opposition to Essun, who has adopted an essentialist conception of masculinity due to her experiences in a racist patriarchy that dominates orogenes or, as they are derisively labeled, "roggas," Ykka outlines a radical, materialist understanding of masculinity and race: "You're saying they're nothing. That they're not people at all, just beasts whose nature it is to kill. You're saying roggas are nothing but, but *prey* and that's all we'll ever be! No! I won't accept that" (Jemisin 2016, 295). Central to the alternative masculinities favored by Castrima-under and represented by Ykka is a materialist conception of masculinity that allows for traditional, patriarchal men to transform themselves through the adoption of feminist-oriented masculinities.

Through Castrima-under and its materialist understanding of masculinities, Jemisin continues the work of Butler, emphasizing the role of compromise and the experiences of women of color in the improved society. Jemisin critically examines early, isolated feminist utopias in her portrayal of Meov and therefore draws from the work of Bryant, Le Guin, and Piercy in constructing this impractical, endangered, and imperfect polity. She continues other feminist utopian trends via her presentation through Castrima-under of a feminist utopia that, like the Louisiana Plantation colony Anyanwu leads in *Wild Seed*, is marked by compromise and the constant threat of citizens adopting patriarchal ideologies. Essun recognizes this threat upon hearing the comments of a male utopian citizen who, in response to the fear of orogenic power, advocates the marginalization of these subjects according to their racial identities: "Too Earthfired many of 'em…Ykka's all right, earned her place, didn't she? Gotta be a few good ones. But the rest? We only need *one*—" (Jemisin 2016, 125). Recognizing a threat among the citizens of this fragile utopia, Essun understands that subjects made vulnerable according to their racial identities must anticipate possible attacks from their fellow citizens belonging to the privileged racial group. Following Essun as she navigates this imperfect utopia, *The Fifth Season* and *The Obelisk Gate*, like *Wild Seed* and *Dawn*, illuminate the experiences of women belonging to marginalized racial groups, emphasize the intersectional forces impacting their lives, and highlight the necessity of compromise in the feminist utopia. Unique to the utopias of Butler and Jemisin are their emphases upon the limited victories and compromises of individuals marked by their race, biological sex, and gender among other identity elements. What makes Jemisin unique within the feminist utopian genre, however, is her focus upon how historically contextualizing patriarchal masculinities and societies cultivates alternative conceptions of manhood.

A notable strength of Jemisin's trilogy is its interest in how historical, patriarchal networks of power contribute to ongoing inequalities and how knowledge of these past injustices is therefore necessary for positively transforming masculinities. The final novel of the series, *The Stone Sky*, for example, delineates the historical events that caused the absence of the moon and began the cycle of fifth seasons. Central to the earlier nation responsible for this catastrophe, Syl Anagist, are the masculinities it normalized, which favor the subjugation of others in order to consolidate power. A subjugated member of this former polity, Hoa, who lives in the present setting of the novel since his existence as a so-called stone eater is tied to that of the Earth, explains the hierarchical networks of Syl Anagist. As Hoa recounts, this earlier nation's interest in the exploitation of *the other* extends to the environment and masculine interests in harnessing natural assets such as the energy or "magic" derived from past lives contained in the Earth. They utilize this magic to develop technological mechanisms and improved societal infrastructure but soon covet greater amounts of this energy for the sake of luxury and convenience. Through this Sylanagistine misuse of natural resources and the nation's violent efforts to produce a tool for extracting the total of the Earth's magic, Jemisin creates a distorted representation of American culture and illuminates the historical dependence of patriarchies upon ecological exploitation. As Jemisin emphasizes, illuminating how patriarchal and environmentally exploitative ideologies have historically worked to fortify hierarchies existing in the present are pivotal to current efforts at disrupting traditional masculinities and the networks of power they favor.

The *Broken Earth* trilogy presents, through its delineation of past efforts to create the so-called Plutonic Engine, connections between two subjugating ideologies, racism and ecological exploitation, as the products of traditional masculinities that require revision for the better society to be realized. Devised as a means of mining the Earth's magic, the Plutonic Engine, an extraction tool, is made up of obelisks, which are utilized to store energy. Channeling this energy through the largest obelisk, the Onyx, and into the Earth, the Sylanagistine engineers estimate that expelling energy or "magic" from the Earth's core as a result will exceed the amount pumped into it, resulting in a continuous surplus of energy. As Jemisin emphasizes, the Plutonic Engine therefore acts as a tool by which the patriarchy, Syl Anagist, may gather power from the subjugation of the natural world. Due to its hierarchical values, this dystopian patriarchy relies upon the subjugation of what is deemed nonhuman, such as the natural world. This subjugation of the Earth enables the nation to limit its exploitation of human lives, which is arduous since the human category of *other* is constantly revised as a result of evolving prejudices: "But for a society built on exploitation, there is no greater threat than having no one left to oppress. And now, if nothing else is done, Syl Anagist must again find a way to fission its people into subgroupings and create reasons for conflict among them. There's not enough magic to be had just from plants and genegineered fauna; *someone* must suffer, if the rest are to enjoy luxury. Better the earth, Syl Anagist reasons" (Jemisin 2017, 333–334). As Jemisin illustrates, this exploitative view of the Earth is related to other oppressive ideologies such as racism and is the product of traditional masculinities and their interests in power and control. The *Broken Earth* series stresses the necessity of tracing the historical roots of oppression to transform contemporary patriarchies and their masculinities, which fortify other oppressive ideologies such as those undergirding environmental exploitation.

This connection between historical, patriarchal ideals of manliness and ecological subjugation is made clear through the use of rape imagery. In recounting the attempted implementation of the Plutonic Engine, the stone eater Hoa, representing alternative masculinities, describes the project of which he took part in terms of sexual violence: "My mouth opens (our mouths open) as the onyx aligns itself perfectly to tap the ceaseless churn of earth-magic where the core lies exposed far, far below. Here is the moment that we were made for. *Now*, we are meant to say. This, here, *connect*, and we will lock the raw magical flows of the planet into an endless cycle of service to humankind" (Jemisin 2015, 333–334). By drawing this parallel between sexual violence and the ecological exploitation of the Earth, Jemisin trenchantly outlines connections between traditionally masculine attitudes toward sexuality and the environment. Where the Sylanagistines "should have seen a living being, they saw only another thing to exploit. Where they should have asked, or left alone, they raped" (Jemisin 2017, 247–249). These historical masculinities devalue living things labeled *other* and systematically exploit them in order to accumulate power. The *Broken Earth* series emphasizes through its incorporation of rape imagery the necessity of considering historical power systems and masculinities and their attitudes toward the environment to transform society and ideals of manhood.

As Jemisin illustrates, tracing the historical context of traditional masculinities extends beyond environmental effects to consider the ways normative masculinities and the nation engender the racist ideologies of earlier, similarly patriarchal polities. As a traditionally gendered society, the former nation, Syl Anagist, builds its success upon the exploitation of those labeled *other* according to, among other identity markers, race. This aspect of Sylanagistine culture is presented most clearly in the image of the obelisks positioned within the so-called briar patch prior to the Plutonic Engine experiment.

As Hoa learns, the briar patch illustrates the intrinsic binding of Sylanagistine mining and energy accumulation efforts to the oppression of other racial groups. It is a network of sink lines connecting unwilling hosts who provide magic to the obelisks, enabling these mechanisms to begin the generative cycle. Foreshadowing so-called node maintainers of the present-day Stillness who are similarly subjugated so their biological assets may be seized and controlled, these captives are exploited according to the racist ideologies of Syl Anagist. These enslaved individuals belong to one of two marginalized racial categories: they are either the only survivors of a terrorized race, the Thniess, or tuners such as Hoa who were engineered by the Sylanagistines as ideal slaves. Jemisin illustrates, through the systemically racist oppression of these two identity categories in Syl Anagist, how exploitative ideologies are informed by traditionally masculine interests in power and control and historical understandings of patriarchy are necessary for combating current, normative masculinities and transforming the nations engendering them.

In presenting this historical oppression through the memories of Hoa, *The Stone Sky*, like *Woman on the Edge of Time* and *Lilith's Brood*, identifies as a crucial step toward positive social and gender transformation the valuation of historical accounts provided by those existing on the margins of society. Similar to Connie in Piercy's novel, Hoa is a subject who, while not subjugated according to his biological sex, is distanced from power within a patriarchal dystopia due to his racial and gender makeup. Unwilling to accept his place within a distorted version of the Western gender order and its patterns of hegemony, subordination, complicity, and marginalization, Hoa, like Connie, drastically disrupts traditionally masculine efforts to consolidate power over others and the natural world. Similar also to Jodahs in Butler's *Imago*, Hoa does not fit within conventional categories of gender, race, and sexuality. For this reason, he is uniquely able to comment on hierarchical social systems plaguing the patriarchal dystopia. Jemisin, like Piercy and Butler, prompts her audience to recognize the value of historical accounts provided by societal members whose intersectionality uniquely impacts their perspectives. Through the *Broken Earth* trilogy, Jemisin expands a trend within speculative fiction to incorporate the perspectives of subjects marginalized according to their unique combinations of identity markers and illustrates the importance of accounts provided by such subjugated individuals when tracing the historical context of normative masculinities.

Marginalized perhaps most overtly according to his racial identity, Hoa provides invaluable context for the current racist ideologies of the Stillness, tracing their origins to the historical oppression of the Thniess and obelisk tuners. As Hoa describes, the Stillness was historically made up of three lands, Maecar, Kakhiarar, and Cilir but Syl Anagist, initially a part of Kakhiarar, gradually accumulated power and control over each of the three lands. The Sylanagistine siege of Cilir, however, resulted in a conflict with the people inhabiting a section of this land, the Thniess, whom the colonizers label the "Niess." Following a conflict between these groups, the Thniess are compelled to respond "like any living thing under threat—with diaspora" (Jemisin 2017, 208–209). As Hoa recounts, the Stillness and its current hierarchical order derive from an ancient conflict between Syl Anagist and the persecuted Thniess.

As Jemisin emphasizes, a central component of this conflict and the racism produced by this patriarchal treatment of others is the advanced ability of the Thniess to utilize magic to improve their society, an ability grounded within an anti-patriarchal valuation of life. The Thniess recognize life and the magic it produces as things that should not be controlled or exploited. This perspective contrasts strikingly with their Sylanagistine patriarchal counterparts who view life as merely as a resource to be used. The Thniess represent a significant threat to Syl Anagist since they reject the oppressive logic justifying this patriarchal dystopia's subjugation of *othered* life forms. This marginalized group instead dedicates magic and their own lives to beauty and construct plutonic engines and other mechanisms for the simple purposes of provoking thought, producing art, and enjoying the process of creation (Jemisin 2017, 210). This conflict escalates when Thniess works of art prove to be more efficient and powerful than the mechanisms developed by the Sylanagistines. As Jemisin outlines, the resulting, racist violence is produced by a patriarchal society whose traditional masculinities value power and control and therefore fear their own subjugation: "They conjure phantoms endlessly, terrified that their victims will someday do back what was done to them—even if, in truth, their victims couldn't care less about such pettiness and have moved on" (Jemisin 2017, 210). Racist ideologies, which are later demonstrated to continue in the present-day Stillness, are therefore rooted in this patriarchal dystopia and the masculinities it normalizes.

As Jemisin illustrates through the Sylanagistine treatment of the Thniess, a crucial step toward realizing alternative masculinities in the present is recognizing how racist, patriarchal polities have historically consolidated control and power over their anti-patriarchal alternatives through scientific racism and comparative anatomy. Living in diaspora, the Thniess are identified by their "icewhite eyes and ashblow hair," which "carry a certain stigma" and are socially distanced from power (Jemisin 2017, 209). Fearing and brutalizing the Thniess for their superior abilities to wield magic, the Sylanagistines co-opt scientific language, labeling such Thniess anatomical attributes as signifiers of inferiority. Beginning with cultural bullying including claims that their split tongues compel them to lie and their unique irises cause them to have poor eyesight and perverse desires, the systemic and scientific racism of Syl Anagist is gradually normalized (Jemisin 2017, 210). A significant step toward the legitimization of these racist beliefs is taken when the scientific community adopts the language of comparative anatomy to reinforce these prejudiced claims: "It became easy for scholars to build reputations and careers around the notion that Niess sessapinae were fundamentally different, somehow—more sensitive, more active, less controlled, less civilized—and that this was the source of their magical peculiarity. This was what made them not the same kind of human as everyone else. Eventually: not as human as everyone else. Finally: not human at all" (Jemisin 2017, 210–211). Valuing the lives and magical abilities of the Thniess as assets to be manipulated and used, the Sylanagistines appeal to traditionally masculine conceptions of rationality and scientific knowledge. Though it is found after the Thniess are eliminated and subjugated that the rumored Niess sessapinae does not exist, the racist and patriarchal beliefs undergirding this falsified claim are not disputed and continue into the present setting of the novel (Jemisin 2017, 211). Pivotal to the systemic racism foundational and endemic to the Stillness is a historical use of scientific endeavors and comparative anatomy that parallels that of the twentieth-century United States. Central to Jemisin's valuation of historical accounts provided by marginalized subjects is their ability to disrupt metanarratives such as comparative anatomical frameworks founded upon and serving racist, patriarchal perspectives and conceptions of manhood.

The trilogy further emphasizes the importance of historically contextualizing the patriarchal co-opting of science, focusing upon the use of comparative anatomy to stabilize the racist patriarchy. Jemisin emphasizes the importance of historical accounts from the societal margins through Hoa, who recounts the Sylanagistine exploitation of another racial group, the so-called obelisk tuners. Exploited like the Earth for the sake of power and energy consolidation, the tuners are treated as tools of the Sylanagistine scientific community to manufacture the Plutonic Engine. Designed and manufactured as improved, subservient versions of the Thniess, Hoa and his fellow tuners are given racist, stereotypical features of this subjugated race and these characteristics, endowed by Sylanagistine, racist schools of comparative anatomy, ensure the tuners' continued marginalization. Since the tuners "must be not just tools, but myths," or racist, social fictions, they are "given exaggerated Niess features—broad faces, small mouths, skin nearly devoid of color, hair that laughs at fine combs," and short statures (Jemisin 2017, 211). Hoa soon realizes how the distinct features of the tuners are utilized to isolate them socially. He and his fellow tuners are harassed, their bodies and hair are examined and touched as a source of amusement for onlookers, and they are disparaged through the use of epithets focused upon their bodies such as "forktongue" (Jemisin 2017, 203). As Hoa realizes during this public excursion, these embellished characteristics promulgate the exoticization and dehumanization of the tuners. The *Broken Earth* trilogy outlines the importance of historically situating traditional conceptions of manliness to better understand how patriarchal masculinities utilize tools such as scientific racism to justify unequal power networks.

Jemisin further illuminates the centrality of historically contextualizing masculinities to current efforts to transform gendered networks of power by illustrating how racist ideologies, produced by patriarchy and legitimized by scientific racism and comparative anatomy, lead to political violence. As the trilogy illustrates, patriarchal, hierarchical conceptions of the *other* as tools and life as merely a valuable resource are utilized by those occupying the higher echelons of patriarchal power networks to justify the marginalization or murder of these individuals (Jemisin 2017, 209). Recognizing his social position, Hoa, for example, considers the likelihood that he and his fellow tuners will be completely subjugated after the Plutonic Engine experiment is completed. Since their lives and the energy they produce will remain valuable to the patriarchy, this subjugation entails instead of death the perpetual exploitation of their immobilized bodies in the briar patch with the myriad other tuners and Thniess estimated by Hoa to number in the millions. As Jemisin emphasizes, understanding the historical background of patriarchal masculinities aids contemporary activists in better comprehending how traditionally masculine gender scripts promulgate the subjugation of, among other categories, those belonging to unfavored racial groups.

As *The Stone Sky* illustrates, accounts from the margins of historical patriarchies are pivotal to current efforts to transform masculinity since they illuminate how power is distributed across the four patterns of masculinity. Through Hoa's account, for example, these patterns—complicity, hegemony, marginalization, and subordination—and their functioning as the power mechanisms of the racist patriarchy are outlined. As Hoa recounts, the man leading the Plutonic Engine project, Conductor Gallat, for example, opts to be compliant to the patriarchal power network of Syl Anagist since hegemonic positions of authority are denied him due to his racial makeup. Though an adopter of traditional masculinities and their interests in power and control, Gallat is unable to reach higher echelons of power since, as his white eyes and pale skin emphasize, Gallat has Thniess genealogy. Distorting the historical, racist policies of American culture, Jemisin presents Syl Anagist as a racist patriarchy that ostracizes individuals according to these racial signifiers with particular emphasis placed upon nonnormative eye colors. Though other races possess pale skin, Gallat's eyes "suggest . . . that somewhere in his family's history—distant, or he would not have been permitted schooling and medical care and his prestigious current position—someone made children with a Niesperson" (Jemisin 2017, 253–254). Hoa's shock at learning of Gallat's authoritative position illustrates the rarity of a person possessing such traits to gain power in Syl Anagist. Such power is shown to be limited, however, and Gallat, distanced from hegemony, experiences another key pattern of masculinity, subjugation. His racial identity is why, though Gallat is a dedicated and productive leader, he is denied respect and dignity. While not possessing enough Thniess racial markers to experience extensive social marginalization, Gallat is subjugated within a network of patriarchal hegemony. Navigating these patterns of masculinity, Gallat opts to be compliant to this system of power. Through Hoa's account, Jemisin emphasizes the importance of recognizing the historical roots of patriarchal masculinities to the project of transforming conceptions of manhood.

Jemisin further emphasizes the importance of such historical accounts by outlining, through Hoa's recollections, the functioning of the other patterns of masculinity within this earlier society: complicity, subjugation, and marginalization. As Hoa outlines, Gallat is complicit to the racist patriarchy that subjugates him and, as a result, subjugates and marginalizes those occupying lower echelons of power such as the tuners whom he considers subhuman. Central to Gallat's dehumanization of the tuners is his conception of them as tools for scientific endeavor. Any tuner who disobeys, is unproductive, or possesses human-like emotions is relegated to the briar patch, which represents the total submission of their lives to the Sylanagistine project. The normative perspective toward the tuners Gallat adopts as a compliant subject of this racist patriarchy is illuminated during a visit to the briar patch. His detached demeanor as he tours the area demonstrates his view of these componentized lives stored for their exploitation as mere assets, valuable but not human. As Hoa considers, Gallat possesses complete control over the lives of those situated beneath him socially and has sent tuners such as Tetlewha, a friend of Hoa and his fellow tuners, to the briar patch. As Essun learns through Hoa's account of Gallat, the compliance of those in closer positions to power in patriarchies such as the Stillness and Syl Anagist reinforces these oppressive, racist systems of power. By emphasizing Hoa's historical record as a tool for illuminating such patterns of masculinity, Jemisin underscores how historical data produced at the margins of the patriarchy are pivotal to destabilizing contemporary, traditional masculinities.

Further emphasizing the pivotal role of marginalized historical accounts in transforming masculinities, Jemisin delineates how Hoa adopted new, feminist-oriented conceptions of manhood as a result of his exposure to such historical records. As Hoa explains, during the Plutonic Engine project in Syl Anagist, he was introduced to Kelenli, a powerful female tuner who exemplifies improved conceptions of masculinity and seeks to destabilize patriarchal systems of power and control grounded in fear. As a mentor, Kelenli exemplifies such courage in explaining her response to prejudice: *"They're afraid because we exist . . . so we can either die like they want, or laugh at their cowardice and go on with our lives"* (Jemisin 2017, 109). As a key model of new masculinities, Kelenli also acts as a teacher, providing the tuners with historical context for their subjugation. Viewing herself as a truth-teller, "the last Niess lorist" whose duty is to teach others of the patriarchal, racist subjugation of these people, Kelenli transmits to Hoa the historical account of the Thniess people and, through this account, pushes Hoa toward alternative, anti-racist ideals of manhood and activism (Jemisin 2017, 214). As Hoa recounts in the present, the historical account Kelenli provides them of the Thniess causes them to reconsider their own subjugation and denial of peoplehood and the possibility of revolution. Jemisin highlights through the transformation of Hoa under the guidance of Kelenli the impact of personal narratives from marginalized subjects and their importance as tools for contextualizing patriarchal masculinities, galvanizing similarly suppressed subjects, and transforming ideals of manhood.

As the *Broken Earth* series illustrates through Hoa's actions during the Plutonic Engine experiment, historical accounts from the margins of the patriarchy, in producing alternative, feminist-oriented masculinities, desta-bilize systems of patriarchal power. More specifically, Hoa's adoption of new, egalitarian masculinities, which oppose racist ideologies, enables him to wield a weapon powerful enough to topple the Sylanagistine patriarchy. Charged with the use of the most powerful obelisk, the onyx, to initiate the obelisk gate and kickstart the Plutonic Engine that will strip Earth of its most valuable natural resources, Hoa desires instead to wield this immense tool to destroy the racist patriarchy and it is this desire that enables him to wield the obelisk. Making contact with the Onyx, Hoa realizes the historical source of its power; it is given life by the countless individuals who were subjugated according to their race and whose magic was forcefully appropriated and fun-neled into it: "Put enough magic into something nonliving, and it becomes alive. Put enough lives into a storage matrix, and they retain a collective will, of sorts. They *remember* horror and atrocity, with whatever is left of them—their souls, if you like" (Jemisin 2017, 332). In order to wield the power of the obelisk and disrupt the traditionally patriarchal experiment of the Sylanagistines, he must be granted access by those possessing the onyx. Sensing Hoa's intention and subjugated status, the obelisk consents. Through historically contextualizing this powerful tool, which is made alive by the countless, subjugated lives it possesses, Hoa recognizes his similar mar-ginalization and is galvanized as a new man who values feminist-oriented, revolutionary conceptions of manhood.

Through this partnership between Hoa and the obelisk, Jemisin emphasizes the power of historical accounts to reveal parallels between groups similarly oppressed by patriarchal masculinities and opportunities for them to therefore work together in challenging these gender scripts and the networks of power they strengthen. The pivotal connection made between Hoa and the onyx is made possible by the transmission to Hoa of Kelenli's historical account of the Thniess genocide and her modeling of alternative, egalitarian masculinities. Recognizing through Kelenli's account, the similarities between the subjugation of the Thniess and the tuners, Hoa notes their mutual subjugation to the racist patriarchy and adopts a radical form of manliness that values activism, justice, and equality. Like the Thniess possessing the obelisk, Hoa and his fellow tuners desire for their peoplehood to be recognized and believe that their actions will bring about such recognition (Jemisin 2017, 329–330). This desire further enables an invaluable partnership between the similarly subjugated racial groups of the tuners and Thniess. Unique to the *Broken Earth* trilogy is Jemisin's contention that changes to current patriarchal systems require such meaningful alliances across space and time between oppressed groups and that such alliances are made possible by historical accounts produced on the societal margins.

This distinctive focus of Jemisin's novels upon how accounts from the historical, social margins enable the transformation of current, patriarchal masculinities and the nations they influence is emphasized by Hoa's development as, like Kelenli, an activist and historian. The revolutionary efforts of Essun to destabilize the racist patriarchy and the masculinities it favors are influenced by Hoa's historical account of an earlier disruption of patriarchal power, the Shattering, which occurred as a result of the sabotaged Plutonic Engine experiment. As Hoa recounts, during this experiment, he, adopting the new, egalitarian masculinities modeled by Kelenli and influenced by her own historical accounts, uses the obelisk gate to destroy Sylanagistine power networks. By introducing a power surge after the launching of the fragments, he and his fellow tuners cause the stored magic to flood back into the systems of Syl Anagist, causing the destruction of this power system and the death of those individuals populating the briar patch and the tuners operating the Plutonic Engine (Jemisin 2017, 320–321). Willing to sacrifice himself to disrupt the complete subjugation of the Earth and those racial groups marginalized in Syl Anagist, Hoa performs an alternative masculinity opposed to power and control. During the initiation of the Plutonic Engine experiment, however, the Earth takes control of twenty-seven of the obelisks and the engine itself. Seeking to eliminate humankind, which has exploited it for its natural resources, it initiates a "burndown" of the obelisks that will, if not corrected, result in the melting of the Earth's crust and the elimination of almost all life on the planet. A new man interested in the preservation and cultivation of life and the well-being of others, Hoa counters this attack and redirects the volatile energy into space, resulting in the displacement of the moon into a high elliptical orbit (Jemisin 2017, 340). Modeling alternative masculinities that value and do not seek power over the lives of others, Hoa navigates the conflict between the Earth and Syl Anagist, minimizes the amount of lives lost in this exchange, and eventually transmits this pivotal historical account to later activists similarly opposing a racist, patriarchal nation. Influenced by the historical accounts of Kelenli, Hoa adopts a new masculinity that replaces interests in power and control with desires for equality and fraternity and likewise passes down historical accounts from the margins to younger generations.

As Jemisin emphasizes, a pivotal aspect of new, feminist-oriented masculinities must be an interest in producing, emphasizing, and valuing accounts that historically contextualize patriarchy and the masculinities it favors. By preserving such historical accounts of patriarchal oppression and sharing them with similarly subjugated individuals, Hoa adopts, as a new man, the role of a lorist that, like Kelenli, historically contextualizes traditional masculinities and the racist patriarchy. As Jemisin emphasizes, attempts to destabilize patriarchal hierarchies require alliances between similarly oppressed groups and these coalitions are enabled significantly by the communication of historical accounts from individuals similarly positioned at the social margins. Through Hoa and his position as a tuner lorist who, like Kelenli, contextualizes for present-day audiences the marginalization of others, Jemisin emphasizes how such accounts from the historical, social margins enable the transformation of current, patriarchal masculinities. As Hoa explains to Essun, utilizing historical accounts to end the complacency of subjugated citizens increases the likelihood of revolution and meaningful change (Jemisin 2017, 312). As a lorist, Hoa, like Kelenli before him, seeks to disrupt complacency surrounding patriarchal social systems and accomplishes this goal through the preservation and recitation of historical systems of subjugation. Adopting this position, Hoa illuminates for Essun the connections between the ancient subjugation of the tuners and that of the present-day orogenes by emphasizing their kinship. The orogenes are distant relatives of the tuners and "are the shallower, more specialized, more natural distillation of" the powers of these ancestors (Jemisin 2017, 50). As Hoa explains, understanding the systemic oppression of the orogenes requires an understanding of the historical oppression of their ancestors, the obelisk tuners. Through Kelenli and Hoa and their roles as lorists, the *Broken Earth* trilogy emphasizes the ways historical accounts from the social margins enable the rethinking of racist, patriarchal nations, and the masculinities they normalize.

In addition to its distinct focus upon the role of historical records from the margins of the patriarchy in the transforming of masculinities, the *Broken Earth* trilogy also represents a significant departure from Butler's *Lilith's Brood* series in its final emphasis, which ventures away from Butlerian themes of compromise and improved but imperfect social systems and toward the hope that a difficult, necessary, and sizable reconstruction of society and gender is possible. Central to this reconstruction is the revision of the former society's masculinities, which mold and are molded by this racist patriarchy. By presenting as vital to this transformation and the conclusion of the fifth seasons characters who reject traditionally masculine interests in power and control and instead favor equality and community, Jemisin emphasizes the necessity of transforming masculinities to positively alter the contemporary United States.

Jemisin outlines through the transformation of Schaffa, for example, the pivotal role transformed hegemonic men play in the alteration of masculinities and the nation. As previously outlined, Jemisin stresses through Schaffa's initial programming and the implementation of a corestone into the left lobe of his sessapinae the socially situated nature of masculinity. This programming, Jemisin's distorted presentation of patriarchal indoctrination, equips Guardians both ideologically and physically to subjugate orogenes according to their racial identities. When this programming is contaminated and the Earth gains control of these corestones, Guardians who experience this alteration "switch teams. Stop working for the status quo and Guardian interests, and start working for the Earth's interests instead" (Jemisin 2016, 207). Schaffa, facing the likelihood of death, allows the Earth to take control of his corestone and becomes a subject of its will. Yet, he proves capable of withstanding the Earth, maintaining his own autonomy, and realizing an alternative form of manliness. This new conception of manhood is socially situated and molded by his interactions with others, namely Nassun, and reflects Hoa's observations, acting as the narrator, that "a person is herself, and others. Relationships chisel the final shape of one's being" (Jemisin 2016, 1). As Jemisin emphasizes through the new conceptions of manhood Schaffa adopts, the new masculinities required for comprehensively transforming society must value the autonomy and freedom of others.

As the *Broken Earth* trilogy presents through Schaffa, the positive transformation of masculinities and the comprehensive dismantling of the patriarchy necessitate men recognizing the toxic effects of patriarchy upon others and rejecting interests in control and power, which, as Jemisin delineates, are often adopted as a result of fear. Diagnosing the patriarchal gender performances of Nassun's father, Jija, for example, Schaffa identifies a fear of orogenes as the motivating force behind this adoption of toxic masculinity: "Something causes a fear like that, Nassun. Something that has nothing to do with you, or your brother, or your mother's lies. Whatever it is has left its wound in your father—a wound that obviously has festered. He will lash out at anything that touches upon or even near that reeking old sore . . . as you have seen" (Jemisin 2016, 186–187). As Schaffa outlines, Jija murdered his son and consistently intimidates and violently attacks his daughter because of his racist attitude and fear of orogenes, which fortify his patriarchal perspective and masculinity. Schaffa similarly diagnoses his own fear of orogenic genocide and self-perception as a benevolent patriarch as the primary motivators for his previous adoption of traditional masculinities. Accepting Nassun's implication that the supposedly benevolent, patriarchal leadership of the Guardians has instigated a genocide, Schaffa explains how the Guardians' treatment of orogenes is motivated by fear, guided by racist, patriarchal ideologies, and focused upon killing the individual by transforming them into a tool. Fear justifies the patriarchal dehumanization of orogenes and the adoption of patriarchal masculinities. Central to Schaffa's departure from such traditional conceptions of manhood is his recognition of the unjust, subjugating nature of racist, patriarchal power systems and the gender roles they legitimize. As Jemisin illustrates through Schaffa, the comprehensive transformation of the patriarchy and its attending masculinities necessitates the recognition of fear as a primary motive for adopting traditional gender roles.

Jemisin similarly identifies as pivotal for the dismantling of racist, sexist systems of power challenges to the patriarchal conditioning of men. The necessity of deprogramming men is most directly outlined in the transformation of Schaffa. A former hegemonic male who was indoctrinated as a Guardian, Schaffa must withstand the influences of his training and, later, the Earth, which, after gaining control of his corestone, attempts to force him to kill Nassun since she desires to use the obelisks to destroy the world. Schaffa's struggle to withstand his training and the will of the Earth act as a distorted portrait of men rejecting patriarchal gender scripts. Once free of the aforementioned terrorizing, racist ideologies of the Guardian order, Schaffa resists the Earth's desire for him to adopt a patriarchal approach to Nassun: there is a pain along his spine. "Something disagrees with his resolve. Automatically his hand twitches toward the back of Nassun's neck . . . and then he stops himself. No. She is more to him than just relief from pain. *Use her,* commands the voice. *Break her. So willful, like her mother. Train this one to obey. No,* Schaffa thinks back, and braces himself to bear the lash of retaliation. It is only pain" (Jemisin 2016, 180). Maintaining the traditionally masculine quality of courage, Schaffa actively resists patriarchal programming and chooses to value connection and equality over power consolidation and subjugation. Importantly, Schaffa, drawn to such intimacy and fraternity, problematically does not confront Nassun about her intentions to destroy the Earth through the use of the obelisks. By presenting through Schaffa an imperfect, transformed man who must learn to value intimacy and equality while also challenging efforts to harm others, Jemisin, like Bryant, Butler, Piercy, and Butler, emphasizes the imperfect qualities of transformed men. Jemisin presents in Schaffa's struggle to perform alternative masculinities a radical, materialist conception of gender and a hopeful portrait of how this difficult, necessary transformation may positively shape the patriarchal, gendered society.

The *Broken Earth* series delineates the pivotal role nonconforming, subjugated men play in the comprehensive alteration of masculinities and the nation. Having experienced a feminist-oriented, utopian polity, Meov, and its corresponding masculinities, embodied by Innon, Alabaster reacts to the murder of his lover and the destruction of this polity with a resolve to dramatically destabilize the racist patriarchy and its patterns of masculinity. Relocated to Corepoint by the stone eater Antimony after the fatal attack upon Meov, Alabaster understands connections between the inequalities of the past to those of the present and sets out to destroy the center of political influence, Yumenes, and disrupt these current societal power networks. Jemisin once again emphasizes, through Alabaster, the importance of historical accounts in recognizing past injustices that inform current hierarchies of power as well as the centrality of metanarratives in fortifying these inequalities. Referencing the aforementioned Second Yumenescene Lore Council's Declaration on the Rights of the Orogenically Afflicted, Alabaster rejects this grand narrative utilized to legitimize systemic racism: "I don't give a shit what the something-somethingth council of big important farts decreed, or how the geomests classify things, or any of that. That we're not human is just the lie they tell themselves so they don't have to feel bad about how they treat us" (Jemisin 2015, 354). As a man modeling new, feminist-oriented masculinities, Alabaster disrupts patriarchal, racist metanarratives and seeks to cause the destruction of the Sanzed-influenced, patriarchal city-states that populate the Stillness. He therefore embodies the new masculinities Jemisin's trilogy presents as necessary for the deconstruction of traditional gender scripts and the comprehensive transformation of the gendered nation.

Jemisin emphasizes as central to the comprehensive transformation of the patriarchal nation an understanding of gender as socially situated and a conception of new masculinities that value connection and community while rejecting efforts to consolidate power. Exemplifying such a radical reconception of manhood, Hoa values others regardless of their identity makeup. He, for example, condemns the racist, patriarchal power networks of the Guardians and emphasizes the possibility of transforming society. Opposing these societal networks that subjugate and marginalize citizens based upon their identity markers, Hoa instead values connection and community. In conversation with Essun, who, after the events of the trilogy, awakens as a stone eater and must relearn her identity and life, Hoa explains that his core desire is for "Friends. Family. Moving with them. Moving forward'" (Jemisin 2017, 397–398). As outlined by Hoa, a key representative of the alternative masculinities Jemisin presents, the new man values connection and community and desires to move society forward through the transformation of its networks of power and corresponding ideals of manhood.

Pivotal to this societal transformation is the impact of men moving from traditional to feminist-oriented masculinities upon the two characters responsible for the conclusion of the fifth seasons, Nassun and Essun. In the climax of *The Stone Sky*, Nassun and Essun battle for the control of the obelisks. Nassun, scarred by her experiences within the racist, patriarchal city-states populating the Stillness, desires to draw the moon into a collision course with Earth and thereby destroy all life upon it. This plan is altered when the Earth, possessing Schaffa, removes his corestone, which ensures the former Guardian will rapidly age and die in the near future. As a result, Nassun revises her plan and decides to use the Obelisk Gate to transform humankind into stone eaters so that Schaffa's life may be extended. In opposition to her daughter, Essun intends to return the moon to its original orbit and, if the Earth accepts this peace offering, bring an end to the cycle of fifth seasons. During the ensuing conflict, both Essun and Nassun risk death through the continuous use of the obelisks. Fearing for her daughter, Essun releases control of the gate and dies as a result of her sustained injuries. Moved by her mother's sacrifice, Nassun alters her plan and returns the moon to its original orbit, bringing an eventual end to the fifth seasons. By emphasizing the origins of these disparate desires to shape the nation, Jemisin highlights the impact of men and the masculinities they adopt upon women of color and society.

The *Broken Earth* trilogy illuminates how masculinities impact individuals marginalized according to their identity markers such as women of color and the centrality of transforming masculinity to the elimination of hierarchical social systems. Jemisin uniquely highlights a significant aspect of the mutually constitutive relationship binding gender and the nation: the manner via which masculinities, in impacting the lives of women, affect the future of the polity. In the trilogy, Essun and Nassun, as a result of their traumatic experiences with patriarchal men, adopt toxic approaches to reshaping society and must learn to again value a hopeful, feminist, utopian approach to societal planning. Initially critical of feminist interests in community and valuing instead traditionally masculine interests in individualism, Essun learns through her experience in two feminist-oriented nations, Meov, and Castrima under, to expunge the influence of patriarchal masculinities from her perspective and vision of a future, improved polity. Traumatized by patriarchal men such as Jija and Schaffa, Essun recognizes the socially situated nature of gender through her interactions with nonnormative men such as Innon, Alabaster, and Hoa, and these positive interactions contribute to her transformation and revitalized interest in equality, community, and efforts to develop a new, improved society.

Jemisin similarly outlines through Nassun how normative and alternative masculinities impact her life and influence her temporary adoption of patriarchal interests in subjugation and power and ultimate rejection of these toxic, traditionally masculine qualities. Nassun's initial plan to destroy life on Earth stems from two sources of trauma: the abuse of her father, which culminates in the aforementioned attempted murder of Nassun, and the draconian punishment methods her mother utilized when training Nassun to hide her orogenic powers. Nassun must learn to reject the traditionally masculine desire to control and overpower others she adopted to defend herself from a patriarchal, racist father. In addition, she must recognize the origins of her mother's abuse, the subjugation of Essun by a patriarch, Schaffa, who, since divorcing himself from traditional masculinities, has been a pivotal, positive influence in Nassun's life. Breaking her daughter's hand to instill in her a fear of revealing her orogenic powers, Essun repeats the abusive cycle begun by Schaffa and the hegemonic, patriarchal Guardian class. During a visit to the Antarctic Fulcrum, Nassun recognizes this connection between her familial trauma and the hegemonic pattern of masculinity embodied by the Guardians: "The Fulcrum is why her mother never loved her. Is why her father does not love her anymore. Is why her brother is dead" (Jemisin 2016, 268). In reaction to this knowledge, Nassun kills the Guardians and orogenes inhabiting this community and, under the advice of the patriarchal stone eater, Steel, decides to take control of the obelisks and destroy the Earth. As the *Broken Earth* trilogy delineates through Nassun, her subjugation to the patriarchal masculinities of Jija and Schaffa through Essun, and her resulting adoption of traditionally masculine interests in gaining power and control over others, men and their masculinities significantly impact women of color and the future of the nation.

A final pivotal aspect of Jemisin's series, outlined in the choices and decisions of Nassun and Essun, is its optimistic portrayal of individuals who comprehensively transform society and its corresponding masculinities. Presenting a radically materialist account of gender that extends the work of Bryant, Le Guin, Piercy, and Butler, Jemisin presents a feminist critical utopia that "negates the negation of utopia" and uniquely and optimistically emphasizes the possibility of developing a feminist-oriented, improved society from the ashes of the dystopian patriarchy (Moylan 1986, 10). Due to her traumatization under patriarchy, Nassun initially desires to destroy humankind. As a result of her experiences with Schaffa and witnessing the sacrifice made by her mother, however, Nassun adopts a materialist account of masculinities, recognizes the possibility of transforming gender scripts, and seeks to transform society by using her powers to end the fifth seasons. Similarly, Essun, through her experiences with nonnormative men, accepts the socially situated nature of masculinities and seeks to transform society and its corresponding gender ideologies. At the conclusion of the series, Hoa, the key male representative of feminist-oriented masculinities, speaks with Essun about the possibility of developing a better, more utopian society:

> "What do *you* want?" You consider. I listen to the slow ongoing roar of the volcano, down here in the deep. Then you say, "I want the world to be better." I have never regretted more my inability to leap into the air and whoop for joy. Instead, I transit to you, with one hand proffered. "Then let's go make it better." You look amused. It's you. It's truly you. "Just like that?" "It might take some time." "I don't think I'm very patient." But you take my hand. Don't be patient. Don't ever be. This is the way a new world begins. "Neither am I," I say. "So let's get to it." (Jemisin 2017, 397–398)

In this final passage of the series, Jemisin extends the work of the feminist utopian genre to reject anti-utopian sentiment and presents the opportunity to transform society through the adoption of new masculinities. Continuing the work of feminist writers such as Bryant, Le Guin, Piercy, and Butler to present a materialist account of masculinity that calls for its transformation, Jemisin emphasizes the importance of recognizing the historical context of patriarchal masculinities and the manner by which they fortify other subjugating ideologies such as racism and environmental exploitation. Jemisin's intersectional, complex portrait of feminist, utopian masculinities continues the work of broadening the feminist utopian genre to imagine methods by which contemporary American society and its attending gender scripts may be positively transformed and concludes with the hopeful message that such change is indeed possible.

Conclusion

These key characteristics of the utopian man—his interest in liberty, equality, and fraternity—unite the divergent novels upon which this analysis focuses, Dorothy Bryant's *The Kin of Ata Are Waiting for You*, Ursula K. Le Guin's *The Dispossessed*, Marge Piercy's *Woman on the Edge of Time*, Octavia Butler's *Lilith's Brood* trilogy, and N.K. Jemisin's *Broken Earth* series. This analysis illustrates the unique power of feminist writers to imagine new masculinities and the suitability of science fiction as a genre for the presentation of alternative masculinities. A central strength of these texts is their presentation of masculinity as socially situated and shaped by the relationships between men. Masculinity studies scholars often and accurately highlight the importance of male homosocial relationships to men's conceptions and performances of gender and focus upon "the varied way that in different times and places, a man fashions a self—an identity—by linking his own being to other men within a collective social ideal or script that defines manliness" (Sussman 2012, 9). While this relationship between men is central to concepts of manhood, the shaping and configuration of this collective social ideal is similarly crucial. By emphasizing the ways homosocial relationships and societal conceptions of manhood in these texts influence masculinities, this analysis illustrates how feminist writers may potentially impact societal gender conceptions through their utopian texts.

As *A New Man* demonstrates, these feminist utopias and their embedded commentaries on gender are crucial to masculinity studies since they, as narratives developed by women, enable audiences to imagine new, feminist-informed masculinities and recognize current societal mechanisms by which the patriarchal order functions. Defining *narrative* as "not restricted to literary and cultural artifacts but" extending "from the construction of individual gender identity by way of biographical, material and embodied social processes to collective national identities and images" (5n14), Stefan Horlacher (2015) describes this communicative mode as crucial to conceptions of masculinity and the future of masculinity studies. Utilizing their own biographical, material, and embodied knowledge produced within the social processes of the patriarchal United States, Bryant, Le Guin, Piercy, Butler, and Jemisin construct new gender identities for their male and female characters alike. The new conceptions of manhood they posit significantly enrich current masculinity studies scholarship since they are informed by the perspectives of those subjects—women and women of color—who are pointedly impacted by patriarchal gender norms.

In addition to the importance of these works as the extension of these authors' gender identities to the larger collective gender ideologies they imagine, they are crucial to masculinity studies since they highlight the overlooked importance of literature as a site for gender transformation. If, as Horlacher (2015) outlines, gender identity is understood as an "evolving cultural product akin to language and the narrative operations of literature," the literary text "could really be seen as a privileged space and epistemological medium where the manifold mechanisms of configuring ever different and divergent masculinities in the discursive condition becomes readable, knowable, and thereby also rewriteable" (5–6). Due to its generic conventions, science fiction enhances such abilities to imagine new worlds and societies in which new gender scripts may be posited and the traditional gender order may be made readable, knowable, and rewriteable. In presenting the transformability of masculinities, literature and, more specifically, science fiction makes up an invaluable site at which alternative conceptions of manhood may be tested.

As this analysis demonstrates, the flexibility of science fiction grants feminist writers the opportunity to craft worlds reflecting their own social and political interests. While these writers are united in their inclusion of nonnormative masculinities in better, imagined polities, they emphasize distinct elements of the contemporary American capitalistic patriarchy requiring alteration. In addition, they center in their fiction characters who interact uniquely with such dystopian polities and their utopian alternatives, exchanges determined significantly by their identities. Dorothy Bryant stresses the importance of a new consciousness and a social constructionist view of gender. Utilizing the specific characteristics of utopian fiction, she imagines a collectivist anarchy that, in valuing a new consciousness characterized by interests in the nonverbal, mystical, and realm of dreams, enables a new, better masculinity to flourish that is rejected by the United States patriarchy. Centering also non-essentialist theories of gender, she presents to her reader both the radical possibility of transforming hypermasculine, toxic masculinities and the sobering observation that such an alteration requires fundamental changes to the capitalistic patriarchy. Though Bryant's utopia is comparatively limited in its focus upon a white male protagonist, it is powerful in its presentation through his narration of the ways the capitalistic patriarchy both serves and harms hegemonic men. While *The Kin of Ata Are Waiting for You* reflects, therefore, Bryant's sociopolitical interests and only highlights the experiences of subjects marginalized according to their identities to a limited degree, the novel is crucial to discussions concerning gender since it, through a patriarchal narrator, rewrites what it means to be masculine.

These novels are valuable to ongoing discussions of masculinity since they focus upon unique characters that interact distinctly with masculinities, revealing to the audience the myriad ways the patriarchal order impacts its various subjects. Similarly reflecting feminist ideals that, like those of Bryant, depart from radical feminist, essentialist conceptions of gender, Ursula Le Guin's *The Dispossessed* is an important text at the intersection of narrative and masculinity studies due to its emphasis upon the continuously dynamic qualities of gender. Recognizing, like Bryant, the mutually constitutive relationship binding society and gender, she focuses upon the constant danger that feminist-oriented nations and their masculinities may succumb to the temptations of capitalism and patriarchy. By focusing upon a male protagonist desired by the ruling class of a capitalistic patriarchy and granted, therefore, significant access to power should he adopt the values of this nation, Le Guin traces the precarious ways feminist-oriented men interact with American systems of power. In addition, *The Dispossessed* considers how the interactions of such new men with patriarchal ideals produce constant threats to the feminist project. Her identification of the better society as ambiguously utopian highlights her disinterest in presenting a closed off, static, imagined nation and masculinities; instead, she is concerned with the instability of gender as a potential threat to alternative conceptions of manhood. Her novel reveals her political and social interests as a feminist in that it both presents the socioeconomic changes necessary for the transformation of men and warns its audience that such altered nations and masculinities require constant reassessment and interrogation.

By widening the scope of focus to include the experiences of subjects distanced from power within the patriarchal order, the novels upon which the second half of this analysis focuses, Marge Piercy's *Woman on the Edge of Time*, Octavia Butler's *Lilith's Brood* trilogy, and N.K. Jemisin's *Broken Earth* series, reflect the widening sociopolitical interests of feminist authors that are germane to current discussions surrounding masculinity. *Woman on the Edge of Time*, for example, highlights the mechanisms of the American capitalistic patriarchy that marginalize subjects in unique ways predicated upon their identity makeup. Piercy illustrates to her audience how conversations concerning manhood must necessarily recognize the interlocking systems of oppression benefiting and, in turn, supported by traditional gender scripts. Aligning her audience with a female protagonist of color, Piercy compels her reader to vicariously experience the ways the contemporary American socioeconomic system subjugates subjects according to, in the case the novel presents, class, race, and biological sex. In this way, *Woman on the Edge of Time* provides insight to its audience concerning American society and, by illuminating the ways patriarchal masculinities are central to this polity, demonstrates the necessity for concepts of manliness to be rethought and transformed. Piercy further delineates this need for alternative masculinities by presenting their centrality to a feminist, utopian community that grants equal power to subjects such as the protagonist regardless of their identity makeup. *Woman on the Edge of Time* exemplifies, therefore, the value of feminist utopias as a site for mining new masculinities and, through the narrative mode, considering how society and gender ideals must change to realize a world conducive to the needs of both men and women.

The impact of utilizing the narrative mode at the intersection of masculinity studies and science fiction studies is dramatically demonstrated by Octavia Butler's *Lilith's Brood*. Drawing upon her lived experiences as a woman of color, Butler encodes within this trilogy the sociopolitical interests of those most impacted by interlocking sources of oppression within the contemporary American capitalistic patriarchy. Her interests in exploring and highlighting for her audience the distinct ways traditional conceptions of manhood impact individuals possessing nonnormative identity markers are illustrated by the protagonists upon which her novels focus. While centering a female protagonist of color in the first novel of this series, *Dawn*, Butler (like Piercy) aligns her audience with an interspecies hybrid male lead in the second text, *Adulthood Rites*, and an interspecies hybrid whose gender does not fit within the traditional binary in the final entry to the trilogy, *Imago*. Utilizing the narrative mode, Butler explores her own experiences as a woman of color and moves beyond these borders, emphasizing the ways subjects marked by, among other elements, their nonnormative sexualities and gender identities experience intersectionality.

In addition, she, through the experiences of these characters within the ambiguously utopian Oankali communities and the dystopian, separatist, human camps concerned with resurrecting a capitalistic patriarchal polity, asks her audience to consider hierarchical behavior as not essentially human. Deconstructing the interlocking systems of patriarchy, capitalism, and racism among other related ideologies, she reveals to her audience the necessity for humankind to transform socioeconomic systems of power. Presenting a sober warning about the toxicity of patriarchy and a measured hope that traditional masculinities may be transformed, she compels her audience to examine contemporary American intersectional forces and the methods by which they may be challenged. Her trilogy is, therefore, important to discussions concerning masculinity since it radically traces connections between the traditional gender order and other oppressive ideologies and challenges male readers to rewrite their own understandings of manliness.

Demonstrating the power of science fiction to comment on the future of masculinities, N.K. Jemisin emphasizes through the *Broken Earth* trilogy both the necessity of comprehensively dismantling the patriarchy through the adoption of alternative masculinities and the pivotal role historical narratives play in this endeavor. Avoiding the overly optimistic attitude toward a future, better society endemic to the utopian genre, Jemisin offers through her trilogy a subdued presentation of feminist-oriented societies and the possibility that an improved, imperfect polity may be built in the ashes of racist, patriarchal systems of power. Central to the disruption of such patriarchal dystopias is the preservation, transmission, and valuing of historical accounts written by subjects disempowered within the patriarchal economy. As Jemisin's series contends, identifying and rejecting the manipulation of historical accounts by men occupying the hegemonic pattern of masculinity and destabilizing such accounts by centering historical records produced at the societal margins is central to the feminist utopian project. Situated at the intersection of masculinity and science fiction studies, Jemisin's *Broken Earth* trilogy outlines clear strategies for rewriting American masculinity without guaranteeing their success or the success of such a comprehensive societal reformation.

Uniting Jemisin with Bryant, Le Guin, Piercy, and Butler are the diverse, productive ways these female writers frame masculinities. In discussing the roots of masculinity studies in 1960s feminist activism, Peter Murphy (2004) reflects how "men were not alone in this feminist analysis of masculinities. Several women contributed invaluable insights into the discourse of 'men's studies,' a 'feminist masculinity,' and the 'male condition,' and in this dialogue with women, the investigation of what it means to be a man in a patriarchal society became more subtle, more layered, more radical" (10). As the chapters making up my analysis demonstrate, such radical, complex examinations of what it means to be a man are located in a widely overlooked site of feminist activism: utopian fiction. Central to the value of such speculative works is the way they frame ideal and problematic masculinities. These texts more specifically avoid the trend Michael Kimmel (2017) identifies of cultural products such as media and literature blurring the boundary separating positive and problematic masculinities or mislabeling these categories altogether (2). In opposition to such toxic or blurred portrayals of patriarchal masculinities, these feminist writers correctly portray abusive conceptions of manhood and align their readers in opposition to characters subscribing to these gender scripts. A central source of power for *The Kin of Ata Are Waiting for You*, for example, is Bryant's reframing of the violent attributes

of traditional masculinities. Bryant presents a protagonist whose initial patriarchal interests in power and control through violence significantly parallel
those of Stephen Rojack, the protagonist of Norman Mailer's *An American
Dream*, but are framed as horrific by Bryant through her unnamed, remorseful
narrator. Bryant therefore demonstrates the opportunities literature grants for
challenging traditional representations of patriarchal masculinities as ideal.

In positioning in *The Dispossessed*, a male protagonist who rejects the
capitalistic and heteronormative underpinnings of hegemonic American
manhood, Le Guin similarly introduces complexity to discussions surrounding masculinity and this contribution is due significantly to her framing of
manliness. Le Guin aligns her audience with Shevek, who subscribes to
improved, feminist masculinities and positions him and the reader in opposition to the misogynistic male characters inhabiting A-Io. Le Guin therefore
carefully frames as positive radical concepts of manliness. *The Dispossessed*
illuminates how feminist authors may, by carefully framing presentations of
masculinities in their novels, compel their readers to rethink and rewrite their
own perceptions of manliness.

While relocating male characters to the margins of *Woman on the Edge of
Time*, Marge Piercy demonstrates how the inclusion in fiction of intersectionality enables the development of more complex, compelling representations
of masculinity. Moving beyond Le Guin's approach of positively framing a
queer male character while only briefly exploring his nonnormative sexuality,
Piercy places on the sidelines of her utopia male characters possessing diverse
racial, sexual, gender, and class identities. She, for example, presents with
rich detail problematic men such as Everett Silvester, a professor and former
employer of the protagonist, Connie, who benefits due to his class position,
sex, and race. In outlining how Silvester hired a new Spanish-speaking sec-
retary, whom he refers to as "Chiquita, like bananas" (50), Piercy (1976)
illustrates how interlocking systems of subjugation based upon class, race,
and biological sex uniquely harm women like Connie who are fired each year
simply to please a hegemonic man. Piercy presents myriad male characters
at the margins of her novel who are complex in their attitudes toward Connie
and their proximity to power. By aligning her reader with a character who
is a woman of color and using her experience to represent the stark contrast
between toxic and positive masculinities, Piercy illustrates the ways feminist
writers may contribute significantly to conversations surrounding manhood
through their fictional representations of masculinity.

Similarly complicating representations of manliness in *Lilith's Brood*
through increasingly complex and imaginary representations of intersectionality, Octavia Butler demonstrates through blurring identity categories
the ways genre fiction enables critiques of masculinities. Like Piercy, Butler
centers protagonists whose complex identities uniquely justify their social

disempowerment. Butler, however, extends conversations concerning gender and manliness by presenting a host of characters that, while possessing myriad combinations of identity elements including new sexualities and genders, are shown to be equally capable of adopting and transforming masculinities. The manner by which feminist-oriented masculinities are positively framed and noted as not essential to any particular race, biological sex, or other identity category in *Lilith's Brood* illustrates the benefit of science fiction for creating challenges to traditional masculinities.

Extending the efforts of writers such as Piercy and Butler to complicate masculinity, Jemisin similarly presents male and female characters capable of adopting problematic masculinities. Focused upon a cast of characters possessing diverse gender identities, sexualities, racès, and biological sexes, among other identity markers, Jemisin's trilogy illustrates the dramatic developments that have occurred within feminist utopian fiction since 1971. Her emphases upon connections between traditional masculinities and social conditioning, trauma, and abuse illustrate the continuing relevance of feminist utopian fiction to masculinity studies. Her trilogy presents patriarchal masculinities as the produce of intensive social conditioning that men seeking improved, egalitarian masculinities must overcome. In this way, she frames patriarchal masculinities as problematic social constructs completely disconnected from biological sex. In the *Broken Earth* trilogy, Jemisin emphasizes the necessity of replacing such traditional conceptions of manhood with new, feminist-oriented masculinities and thereby illustrates the importance of feminist speculative fiction to ongoing discussions of American masculinity.

Feminist writers add to discussions concerning alternatives to the patriarchal order and its gender scripts, making this analysis relevant to American culture and ongoing concerns about the future of manhood. The relevance of both feminist thought and fiction to discussions surrounding manliness is emphasized at an increasing rate by masculinity studies scholars.[1] Though my research builds upon the interest among these works in feminism and the construction of male identity, it more closely aligns with approaches analyzing cultural products as sources for new masculinities.

In recent years, more scholars have begun to adopt such an approach. The edited collection *Performing American Masculinities: The 21st-Century Man in Popular Culture*, for example, "focuses on the possibilities for identity formation for men in the United States since the mid-1990s" by mining various avenues of popular culture "to posit questions about the processes of gender creation and the contestation of masculinities as constantly changing political forms" (Watson 2011, 1). Still more recent publications narrow this field of inquiry to literature. Exemplifying this trend, Stefan Horlacher (2015) introduces *Configuring Masculinity in Theory and Literary Practice*, made up of essays applying masculinity studies to literature, by pointing "to the problems the construction of male gender identities seems to pose (not only) in the twentieth and twenty-first centuries" and emphasizing "the outstanding contribution that literature can make with regard to male gender identity formation" (1). There is a pattern developing within studies of American culture and, more specifically, at the intersection of literary studies and masculinity studies. This trend points to the ongoing relevancy of discussions concerning American masculinities and the culture shaping them. This analysis emphasizes as an invaluable resource for masculinity studies the voices of feminist utopias. Feminist utopias, informed by the diverse lived experiences of white female writers and female writers of color, make up important sources of alternative, feminist-oriented masculinities.

NOTE

1. Works such as *Feminism and Masculinities*, for example, contain essays that "focus specifically on the ways in which a feminist analysis provides insights into the social, cultural, and political construction of manhood." While this text, which is "about what feminism has to tell us about being a man" (Murphy 2004, 10), focuses upon feminist perspectives on masculinity, it does not utilize fiction as a site for mining such ideals.

References

"About the MacArthur Fellows Program." MacArthur Foundation. Accessed October 15, 2019. https://www.macfound.org/programs/fellows/strategy/.

Ackerman, Erin M. Pryor. "Becoming and Belonging: The Productivity of Pleasures and Desires in Octavia Butler's Xenogenesis Trilogy." *Extrapolation* 49, no. 1 (2008): 24–43.

Annas, Pamela J. "New Worlds, New Words: Androgyny in Feminist Science Fiction." *Science Fiction Studies* 5, no. 2 (1978): 143–156.

Arthur, W. Brian. *The Nature of Technology: What It Is and How It Evolves*. New York: Simon & Schuster, 2009.

Attebery, Brian. *Decoding Gender in Science Fiction*. London: Routledge, 2002.

Badami, Mary Kenny. "A Feminist Critique of Science Fiction." *Extrapolation* 18, no. 1 (1976): 6–19.

Barr, Marleen, and Nicholas D. Smith. Preface to *Women and Utopia: Critical Interpretations*, edited by Marleen Barr and Nicholas D. Smith, 1–2. Lanham: University Press of America, 1983.

Beal, Frances M. "Black Scholar Interview With Octavia Butler: Black Women and the Science Fiction Genre." *The Black Scholar* 17, no. 2 (1986): 14–18.

Bell, David M. "Paying 'Utopia' a Subversive Fidelity; or, An Affective Trip to Anarres." *Utopian Studies* 27, no. 2 (2016): 129–151.

Beneke, Timothy. *Proving Manhood: Reflections on Men and Sexism*. Berkeley: University of California Press, 1997.

Benfield, Susan Storing. "The Interplanetary Dialectic: Freedom and Equality in Ursula Le Guin's *The Dispossessed*." *Perspective on Political Science* 35, no. 3 (2006): 128–134.

Benson, Josef. *Hypermasculinities in the Contemporary Novel: Cormac McCarthy, Toni Morrison, and James Baldwin*. Lanham: Rowman & Littlefield, 2014.

Bierman, Judah. "Ambiguity in Utopia: The Dispossessed." *Science Fiction Studies* 2, no. 3 (1975): 249–255.

Blackmore, Tim. *War X: Human Extensions in Battlespace*. Toronto: University of Toronto Press, 2011.

Blackmore, Tim. "Warring Stories: Fighting for Truth in the Science Fiction of Joe Haldeman." *Extrapolation* 34, no. 2 (1993): 131.

Bollinger, Laurel. "Symbiogenesis, Selfhood, and Science Fiction." *Science Fiction Studies* 37, no. 1 (2010): 34–53.

Booker, M. Keith. "Woman on the Edge of a Genre: The Feminist Dystopias of Marge Piercy." *Science Fiction Studies* 21, no. 3 (1994): 337–350.

Bryant, Dorothy. *Ella Price's Journal*. Philadelphia: Lippincott, 1972.

Bryant, Dorothy. *The Kin of Ata Are Waiting for You*. New York: Random House, 1971.

Buchbinder, David. *Studying Men and Masculinities*. London: Routledge, 2012.

Burns, Anthony. *Political Theory, Science Fiction, and Utopian Literature: Ursula K. Le Guin and the Dispossessed*. Lanham: Lexington Books, 2008.

Butler, Judith. *Gender Trouble: Feminism and the Subversion of Identity*. London: Routledge, 1990.

Butler, Octavia. "Bloodchild." In *Bloodchild and Other Stories*, 1–29. New York: Seven Stories Press, 1996.

Butler, Octavia. *Clay's Ark*. New York: St. Martin's Press, 1984.

Butler, Octavia. *Lilith's Brood*. New York: Grand Central Publishing, 2000.

Butler, Octavia. *Wild Seed*. New York: Warner Books, 1980.

Canfield, David. "Fantasy's New Queen." *Entertainment Weekly*, September 2018.

Carmichael, Deborah. "The American West in Film, Television, and History." *Film & History* 33, no. 1 (2003): 6–8.

Chan, Edward K. "Utopia and the Problem of Race: Accounting for the Remainder in the Imagination of the 1970s Utopian Subject." *Utopian Studies* 17, no. 3 (2006): 465–490.

Clark, Keith. *Black Manhood in James Baldwin, Ernest J Gaines, and August Wilson*. Champaign: University of Illinois Press, 2004.

Clute, John. "Ursula K. Le Guin Obituary." Last modified January 24, 2018. www.theguardian.com/books/2018/jan/24/obituary-ursula-k-le-guin.

Connell, Raewyn. *Masculinities*. Crows Nest: Allen and Unwin, 1995.

Connell, Raewyn, and James W. Messerschmidt. "Hegemonic Masculinity: Rethinking the Concept." *Gender and Society* 19, no. 6 (2005): 829–859.

Curtis, Claire P. "Utopian Possibilities: Disability, Norms, and Eugenics in Octavia Butler's *Xenogenesis*." *Journal of Literary and Cultural Disability Studies* 9, no. 1 (2015): 19–33.

Davids, Laurence, and Peter Stillman, editors. *The New Utopian Politics of Ursula Le Guin's The Dispossessed*. Lanham: Lexington Books, 2005.

de Vita, Alexs Brooks. "Descent into the Pit of the Redeemer: The Sacrificial Child in International Film and Literature." *Extrapolation* 55, no. 3 (2014): 369–392.

Deane, Bradley. "Imperial Barbarians: Primitive Masculinity in Lost World Fiction." *Victorian Literature and Culture* 36, no. 1 (2008): 205–225.

Deery, June. "Ectopic and Utopic Reproduction: *He, She and It*." *Utopian Studies* 5, no. 2 (1994): 36–49.

Delany, Samuel R. "To Read The Dispossessed." In *The Jewel-Hinged Jaw: Notes on the Language of Science Fiction*. Middletown: Wesleyan University Press, 2009.

Duchamp, L. Timmel. "'Sun Woman' or 'Wild Seed?': How a Young Feminist Writer Found Alternatives to White Bourgeois Narrative Models in the Early Novels of Octavia Butler." In *Strange Matings: Science Fiction, Feminism, African American Voices, and Octavia E. Butler*, edited by Rebecca J. Holden and Nisi Shawl, 82–95. Seattle: Aqueduct Press, 2013.

Edwards, Tim. *Cultures of Masculinity*. London: Routledge, 2006.

"Ella Price's Journal." Feminist Press. Accessed August 9, 2019. https://www.feministpress.org/books-a-m/ella-price.

Elshtain, Jean. "Against Androgyny." *Telos* 47, no. 4 (1981): 5–21.

Evans, Janelle Marie. "Questing to Understand the Other Without 'Othering': An Exploration of the Unique Qualities and Properties of Science Fiction as a Means for Exploring and Improving Social Inequity." *Meridians: Feminism, Race, Transnationalism* 16, no. 1 (2017): 144–156.

Fancourt, Donna. "Accessing Utopia through Altered States of Consciousness: Three Feminist Utopian Novels." *Utopian Studies* 13, no. 1 (2002): 94–113.

Ferry, Peter. *Masculinity in Contemporary New York Fiction*. London: Routledge, 2014.

Firestone, Shulamith. *The Dialectic of Sex*. New York: William Morrow and Company, 1970.

Fitting, Peter. "Reconsiderations of the Separatist Paradigm in Recent Feminist Science Fiction." *Science Fiction Studies* 19, no. 1 (1992): 32–48.

Fitting, Peter. "'So We All Became Mothers': New Roles for Men in Recent Utopian Fiction." *Science Fiction Studies* 12, no. 2 (1985): 156–183.

Forsey, Helen. "The Kin of Ata Are Waiting for You." *Communities*, no. 104 (1999): 68.

Franklin, H. Bruce. "The Vietnam War as American Science Fiction and Fantasy." *Science Fiction Studies* 17, no. 3 (1991): 341–359.

Freedman, Carl. *Critical Theory and Science Fiction*. Middletown: Wesleyan University Press, 2013.

Freibert, Lucy M. "World Views in Utopian Novels by Women." In *Women and Utopia: Critical Interpretations*, edited by Marleen Barr and Nicholas D. Smith, 67–84. Lanham: University Press of America, 1983.

Furlanetto, Elton. "'There Is No Silence': An Interview with Marge Piercy." *Utopian Studies* 25, no. 2 (2014): 416–430.

Haggard, H. Rider. *She: A History of Adventure*. Harlow: Longmans, 1887.

Hall, Peter C. "'The Space Between' in Space: Some Versions of the *Bildungsroman* in Science Fiction." *Extrapolation* 29, no. 2 (1988): 153–182.

Hamming, J. "Nationalism, Masculinity, and the Politics of Climate Change in the Novels of Kim Stanley Robinson and Michael Crichton." *Extrapolation* 54, no. 1 (2013): 21–45.

Hanson, Carter F. "Memor's Offspring and Utopian Ambiguity in Ursula K. Le Guin's "The Day before the Revolution" and *The Dispossessed*." *Science Fiction Studies* 40, no. 2 (2013): 246–262.

Hantke, Steffen. "Surgical Strikes and Prosthetic Warriors: The Soldier's Body in Contemporary Science Fiction." *Science Fiction Studies* 25, no. 3 (1998): 495–509.

Haraway, Donna. "A Cyborg Manifesto: Science, Technology, and Socialist-Feminism in the Late Twentieth Century." In *Simians, Cyborgs, and Women: The Reinvention of Nature*. London: Routledge, 1991.

Hobbs, Alex. *Aging Masculinity in the American Novel*. Lanham: Rowman & Littlefield, 2016.

hooks, bell. *We Real Cool: Black Men and Masculinity*. London: Routledge, 2003.

Horlacher, Stefan. "Configuring Masculinity." In *Configuring Masculinity in Literary Theory and Practice*, edited by Stefan Horlacher, 1–10. Leiden: Brill, 2015.

Horn, Barbara. Afterword to *Ella Price's Journal*, edited by Dorothy Bryant, 230–259. New York: The Feminist Press, 1997.

Huebner, Andrew. J. *The Warrior Image: Soldiers in American Culture from the Second World War to the Vietnam Era*. Chapel Hill: The University of North Carolina Press, 2008.

Jaeckle, Daniel P. "Embodied Anarchy in Ursula K. Le Guin's *The Dispossessed*." *Utopian Studies* 20, no. 1 (2009): 75–95.

Jaeckle, Daniel P. "Interpersonal Ethics in Ursula K. Le Guin's *The Dispossessed*." *Anarchist Studies* 20, no. 1 (2012): 61–79.

Jameson, Fredric. *Archaeologies of the Future: The Desire Called Utopia and Other Science Fictions*. New York: Verso, 2005.

Jaramillo, Deborah L. "Narcocorridos and Newbie Drug Dealers: The Changing Image of the Mexican Narco on US Television." *Ethnic and Racial Studies* 37, no. 9 (2014): 1587–1604.

Jemisin, N. K. *The Fifth Season*. London: Orbit, 2015.

Jemisin, N. K. *The Obelisk Gate*. London: Orbit, 2016.

Jemisin, N. K. *The Stone Sky*. London: Orbit, 2017.

Jesser, Nancy. "Blood, Genes, and Gender in Octavia Butler's *Kindred* and *Dawn*." *Extrapolation* 43, no. 1 (2002): 36–61.

Johns, Adam J. "Becoming Medusa: Octavia Butler's *Lilith's Brood*." *Science Fiction Studies* 37, no. 3 (2010): 382–400.

Jonas, Gerald. "Ursula K. Le Guin, Who Elevated Sci-Fi and Fantasy Fiction, Dies at 88." *The New York Times*, January 23, 2018, B15.

Kapell, Matthew Wilhelm. *Exploring the Next Frontier: Vietnam, NASA, Star Trek and Utopia in 1960s and 70s American Myth and History*. Milton Park: Taylor and Francis, 2016.

Kaplan, David M. *Ricoeur's Critical Theory*. Albany: SUNY Press, 2003.

Kilgore, De Witt Douglas, and Ranu Samantrai. "A Memorial to Octavia E. Butler." *Science Fiction Studies* 37, no. 3 (2010): 353–361.

Kimmel, Michael. *Angry White Men: American Masculinity at the End of an Era*. New York: Nation Books, 2017.

Kimmel, Michael. *Manhood in America: A Cultural History*. Oxford: Oxford University Press, 2006.

King, Roger J. H. "Utopian Fiction as Moral Philosophy: Imagination and Critique." *Utopian Studies* 2, no. 3 (1991): 72–78.

Klarer, Mario. "Gender and the 'Simultaneity Principle': Ursula Le Guin's *The Dispossessed*." *Contemporary Literary Criticism Select* 136 (1992): 107–121.

Kramarae, Cheris, and Jana Kramer. "Feminist's Novel Approaches to Conflict." *Women and Language* 11, no. 1 (1987): 36–40.

Larbalestier, Justine. *The Battle of the Sexes in Science Fiction*. Middletown: Wesleyan University Press, 2002.

Le Guin, Ursula K. "American SF and the Other." *Science Fiction Studies* 2, no. 3 (1975): 208–210.

Le Guin, Ursula K. *The Dispossessed: An Ambiguous Utopia*. New York: Harper & Row, 1974.

Lindow, Sandra J. "Mapping the Walls of *The Dispossessed*." *Extrapolation* 52, no. 2 (2011): 174–191.

Lorde, Audre. "The Master's Tools Will Never Dismantle the Master's House." In *Sister Outsider: Essays and Speeches*, 111–113. Toronto: Crossing Press, 1984.

Magarey, Susan. "Dreams and Desires: Four 1970s Feminist Visions of Utopia." *Australian Feminist Studies* 22, no. 53 (2007): 325–350.

Mamola, G. "Walking Towards Elfland: Fantasy and Utopia in Ursula K. Le Guin's 'The Ones Who Walk Away from Omelas.'" *Extrapolation* 59, no. 2 (2018): 149–162.

Mann, Susan Archer. *Doing Feminist Theory: From Modernity to Postmodernity*. Oxford: Oxford University Press, 2012.

Martinson, Anna M. "Ecofeminist Perspectives on Technology in the Science Fiction of Marge Piercy." *Extrapolation* 44, no. 1 (2003): 50–68.

Marx, Leo. "Technology: The Emergence of a Hazardous Concept." *Technology and Culture* 51, no. 3 (2010): 561–577.

Matarese, Susan. "Death and Community: Insights from the Utopian Vision of Marge Piercy." *Utopian Studies* 1, no. 3 (1991): 106–109.

Mathisen, Werner Christie. "The Underestimation of Politics in Green Utopias: The Description of Politics in Huxley's *Island*, Le Guin's *The Dispossessed*, and Callenbach's *Ecotopia*." *Utopian Studies* 12, no. 1 (2001): 56–78.

McBean, Sam. "Feminism and Futurity: Revisiting Marge Piercy's *Woman on the Edge of Time*." *Feminist Review* 107 (2014): 37–56.

McKenna, Erin. *The Task of Utopia: A Pragmatist and Feminist Perspective*. Lanham: Rowman & Littlefield, 2001.

Mebane-Cruz, Anjana, and Margaret Wiener. "Imagining 'The Good Reality': Communities of Healing in Two Works of Utopian Fiction." *Contemporary Justice Review* 8, no. 3 (2005): 307–320.

Merchant, Carolyn. *The Death of Nature: Women, Ecology and the Scientific Revolution*. New York: Harper & Row, 1989.

Mirandé, Alfredo. *Hombres y Machos: Masculinity and Latino Culture*. Boulder: Westview Press, 1997.

Moylan, Tom. *Demand the Impossible: Science Fiction and the Utopian Imagination*. North Yorkshire: Methuen, 1986.

Moylan, Tom. "The Locus of Hope: Utopia Versus Ideology." *Science Fiction Studies* 9, no. 2 (1982): 159–166.

Murphy, Peter F. Introduction to *Feminism and Masculinities*, edited by Peter F. Murphy, 1–21. Oxford: Oxford University Press, 2004.

Nanda, Aparajita. "Power, Politics, and Domestic Desire in Octavia Butler's *Lilith's Brood.*" *Callaloo* 36, no. 3 (2013): 773–788.

Netolicky, Deborah M. "Cyborgs, Desiring-Machines, Bodies Without Organs, and *Westworld*: Interrogating Academic Writing and Scholarly Identity." *KOME: An International Journal of Pure Communication Inquiry* 5, no. 1 (2017): 91–103.

Neverow, Vara. "The Politics of Incorporation and Embodiment: *Woman on the Edge of Time* and *He, She and It* as Feminist Epistemologies of Resistance." *Utopian Studies* 5, no. 2 (1994): 16–35.

Nishime, LeiLani. "The Mulatto Cyborg: Imagining a Multiracial Future." *Cinema Journal* 44, no. 2 (2005): 34–49.

Obourn, Megan. "Octavia Butler's Disabled Futures." *Contemporary Literature* 54, no. 1 (2013): 109–138.

Olderman, Raymond. "American Fiction 1974–1976: The People Who Fell to Earth." *Contemporary Fiction* 19, no. 4 (1978): 497–530.

Olster, Stacey Michele. *The Cambridge Introduction to Contemporary American Fiction.* Cambridge: Cambridge University Press, 2017.

O'Neale, Sondra. "Inhibiting Midwives, Usurping Creators: The Struggling Emergence of Black Women in American Fiction." In *Feminist Studies/Critical Studies*, edited by Teresa de Lauretis, 139–156. Bloomington: Indiana University Press, 1986.

Osherow, Michele. "The Dawn of a New Lilith: Revisionary Mythmaking in Women's Science Fiction." *NWSA Journal* 12, no. 1 (2000): 68–83.

Payne, Diana L., Kimberly A. Lonsway, and Louis F. Fitzgerald. "Rape Myth Acceptance: Exploration of Its Structure and Its Measurement Using the *Illinois Rape Myth Acceptance Scale.*" *Journal of Research in Personality* 33, no. 1 (1999): 27–68.

Pearson, Carol S. "Coming Home: Four Feminist Utopias and Patriarchal Experience." In *Future Females: A Critical Anthology*, edited by Marleen S. Barr, 63–70. Madison: Popular Press, 1981.

Pearson, Carol S. "Of Time and Revolution: Theories of Social Change in Contemporary Feminist Science Fiction." In *Women in Search of Utopia: Mavericks and Mythmakers*, edited by Ruby Rohrlich and Elaine Baruch Hoffman, 260–268. New York: Schocken Books, 1984.

Pearson, Carol S. "Towards a New Language, Consciousness and Political Theory: The Utopian Novels of Dorothy Bryant, Mary Staton and Marge Piercy." *Heresies* 4, no. 1 (1981): 84–87.

Pearson, Carol S. "Women's Fantasies and Feminist Utopias." *Frontiers* 2, no. 3 (1973): 48–65.

Pearson, Wendy Gay, Veronica Hollinger, and Joan Gordon, editors. *Queer Universes: Sexualities in Science Fiction.* Liverpool: Liverpool University Press, 2008.

Peppers, Cathy. "Dialogic Origins and Alien Identities in Butler's *Xenogenesis.*" *Science Fiction Studies* 22, no. 1 (1995): 47–62.

Pfaelzer, Jean. "The Changing of the Avant Garde: The Feminist Utopia." *Science Fiction Studies* 15, no. 3 (1988): 282–294.

Piercy, Marge. *He, She and It.* New York: Alfred A. Knopf, 1991.

Piercy, Marge. *Woman on the Edge of Time.* New York: Ballantine Books, 1976.

Pierson, David. *Breaking Bad: Critical Essays on the Contexts, Politics, Style, and Reception of the Television Series.* Lanham: Lexington Books, 2013.

Plisner, Andrew. "Arboreal Dialogics: An Ecocritical Exploration of Octavia Butler's *Dawn.*" *African Identities* 7, no. 2 (2009): 145–159.

Potts, Stephen W. "'We Keep Playing the Same Record': A Conversation with Octavia Butler." *Science Fiction Studies* 23, no. 3 (1996): 331–338.

Reeser, Todd W. *Masculinities in Theory: An Introduction.* Hoboken: Wiley-Blackwell, 2010.

Rios, Victor M. *Punished: Policing the Lives of Black and Latino Boys.* New York: New York University Press, 2011.

Roberts, Robin. *A New Species: Gender and Science in Science Fiction.* Champaign: The University of Illinois Press, 1993.

Robinson, Sally. *Marked Men: White Masculinity in Crisis.* New York: Columbia University Press, 2000.

Robinson, Spider. "Galaxy Bookshelf." *Galaxy Science Fiction* 38, no. 5 (1977): 97.

Rosinsky, Natalie Myra. *Feminist Futures: Contemporary Women's Speculative Fiction.* Ann Arbor: UMI Research Press, 1982.

Ruether, Rosemary Radford. *New Woman/New Earth: Sexist Ideologies and Human Liberation.* New York: The Seabury Press, 1975.

Russ, Joanna. "*Amor Vincit Foeminam*: The Battle of the Sexes in Science Fiction." *Science Fiction Studies* 7, no. 1 (1980): 2–15.

Russ, Joanna. *The Female Man.* New York: Bantam, 1975.

Russ, Joanna. "The Image of Women in Science Fiction." In *Country You Have Never Seen: Essays and Reviews*, 205–218. Liverpool: Liverpool University Press, 2007.

Sale, Roger. "Woman on the Edge of Time." *The New York Times*, June 20, 1976, 189.

Sargent, Lyman Tower. "A New Anarchism: Social and Political Ideas in Some Recent Feminist Eutopias." In *Women and Utopia: Critical Interpretations*, edited by Marleen Barr and Nicholas D. Smith, 3–33. Lanham: University Press of America, 1983.

Sargent, Pamela. "Women in Science Fiction." *Futures* 7, no. 5 (1975): 433–441.

Sargisson, Lucy. *Contemporary Feminist Utopianism.* London: Routledge, 1996.

Seidler, Victor J. *Transforming Masculinities: Men, Cultures, Bodies, Power, Sex, and Love.* London: Routledge, 2006.

Shaw, Marc E., and Elwood Watson. "Introduction: From Seinfeld to Obama: Millennial Masculinities in Contemporary American Culture." In *Performing American Masculinities: The 21st-Century Man in Popular Culture*, edited by Marc E. Shaw and Elwood Watson, 1–6. Bloomington: Indiana University Press, 2011.

Shklovksy, Victor. "Art as Technique." In *Russian Formalist Criticism: Four Essays*, edited by Lee T. Lemon and Marion J. Reis, 3–24. Lincoln: University of Nebraska Press, 1965.

Smith, Curtis. *Twentieth-Century Science Fiction Writers*. London: St. James Press, 1986.

Smith, Harrison. "Ursula K. Le Guin, Grande Dame of Science Fiction, Dies at 88." Last modified January 24, 2018. www.washingtonpost.com/local/obituaries/ursula-k-le-guin-grand-dame-of-science-fiction-dies-at-88/2018/01/23/8842ceb8–0087–11e8–8acf-ad2991367d9d_story.html?noredirect=on&utm_term=.38e2ae28c5fe.

Somay, Bülent and RMP. "Towards an Open-Ended Utopia." *Science Fiction Studies* 11, no. 1 (1984): 25–38.

Starhawk. *The Fifth Sacred Thing*. New York: Bantam, 1993.

Stein, Karen F. "Inclusion and Exclusion in Some Feminist Utopian Fictions." In *Women's Utopian and Dystopian Fiction*, edited by Sharon R. Wilson, 112–132. Cambridge: Cambridge Scholars Press, 2013.

Stickgold-Sarah, Jessie. "'Your Children Will Know Us, You Never Will': The Pessimistic Utopia of Octavia Butler's *Xenogenesis Trilogy*." *Extrapolation* 51, no. 3 (2010): 414–430.

Stimpson, Catharine R. "Feminisms and Utopia." *Utopian Studies* 2, no. 3 (1991): 1–6.

Stratton, Susan. "The Messiah and the Greens: The Shape of Environmental Action in *Dune* and *Pacific Edge*." *Extrapolation* 42, no. 4 (2001): 303–316.

Sussman, Herbert. *Masculine Identities: The History and Meanings of Manliness*. Santa Barbara: Praeger, 2012.

Suvin, Darko. "Of Starship Troopers and Refuseniks: War and Militarism in U.S. Science Fiction, Part 2." *Extrapolation* 48, no. 1 (2007): 9–34.

Swyngedouw, E. "Apocalypse Forever? Post-Political Populism and the Spectre of Climate Change." *Theory, Culture, and Society* 27 (2010): 213–232.

Teslenko, Tatiana. *Feminist Utopian Novels of the 1970s: Joanna Russ and Dorothy Bryant*. London: Routledge, 2003.

Tucker, Jeffrey A. "'The Human Contradiction': Identity and/as Essence in Octavia E. Butler's *Xenogenesis*." *The Yearbook of English Studies* 37, no. 2 (2007): 164–181.

Vint, Sherryl. "Becoming Other: Animals, Kinship, and Butler's 'Clay's Ark.'" *Science Fiction Studies* 32, no. 2 (2005): 281–300.

Wald, Priscilla. "Science, Technology, and the Environment." In *The Cambridge Companion to American Science Fiction*, edited by Gerry Canavan and Eric Carl Link, 179–193. Cambridge: Cambridge University Press, 2015.

Wallace, Maurice O. *Constructing the Black Masculine: Identity and Ideality in African American Men's Literature and Culture*. Durham: Duke University Press, 2002.

Warren, Karen J. "Ecological Feminist Philosophies: An Overview of the Issues." In *Ecological Feminist Philosophies*, edited by Karen J. Warren, ix–xxvi. Bloomington: Indiana University Press, 1996.

Wasson, Sara. "Love in the Time of Cloning: Science Fictions of Transgressive Kinship." *Extrapolation* 45, no. 2 (2004): 130–144.

Waters, Alice E. "Hoping for the Best, Imagining the Worst: Dystopian Anxieties in Women's SF Pulp Stories of the 1930s." *Extrapolation* 50, no. 1 (2009): 61–79.

White, Eric. "The Erotics of Becoming: *Xenogenesis* and *The Thing.*" *Science Fiction Studies* 20, no. 3 (1993): 394–408.

Wilchins, Riki. *Queer Theory, Gender Theory: An Instant Primer.* Boston: Alyson Books, 2004.

Wilson, D. Harlan. "Technomasculine Bodies and Vehicles of Desire: The Erotic Delirium of Michael Bay's *Transformers.*" *Extrapolation* 53, no. 3 (2012): 347–364.

Winckler, Reto. "This Great Stage of Androids: *Westworld*, Shakespeare, and the World as Stage." *Journal of Adaptation in Film & Performance* 10, no. 2 (2017): 169–188.

"Woman on the Edge of Time." *Kirkus Review*, May 7, 2019. https://www.kirkusre views.com/book-reviews/marge-piercy-7/woman-on-the-edge-of-time/.

Yaszek, Lisa. *Galactic Suburbia: Recovering Women's Science Fiction.* Columbus: Ohio State University Press, 2008.

Yaszek, Lisa. "The Women History Doesn't See: Recovering Midcentury Women's SF as a Literature of Social Critique." *Extrapolation* 45, no. 1 (2004): 34–51.

Zaki, Hoda M. "Utopia, Dystopia, and Ideology in the Science Fiction of Octavia Butler." *Science Fiction Studies* 17, no. 2 (1990): 239–251.

Index

Index

About the Author

Michael Pitts is an assistant professor at the University of South Bohemia. His research, which has been published in *Extrapolation* and the *European Journal of American Studies*, is positioned at the intersection of masculinities studies, queer theory, speculative fiction, and feminist theory.

www.ingramcontent.com/pod-product-compliance
Lightning Source LLC
Chambersburg PA
CBHW022321280326
41932CB00010B/1184